# HOW TO
# PUBLISH
## ON THE
# INTERNET

**ANDREW L. FRY** is cofounder and director of projects for Free Range Media, Inc., a multimedia publishing company that focuses on Internet. Formerly a project manager at Microsoft, Inc., he has also worked in television at a Seattle CBS affiliate station, owned and operated his own video production company, published magazine articles, and written scripts for everything from business videos to public service announcements.

**DAVID PAUL** is a technical writer as well as a published film critic and a former political scientist. He is the editor of and a contributor to *Politics, Art and Communication in the East European Cinema* and he is the author of *Czechoslovakia: Profile of a Socialist Republic at the Crossroads of Europe*. He is the coauthor, with Paul V. Warwick and Davis F. Roth, of *Comparative Policies: Diverse States in an Independent World*. For the past seven years he has earned his living writing and editing software documentation, both printed and on-line, and he cruises the Internet from his current home in Seattle.

# HOW TO
# PUBLISH
## ON THE
# INTERNET

### A Comprehensive Step-by-Step
### Guide to Creative Expression
### on the World Wide Web

# by Andrew Fry
# and David Paul

**WARNER BOOKS**

A Time Warner Company

Warner Books, Inc., 1271 Avenue of the Americas, New York, NY 10020

 A Time Warner Company

Printed in the United States of America
First Printing: June 1995
10   9   8   7   6   5   4   3   2   1

Library of Congress Cataloging-in-Publication Data
Fry, Andrew.
    How to publish on the Internet : a comprehensive step-by-step
guide to creative expression on the World Wide Web / Andrew Fry and
David Paul.
        p.   cm.
    Includes index.
    ISBN 0-446-67179-7 (trade pbk.)
    1. World Wide Web (Information retrieval system)   2. Internet
(Computer network)   I. Paul, David W.   II. Title.
TK5105.888.F79   1995
025.04—dc20                                              95-2286
                                                          CIP

Cover design by Rachel McClain
Book design by Stanley S. Drate/Folio Graphics Co., Inc.

# Acknowledgments

The prophet Mohammed and the sage Henry David Thoreau wrote their most famous works with divine help and the inspiration of nature, respectively. *How to Publish on the Internet* makes no claims to such lofty ideals, but we suppose we, too, should acknowledge whatever transcendent force has helped us with our writing. We also happily and gratefully acknowledge the help and wisdom of numerous humans without whom we could not have completed our work (or at least would have had an extremely hard time of it). In particular, we'd like to thank Todd Tibbetts and Kristin Adams, who applied their expertise and patience to the construction of the illustrations throughout this book; Mike Samsel, whose encouragement and cooperation made a lot of things possible; Caroline McGovern, who cheerfully read and tested some of the material; Chris Wilson, who told us much about the early days of Mosaic at NCSA; John Houston, who shared with us some interesting insights into the effectiveness of interactive learning; and the entire staff of Free Range Media, for their enthusiasm and support. We also thank SPRY Inc. for access to their facilities and technical expertise. We are grateful to the following for permission to publish illustrations based on screens from their Web sites: Prof. Michael Greenhalgh of the Australian National University, Mike Peters of Stanford University, Todd Tibbetts, SPRY Inc., DealerNet, and Free Range Media. We thank our editor, Anne Douglas Milburn, for her hard work, good humor, and support; and Laura Fillmore, our agent, for her enthusiasm and attention to the nitty gritty. Finally, Andrew would personally like to thank Julie and Savannah for their love and support.

ANDREW FRY AND DAVID PAUL
*Seattle, 1995*

# Contents

## PART THREE

### INTERACTING WITH THE SERVER

# Preface

Everybody's talking about the Internet, the "electronic highway" that leads to information, education, and entertainment. You've heard the talk, felt the enthusiasm—and now you want to learn to drive that highway.

Or maybe you've already discovered the Net. You use electronic mail. You follow a newsgroup on the arts or boats or homeowners' tips. Maybe you've participated in an on-line forum, browsed the electronic bulletin boards, checked the State Department's travel advisories, or looked at job listings. Maybe you've even carried on an argument with someone halfway around the world about politics or soccer or the meaning of life. If so, you've seen how the Net can bring people and their ideas together.

You may have discovered that the Net can also be used to distribute information about products you can buy, from software to real estate, or that some pretty good writers have begun circulating their poems—and you've begun to suspect that you, too, could reach an audience, find a market, present ideas you're passionate about in your own way, maybe even create a name for yourself. If only you could get your stuff out on the Net effectively.

Well, you can.

You can use the Internet to:

- Post a copy of that essay you've written—and interested readers, browsing the Net, will be able to read it. Maybe they'll give you feedback or offer their own essays on similar subjects.
- Use the appropriate newsgroups to post announcements about your editorial services, your catering business, your acupuncture practice, your landscaping company, your law firm—or whatever you sell, buy, create, or produce. Internet users who are looking for what you have to offer will be able to find you.

- Develop your creative potential, whether it be through words or graphic art or both, and share your work with others.
- Create an electronic study group, literary circle, fan club, or discussion group that attracts people from around the world: people who share your interests and want to share their ideas, research, and work.

How?

By publishing your material on the Internet.

You've probably seen examples of what's circulating on the Net. You know that the technology already exists for you to publish your text and graphics on the Net, and to design electronic pathways that lead your potential audience to your information. In the future, you'll be able to do even more, as the developing technologies make it increasingly more efficient for you to add sound and moving video images to your material.

Perhaps you're saying, "Okay, sounds good. But what does it mean to *publish* on the Internet? After all, the Internet isn't a book or a magazine."

Good question. Traditionally, we think of publishing as a *print medium*. We think of sheets of paper covered with text and pictures, numbered consecutively and bound together, packaged, shipped, and sold to the public. For more than five hundred years, going back to the time of Gutenberg, publishing has meant circulating printed words and pictures on paper.

But publishing took place before the invention of movable type, and long before the invention of phototypography. Before Gutenberg, publishing meant scribes, monks, and others of the learned elite who painstakingly worked with quill and ink on paper, papyrus, parchment, or vellum. And publishing continues to evolve along new lines and through new media.

We can think of the Internet as the newest medium of publishing. It is an *electronic* medium, with some of the features familiar to us in other electronic media, for example television (a *broadcasting* medium) or fax machines (a *digital facsimile transmitting* medium). But the Internet is far more than a digital transmitting medium. And it is not truly a broadcasting medium, because information on the Net is not transmitted widely (*broadly*) over the airwaves; Net readers have to find the information they're looking for by making a specific connection that brings them the specific materials.

Publishing on the Internet means publishing on-line—that is, circulating information electronically via computer networks. Over these networks, information flows from one computer screen to other computer screens, potentially thousands of computer screens. Let's say, for example, that you live in Omaha. A document you create and put out on the Net can be read by people in Seattle, Buenos Aires, Kiev, Nairobi, Bombay, and Melbourne—anywhere there are users with computers and network connections.

Just as important as the way published material circulates on the Internet is the *form* its content takes. Publishing on the Internet means creating and distributing content that's flexible and dynamic, that changes in real time, and that can be logically linked in a number of different sequential fashions to make the information interactive.

In simpler language, what you publish on the Internet can take on different forms, and it can be easily and quickly updated. Unlike a magazine or book, which requires weeks or months of production time, Internet content can be circulated immediately upon creation. If something changes, it doesn't take months to adjust the published information.

For example, let's say you've written an article about the political system of Russia, and your article has been accepted by a prestigious quarterly journal. In just nine months, it will be published in a handsome volume. Now suppose that eight months from now, while your article is at press, the Russian president is ousted in a military coup and the Russian parliament is dismissed. It's too late to stop the presses, however, and before your article reaches its intended audience, it may no longer describe the current political system. You might be able to submit an update for publication in the next edition of the journal—three months after your article is published—but who knows what else might change in that additional span of time?

If you publish the article on the Internet, however, you can publish an update at any time, and it will be circulated immediately. You can even edit the original article, if you prefer, to reflect the new situation. You can add or change tables and graphics, and you can even rearrange sections of the article if it helps clarify the work. The content of your article, in other words, is *flexible and dynamic,* and you can change it in *real time*—that is, as events in the real world are unfolding.

And what does it mean that Internet content can be logically linked in different sequential fashions to make the information interactive? It means that what you write, or what you compose, does not have to be read from A to Z, or from Page 1 through to whatever the final page is. Instead, you can organize the material in a number of different pieces and give your reader the possibility to choose what order to read the pieces in.

For example, let's say you are publishing a guide to choose the ideal dog. In a book or printed article, you might discuss dogs by breeds, listed alphabetically. Thus, *Afghan* would come before *Airedale, Beagle, Boxer,* and so on. Some of your readers, however, might not want to page through all of these breed descriptions; they might have certain physical character- istics in mind, such as "large, short-haired dogs," and therefore they'd prefer to go directly to a list of large, short-haired dogs. But they can't read your printed article that way if you've organized the content as an alphabetic listing.

On the Internet, you can present your information in such a way that your audiences can access if from a number of different logical ap- proaches. You can offer them the tried-and-true alphabetic list, from *Af- fenpinscher* to *Yorkshire Terrier,* but you can also give your readers some alternative approaches—including a topic on large, short-haired dogs. This topic would limit the list of breeds to *Boxer, Dalmatian, Labrador Retriever,* and other breeds that meet the reader's preferences.

The key to creating flexible and dynamic information for the Internet is in the way you *link* different pieces of the information to each other. You can link the pieces logically, but not in a fixed sequence. The people who want to find the ideal breed of dog for their family can choose the order in which they read the separate topics that make up your guide. This is one example of what we mean by *interactive* content: the reader "interacts" with the information by making choices from among alterna- tives.

In summary, publishing on the Internet represents a new form of dis- seminating information, combining some features of traditional publishing (distributing text and pictures to a readership) with features that are akin to broadcasting (circulating the information immediately). Going one step further, publishing on the Internet adds something that neither traditional publishing nor broadcasting provides: the potential for interaction be- tween your content and your audience.

This book is your guide to publishing on the Internet. Its starting point is the World Wide Web project, an emerging technology that is expanding the possibilities of communication over the Internet in ways that were hardly imaginable just a few years ago. In the following chapters, you will find an introduction to the Internet and the World Wide Web, a detailed primer on creating content for the Internet, and a conceptual and practical strategy that will help you reach your full potential audience and create an *information community* around the specific interests, ideas, and vision you want to share.

# PART ONE

# AN INTRODUCTION TO THE INTERNET

**P**art One of this book provides a short introduction to the Internet and the World Wide Web. If you are already familiar with the World Wide Web and have a clear picture of the types and forms of information it contains, you might want to skip this section and jump to Part Two. There you'll get right into the nuts and bolts of creating content for the Web.

## WHAT'S IN PART ONE

1. **The Internet and the World Wide Web.** A survey of the new mass media: what they are, how they work, where they came from, how they compare with other communications media, and where they are going.
2. **Sample Sites: A Threepenny Tour of the World Wide Web.** A look at several document sets already published on the World Wide Web, and how they exemplify the different ways you can approach publishing your material.
3. **The World Wide Web: Size, Popularity, and Potential.** How big is the Web? This chapter takes a look at some of the evidence.

# 1 The Internet and the World Wide Web

What is the Internet? How did it come to be what it is today? What is the World Wide Web, and how does it relate to the Internet? And how can you use it to express yourself?

As a jumping-off point, it might be useful to think of the Internet as the *platform* for expressing your ideas, and the World Wide Web as the specific *medium* in which you publish your content.

Let's look first at the Internet.

## THE INTERNET

When we say that the Internet is the *platform* for expressing your ideas, we mean two things. First, it is a basic means for communicating ideas. And second, it is a technology.

*A means for communicating ideas.* To understand the Internet as a platform in the first sense, you might compare it to other platforms for circulating ideas—broadcast, or telephone, or print. These alternative means for communicating can be broken down into specific media. For example, newspapers, magazines, and books are three specific media of print communications. Television and radio are two specific media of broadcasting. Electronic mail, or e-mail, is one medium associated with the Internet, and the World Wide Web, which we shall discuss later in this chapter, is another, perhaps broader one.

*A technology.* The Internet consists of myriad individual computers and many computer networks the world over. These computers and networks transmit information to each other through *gateways,* which are electronic devices that interpret each other's code and make it possible for users of one network to read information sent from another network. This exchange of information very often takes place between networks that are based on different types of computers running different types of programs. What makes it possible for them to communicate with each other are *protocols,* or agreed-upon sets of rules that the networks and their computers can work with.

## What is a protocol?

In technical computer terms, a protocol is a set of rules that programmers apply when writing code. Traditionally, protocol refers to terms of ceremony observed among diplomats. More loosely, it also describes certain patterns of courtesy that we expect of each other in everyday life. When we pick up the telephone, for example, we don't just hold it to our ear and expect the caller to initiate the conversation; we first say, "Hello," or "New Age Technologies, Anderson speaking," or something of that sort. Likewise, when we are introduced to a new acquaintance, we generally offer our hand; this, like the way we answer the telephone, is correct behavior, and it is expected by our counterpart. Internet protocols are analogous; they comprise sets of rules that constitute "correct behavior" between computers and networks—behavior that each side of a network connection expects from the other side.

### The Internet "Language"

Two specific protocols are crucial to all Internet communications: *Transmission Control Protocol (TCP)* and *Internet Protocol (IP)*. They are commonly spoken of together as TCP/IP. And, together, they define the common language of the Internet.

You might think of this in the following terms. When you work with a word processor on your own computer, you type words in standard English. Your word-processing software understands this language and instructs the computer to do what you expect it to do: record your ideas, organize them according to the formats you specify, store them in an electronic file, and transfer them to a printer which will in turn print them on paper.

What goes on in the innards of your computer is a pretty complicated set of processes, and what networks do is also complicated. For one computer to communicate with another, they both have to "speak" the same

**How to Publish on the Internet**

language—a computer language based on code, that is. When two or more computers that speak the same language are connected by cables or telephone links, they form a simple network and can exchange information with each other. A more complex network might be one in which computers are connected to each other through a *server* that controls access to network resources. A file server, for example, stores files that may be used in common by the computers making up the network; a mail server receives and delivers e-mail messages for all computers on the network.

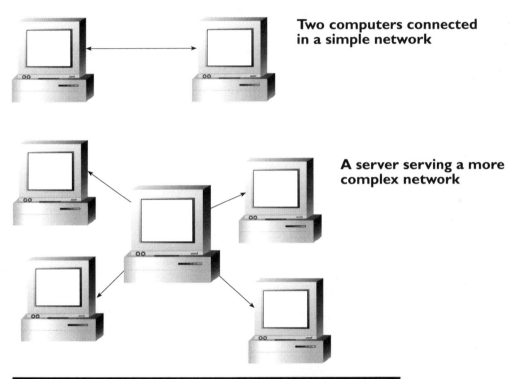

**Two computers connected in a simple network**

**A server serving a more complex network**

FIGURE 1-1   **A simple network and a network with a server.**

A network that exists within a limited geographical space, such as a school or an office complex, is called a *local-area network,* or *LAN.* A network that extends over large distances, connecting geographically separated areas, is called a *wide-area network,* or *WAN.*

We can think of the Internet as a network that spans the entire world, connecting computers and computer networks globally through the international set of standards known as TCP/IP.

## IP and TCP

The Internet actually takes its name from the *Internet Protocol,* or *IP.* Thus, the Internet can be defined as all networks that communicate with each other through codes written according to the rules of the Internet Protocol. The rules of IP govern the movement of information over the Internet. The programming code that they are written in operates within the innards of your computer. You do not see the IP as it works, and unless you are an Internet programmer, you don't need to know much about it.

The second crucial protocol, *Transmission Control Protocol,* or *TCP,* works hand in hand with IP. The rules of TCP govern how computers and networks manage the flow of information among themselves. Functionally, TCP divides information into packets so they can be transmitted over electronic connections between computers. IP does the actual transmitting, making it possible for the information to get through the gateways between the sending computer and the receiving computers(s). And then, at the receiving end, TCP again comes into play, reassembling the packets of information and checking them for errors.

Thus, the Internet is a supernetwork, a "network of networks." It is capable of exchanging information between any computer in the world and any other computer in the world, as long as both computers are connected to the Internet and able to "speak" TCP/IP.

**FIGURE 1-2  The Internet.**

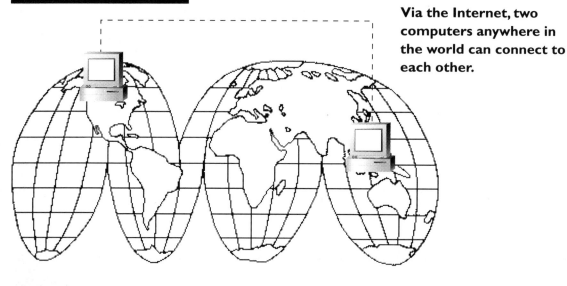

Via the Internet, two computers anywhere in the world can connect to each other.

## Servers and Clients

The networks that constitute the Internet center around servers. A server is a computer (or its software: see the accompanying sidebar) that "serves" other computers by administering network files and network operations. In addition to file servers and mail servers, there are several other familiar types of servers, such as print servers and database servers. A print server processes printing commands from other computers and channels them to one central printer. A database server contains files of information organized within a computer program that permits data retrieval, searching, sorting, and various other relational operations to be performed over a network.

The computers being served contain programs called *clients*. The clients enable a user to work with the information stored on a server—read notices posted in public folders, for example, or perform database operations using records shared by other clients on the network. (See figure 1-1 for an illustration of the connections between a server and its clients.)

The Internet contains servers that perform functions similar to those on a LAN or WAN—file servers, mail servers, database servers, and so on. Internet servers take on their own characteristics because of the nature of the information they contain and the services they perform, and thus certain types of servers are specific to the Internet: Gopher servers, WAISes, and Web servers are three examples. You can use a search tool,

### Servers and clients: computers or programs?

Technically, both servers and clients are software, not hardware. It is server programs that control access to network resources, and client programs that allow users at their own workstations to make use of the information. This definition is clear-cut in the case of mainframe computers, where the clients frequently occupy space on the same machine as the servers, and individual workstations may consist only of terminals rather than full-scale personal computers.

In a LAN environment, however, the terms of reference have become a bit muddied. It is still conventional to think of a client as software, but it has become common to think of a server as more or less synonymous with the computer that is dedicated to running network administration software. Thus it sometimes happens within a work group that a cry is heard echoing down the hallway, "Hey, some idiot turned off the print server in Room 401!"—which, of course, means that someone turned the computer off and messed up the configuration of the server *software*, canceling all pending print jobs. Not a popular thing to do.

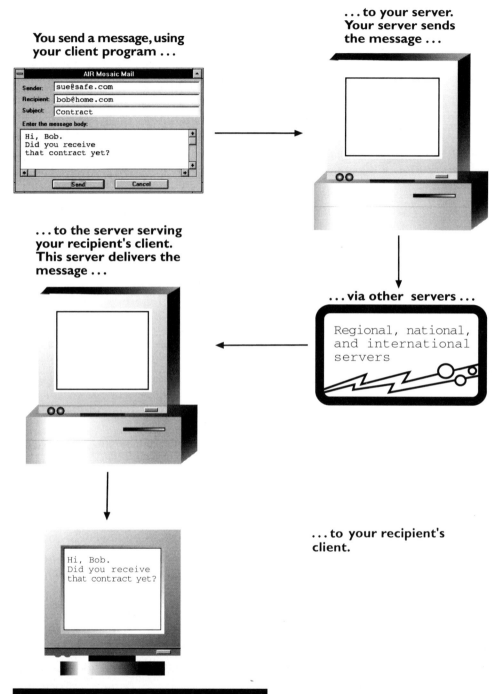

**You send a message, using your client program . . .**

**. . . to your server. Your server sends the message . . .**

| AIR Mosaic Mail |
|---|
| Sender: sue@safe.com |
| Recipient: bob@home.com |
| Subject: Contract |
| Enter the message body: |
| Hi, Bob.<br>Did you receive<br>that contract yet? |
| Send    Cancel |

**. . . to the server serving your recipient's client. This server delivers the message . . .**

**. . . via other servers . . .**

Regional, national,
and international
servers

**. . . to your recipient's client.**

Hi, Bob.
Did you receive
that contract yet?

**FIGURE 1-3    E-mail clients and servers.**

**How to Publish on the Internet**

such as Archie, to find a specific file when you know it exists on the Internet but you don't know which file server it's located on. You use a *WAIS* (Wide Area Information Server) to retrieve information that you can request by subject. *Web servers* are servers on the World Wide Web which offer hypertext-based access to documents. An Internet server can be more than one of these things at once; it can be a file server, an e-mail server, and a WAIS—and it can also be a Web server.

On the Internet there are a great many servers containing an unimaginable amount of information—about government functions, sports products available for purchase, items somebody wants to buy, the weather, unidentified flying objects . . . and on and on. You access this information by running client software on your computer. The client software gets a particular piece of information from a server and displays it for you to view, reply to, or act upon.

An e-mail program is one familiar form of client software. Actually, e-mail programs include both client and server programs, but it's the client that you work with on your computer; the server, ordinarily, is on the computer you log onto when you establish your Net connection. The client program, on your computer, contains the tools you need to read, compose, and store messages; it gets your incoming mail from the server and transfers your outgoing mail to the server for delivery. The mail server then sends your messages over the Internet to other servers. There, similar interactions take place between each server and its clients. Your messages, in other words, reach their intended recipients by the same client-server interaction that brings you your e-mail.

So, too, with other Internet activities: client software interacts with servers to bring information resources onto your computer screen. Thus, we can characterize the Internet as a vast network of networks on which thousands of servers are serving millions of clients the world over.

## Origins of the Internet

The Internet had its origins in the U.S. military-industrial complex. In 1969, the Department of Defense (DOD) initiated a project called ARPANET, a communications network of the Advanced Research Projects Agency (ARPA). ARPA's job was to administer DOD grants to corporations and universities engaged in defense-related research. The ARPANET was designed for two purposes: to facilitate ARPA's administrative work by providing a quick and convenient form of communications, and—perhaps more importantly—as an experiment in military communications that might be resistant to nuclear attack.

Fortunately, the ARPANET was never tested by an actual nuclear attack. However, it demonstrated an impressive capability to deliver information among government, academic, and corporate network sites. The ARPANET's success attracted more and more universities and research institutes, whose members began to use it for civilian purposes. It was now divided into two networks, one strictly for military sites (MILNET) and the other (still called ARPANET) for nonmilitary sites.

It didn't take long before the networks were used for many purposes of communication. Researchers found they could share information

## Broadcast, print, and the Internet: some comparisons

We're all familiar with television and radio networks and their affiliated stations. Programming for the mainstream commercial networks (NBC, ABC, CBS, and Fox) and their stations is paid for mainly by advertisements. Public networks (PBS and NPR) are funded by grants and voluntary audience subscriptions. The audience, referred to as *viewership* or *listenership,* has some limited interaction with the content providers (the networks and local stations), primarily in the form of call-in programs and letters. Measurements of audience size, made through ratings systems such as the Nielsen ratings, are closely watched—especially in the case of the commercial media—in order to win sponsors and fuel the programming.

The commercial print media include publishers creating books, magazines, and newspapers, which are paid for by sales, subscriptions, and advertisement sales. Not-for-profit publishers offer books and journals that are financed mainly by sales, institutional subsidies, and some ad sales. The audience, referred to as *readership,* can interact with content providers through letters to the editor, public forum sections, and e-mail. Audience size, measured in terms of circulation, is important for those publishers who compete for advertisers.

The print media have traditionally been more decentralized than the broadcast media, with hundreds of publishing houses and thousands of local newspapers constantly churning out print. However, there are a number of well-established companies that are roughly analogous to the broadcasting networks: Hearst and Gannett, in the newspaper business, are the best-known names. In recent times there has been a tendency toward the merging of several media forms under one organizational roof, in some cases combining not just different types of print media but non-print media as well: the Time Warner and CBS conglomerates are prime examples.

Most decentralized of all is the Internet, based on thousands of servers around the globe. As yet, the World Wide Web has no equivalent to ABC, NBC, CBS, Hearst, or Gannett; however, there are tools like the Global Network Navigator (GNN) and CommerceNet, developed to organize content on a wide scale. And in addition, many more specialized Web sites are developing service pages that give their readers easy access to organized sets of World Wide Web documents.

How to Publish on the Internet

quickly, and institutional administrators could conduct business through e-mail. Libraries around the U.S. could gain access to each other's resources, especially as card catalogs went on-line, and inter-library loaning was dramatically speeded up. By the mid-1980s, many local networks were connected to each other by the Internet Protocol, and the term "Internet" came into use.

For a few more years, the Internet remained the elite province of academicians, government employees, and a relative few corporate users. In time, however, the Internet was discovered by the public. Commercial and noncommercial service providers made servers available, and both individuals and corporate groups learned how to use TCP/IP to gain access to that large, and constantly growing, world of electronic information. During the 1992 U.S. presidential campaign, the "information superhighway" became a policy issue and a buzzword, and the Internet—or at least a vague, popularized notion of it—became a conversation piece at cocktail parties, in espresso houses, and among corporate marketers. By the mid-1990s, new software featuring graphical user interfaces was making it easy for beginners to navigate and the Net became the hottest new communications platform.

> **N O T E** For an interesting summary of the technological developments that make up the history of the Internet, see Robert H. Zakon's Internet document, "Hobbes' Internet Timeline," at `gopher://is.internic.net/00/ infoguide/about-internet/history/timeline`.

## THE WORLD WIDE WEB

The advent of new, graphical network software opened exciting possibilities for Internet access. The most exciting developments have built upon the original success of the World Wide Web project.

The World Wide Web was first developed at the CERN Research Center in Switzerland by a team led by Tim Berners-Lee. Originally, the World Wide Web was designed as a medium for CERN's physicists to share their research. It soon became clear that this new technology had a far wider potential, and the protocol forming the basis of the Web technology, known as the *Hypertext Transfer Protocol,* or *HTTP,* came to be applied within the context of the Internet.

The World Wide Web has grown rapidly, and those who originally developed it have been joined by others in advancing its technology. Two very important centers for the evolving technology are the National Center for Supercomputing Applications (NCSA), especially its base at the University of Illinois at Urbana-Champaign, and the Massachusetts Institute of Technology (MIT), both in the United States. The main center of the World Wide Web Consortium, or W3C, as it's sometimes known, has recently moved to MIT.

## What Is the Web?

The World Wide Web, familiarly known as "the Web," is a medium of communication built around the goal of seamless information delivery through *hypertext* links—codes that connect to other topics or documents.

The Web's immediately visible feature is its user-friendly look; it's a big improvement over the rather "flat" look of the Internet minus HTTP. Ordinarily, you view the Web through a *browser,* a software program that searches a network, retrieves copies of files, and displays them in an easy-to-read format. Using a browser, you can explore the Internet by clicking on icons or "hot" text; you don't need to master the arcane and compli-

## What is hypertext?

The word hyper*text* is a bit of a misnomer, for it includes not just text but other data, too, such as graphical images. Hypertext is data that is especially coded to contain links to other data. Most frequently, the links are activated by a mouse click. Thus, if you click on a word coded with hypertext, you immediately jump to another topic, or perhaps even another document, that contains the corresponding hypertext coding. For example, if you are reading a topic on the World Wide Web and you click on the word hypertext, you might jump to a topic that discusses the technical qualities of hypertext. Hypertext within a document is generally displayed with formatting that makes it easily recognizable—underlined or highlighted words, for example, or a distinctive border around a graphic.

Similarly, a graphical image might be a hypertext link. Let's say you're interested in buying a new home and you've discovered an ad that a local real estate company has posted on the Internet. There's a picture of a house coded as hypertext, and when you click on it, up pops a screen containing information about the house: price, size in square feet, number of rooms, neighborhood location, the year it was built, type of heating system, and so on.

This is one example of how nontextual data can serve as hypertext. With a little imagination, you can begin to explore the possibilities in combining text and graphics, not just as aesthetic or expository devices but also as elements in a creative strategy for structuring documents.

cated UNIX or DOS text commands that, until recently, were the only way to access the Net's resources.

Figure 1-4 shows how one popular browser looks on a computer screen. We'll come back and discuss browsers again later in this chapter.

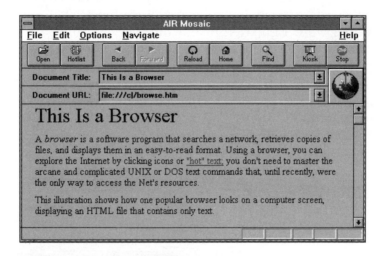

**FIGURE 1-4  A browser.**

## How Does the Web Facilitate Publishing?

One of the byproducts of the World Wide Web technology has been the way it has changed the paradigm of Internet usage. A few years ago, the typical Internet user was a diehard aficionado of Net services, but he or she was generally a consumer more than a producer. While many people flocked to the newsgroups and carried on conversations with each other, very few actually used the Net to post creative work, discuss their business, or share reports and lengthy essays.

Now, in contrast, more and more Internet users are becoming not just consumers but *producers,* or *publishers,* on the World Wide Web. The hypertext technology is smart, reader-friendly, and reasonably easy to learn, the audience potential is enticing, and the market open to practically everyone.

Hypertext is the key to the Web's potential as a publishing medium. Hypertext enables you to organize content on the basis of structured, logical association. Browsing the Web, a reader can jump quickly from one related topic to another. Within a single document, the reader can jump from subtopic to subtopic according to various sequences. The beauty of this capability lies in the fact that you, as publisher, control the content of your material (as in traditional publishing) while at the same time allowing your readers the freedom to navigate through the subtopics in the order of their choice.

Suppose, for example, that you are publishing an article about nuclear physicists and nuclear physics laboratories. You might offer your reader an overview topic that briefly outlines the subject, under the heading Nuclear Physics. Early in the article, you might mention several of the most prominent laboratories, coding each name as hypertext so that the reader can click on it and jump to a subtopic about that lab. Thus, your reader might want to jump to a subtopic about the Fermi Laboratory; from there to a subtopic about Enrico Fermi, the nuclear physicist for whom the Fermi Lab is named; and from there to a topic on the University of Chi-

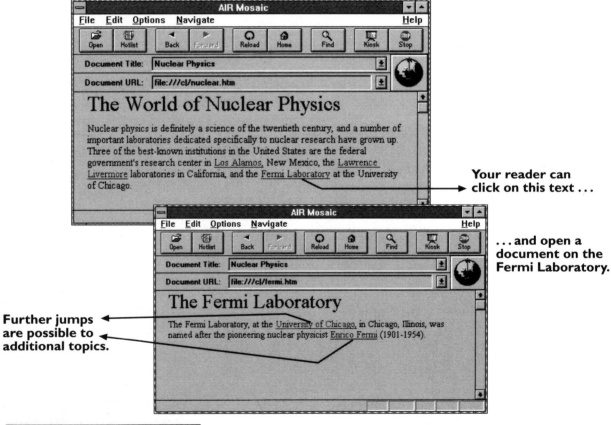

Your reader can click on this text . . .

. . . and open a document on the Fermi Laboratory.

Further jumps are possible to additional topics.

**FIGURE 1-5   Hypertext links.**

cago, where Fermi taught. And eventually, the reader can return to the main overview topic by way of yet another hypertext link.

These choices are possible because *you*, the Internet publisher, have built them into the design of your content. At each point of choice, you can build in alternative selections. Instead of jumping to the Fermi Lab, to stay with our example, the reader might instead jump to the Lawrence Livermore Lab—or not jump at all, if the reader wants to continue reading the overview topic, Nuclear Physics.

This is what we mean by *structured, logical association:* by using hypertext, you have the ability to connect certain ideas conceptually. You also offer the reader choices in making those conceptual connections, so that the reader does not have to read from point *A* to point *B* to point *C* and so on. The reader can instead jump from point *A* to point *Q*, back to point *A*, then to point *F*, and so on, choosing from whatever range of possible sequences you design into the content.

**Not only text.** Another important characteristic of the Web is that it allows you to include nontextual elements in your content. Among other

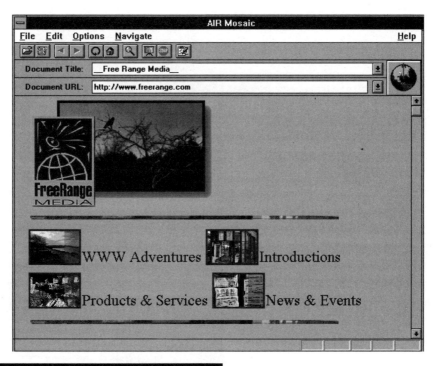

FIGURE 1-6 **Web document containing graphics.**

things, that means graphics, which you'll find a lot in existing Web documents. In fact, if you explore what's already available on the Web, you'll probably see some documents that are primarily composed of graphics.

Nontextual elements also include sound, video, and animation. All of these are integral parts of the rapidly developing computer multimedia world, and all are now available for Internet use. Any of these elements can be added to any text document—and, as you can imagine, they will spice up your presentation tremendously.

## How Do You Use It?

To distribute your material on the Web, you place a file on a server that has been set up as an HTTP server, meaning that it operates according to the Web's specific protocol for transporting hypertext. (We'll discuss hypertext in more detail later in this chapter.) By putting your file on an HTTP server and identifying it for your potential audience, all your readers need to know is the address at which that file exists. They can retrieve it by requesting it from your server's address on the Web. Their client software will present your information on their screens in the form of an interactive document.

---

### HTTP and HTML

These two abbreviations may seem a bit confusing until you're used to them. It might help you keep them straight if you concentrate on the last two letters of each, remembering that the first two letters stand for the same thing, *HyperText.*

Bear in mind that *TP* stands for *transfer protocol.* You can compare it to *IP* (the now-familiar Internet Protocol, which serves to move information over the Internet and through gateways). *TP,* too, refers to information that's being moved along the Internet. The *HT* in HTTP tells you it's hypertext that's being moved. Ergo, HTTP is a protocol, or set of rules operating in the background, that transports hypertext along the Internet.

The *ML* in HTML stands for *markup language.* This is what you use in order to prepare your content for publishing on the World Wide Web. You can compare HTML to the markup codes that editors pencil in as they work on conventionally typed or printed manuscript hard copy. The principle is the same: the marks, or codes, you use with HTML serve as signals to the printer—that is, to the software that electronically converts your markup language into screen display—to treat text marked as headings for display as headings, text marked as italic as italics, and so on.

---

**How to Publish on the Internet**

You don't have to understand the technicalities of how HTTP works or know much about HTTP at all, as long as your client software can process it. The code that transports Internet materials, as well as the code that makes the Web function, already exists—in the software that runs the Internet and in the Internet-access software that you install on your computer.

You do, however, need to learn a simple set of editing codes that make up the *Hypertext Markup Language (HTML).* By using HTML, you build into your content the codes that format your text, design the screen layout for your presentation, and structure the logic and flow of your content.

Learning HTML isn't like learning a foreign language. You can learn the basics of HTML within a few hours, and the sophisticated usage of it through practice. There are even some new software products on the market that can help you—text editors such as HoTMetaL Pro, CyberLeaf, and others—that drop HTML codes into your text as you're writing. You can use one of these programs or not, as you prefer. In Part Two, we'll help you through the mysteries of HTML and give you some lab exercises that will start you on your way to creating Web documents with flair.

> **N O T E**  We realize you may not have access to a Web server yet. That's okay; you can still work with the basic HTML constructions. You can create HTML documents and store them on your local hard disk until you're ready to transfer them to a Web site.

Now let's return to the software that actually displays the information coded with HTML. That software is the *browser.*

## Browsers

A browser is a computer program that provides an easy-to-use interface for scanning ("browsing") files on the Internet and transferring them to your computer. More specifically, a browser is a client software program that accesses content from an Internet server and assembles it in the form of a document that you view on the computer screen.

Put yet another way, a browser is a tool that you use for working with World Wide Web documents. It performs the following tasks:

❑ Displays documents on your computer screen by translating their HTML codes into an easily read, interactive format, with text and in-line graphics. If configured for it, your browser can also display external graphics and video images, in addition to playing sound files.

- Enables you to navigate through a document—and between documents—by way of hyperlinks.
- Takes your instructions about where on the Internet to find a specific file, then goes to that location, negotiates the necessary protocols, and retrieves the file.
- Allows you to custom-design your view of a document, by changing colors and specifying font assignments for the various text elements of a document, for example.

There are a number of different browsers available; three of the most familiar names are Mosaic, Cello, and Netscape. Browsers can be obtained in several ways and from a variety of sources. Here are two Internet addresses you can use to download a copy of Mosaic for Windows:

```
ftp://ftp.spry.com/AirMosaicDemo/AMOSDEMO.EXE
file://ftp.ncsa.uiuc.edu/PC/Windows/Mosaic/
```

and for the Mac:

```
file://ftp.ncsa.uiuc.edu/Mac/Mosaic/
```

You can get one by purchasing an integrated Internet software package (for example, SPRY's Internet In A Box, or even by downloading one from an Internet server using FTP. You can also obtain a simple browser by upgrading to one of the new operating systems (such as Microsoft's Windows 95 or IBM's new version of OS/2) that come with a browser built in. These various browsers all have their own look and feel, but they all share the ability to give you relatively easy access to Internet resources by bypassing the old, complicated text commands.

## Web Sites

Where does the browser find the information? On servers, of course—but not just any Internet server. Web servers are specially set up to deliver information files by using HTTP, which means these servers are able to transport hypertext on the Internet. When a user retrieves a document from a Web server, the document arrives as an ASCII file with HTML codes embedded in it, and the user's browser (the client software) translates these codes into screen images.

When a Web server is connected to the Internet and has information to distribute, it becomes a *Web site.* A Web site is the location of published hypertext content. When you read the electronic magazine *Hot-Wired,* for example, you are visiting a Web site. An auto dealership that advertises its cars over the DealerNet does so from a Web site.

When you are ready to publish your HTML document, whether it be an epic poem, an ad for your plumbing services, or an article for a fan club, you post it on a Web server that has been connected to the Internet as a Web site.

We'll leave the details of how you do this until later in this book. Now let's turn to chapter 2, where we'll take a brief tour of the World Wide Web by visiting some existing Web sites.

# 2

# Sample Sites:

## A Threepenny Tour of the World Wide Web

It would be impossible to describe each of the thousands of Web sites already operating on the Internet, so we've chosen a handful of sites for a quick guided tour. The publications we've selected illustrate the qualities that make the World Wide Web such an exciting and promising medium.

We're going to focus on the variety of ways in which Web publications are being used for both commercial and noncommercial purposes in our sample sites. In some cases, the two purposes overlap within the same Web site.

⚠ Throughout this chapter and elsewhere in this book, we describe the Internet location of a document by giving its *uniform resource locator (URL),* for example `http://www.freerange.com/home/advent.html`. The URL is the specific path to the document, including its file name, on a given World Wide Web server. **Please note** that the URLs we list are complete and accurate *as of the time we write.* We cannot guarantee that a URL will be accurate forever, for it often happens that files are moved or server names are changed.

## SOME NONCOMMERCIAL USES

We'll start our tour with two exhibits created by people who have an obvious love for their subject matter, *The New Guinea Sculpture Garden at Stanford* and *The Palace of Diocletian at Split.*

## The New Guinea Sculpture Garden at Stanford

This Web publication depicts and describes an interesting recent art project at Stanford University. The New Guinea Sculpture Garden comprises a collection of wood and stone sculptures created on the spot in Palo Alto, California, by ten master carvers from Papua New Guinea. The Web publication describing the sculpture project was created by Mike Peters, in cooperation with Bev Simmonds. The full set of documents can be viewed at `http://fuji.stanford.edu/icenter/png/npg.html`.

Figure 2-1 shows the opening, or home, page of this publication. Notice that it begins with the text heading, "The New Guinea Sculpture Garden

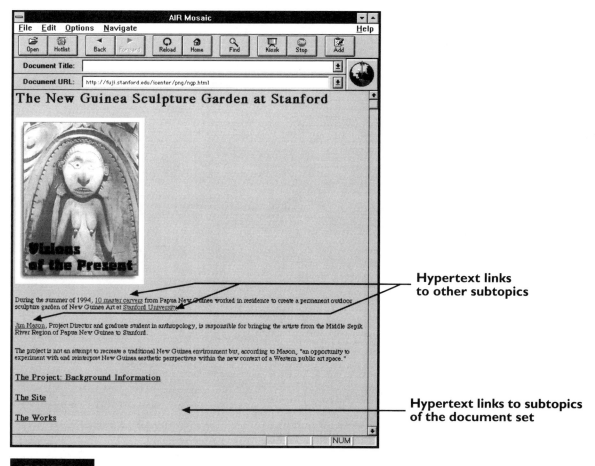

**FIGURE 2-1**

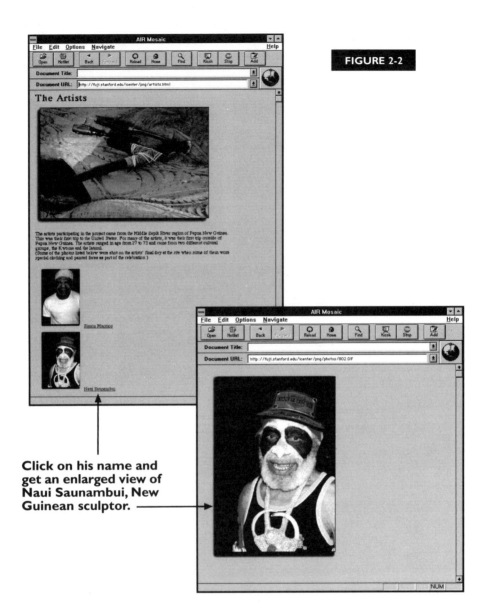

FIGURE 2-2

**Click on his name and get an enlarged view of Naui Saunambui, New Guinean sculptor.**

at Stanford,'' followed by a graphic illustration of what we can assume to be one of the pieces of sculpture. A brief textual introduction contains three hypertext links to subtopics, and then we see a list of the main subtopic headings. By clicking on any of these headings, the reader can jump to a new page containing information on that subject.

Let's click on **The Artists.** This takes us to a screen that briefly describes who the sculptors are (men from the Middle Sepik River region of

FIGURE 2-3

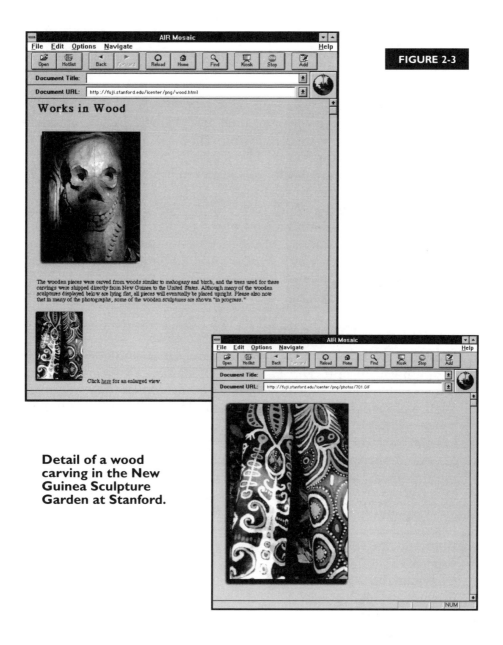

**Detail of a wood carving in the New Guinea Sculpture Garden at Stanford.**

Papua New Guinea), shows a picture of some of their tools, and then displays a small photo of each man. The text explains that some of the men were dressed up in ceremonial costume on the final day of their project. In each case, the man's name is printed beside his photo, and is formatted as a link to something (but it isn't yet clear what it is a link to). Scrolling down this second screen, we come to a photo of a man named **Naui Sau-nambui,** whose face is painted; intrigued by this, we click on his name and, after a short delay while a new graphic file is downloaded, we see a blown-up picture of the man, as in figure 2-2.

Returning to the home page, we decide to try the topic **The Works.** From there, the subtopics branch into **Works in Wood** and **Works in Stone.** We click on **Works in Wood.** The new screen displays small photos of the wood sculptures, and in each case—as with the photos of the artists—there is an opportunity to see an enlarged view. The detail shot illustrated in figure 2-3 is an example.

*The New Guinea Sculpture Garden* is a simply constructed, well-designed publication that accomplishes exactly what it sets out to do: It is an exercise in documenting the work that went into the development of a sculpture garden, as well as some supplementary discussion of the artists and what the work means.

## The Palace of Diocletian at Split

From the exotic arts of New Guinea, our focus shifts to the Adriatic coast of southern Europe. *The Palace of Diocletian at Split* is one of the most interesting and structurally sophisticated publications we've seen on the Web. This set of documents was created by Michael Greenhalgh, a professor of art history at the Australian National University, in cooperation with his software technician, Frans van Hoesel. Professor Greenhalgh's publication comprises a study of a major architectural complex from the Roman period, as well as supplementary discussions of the emperor Diocletian (c. A.D. 245–316) and the political structures of his empire.

The building that serves as the focal point for this set of documents is located in Split (known by the Romans as Spalato), in what is today the Republic of Croatia. Much of the complex was destroyed in the numerous wars of the nineteenth and early twentieth centuries, and further damage was done during the fighting between Croatia and Serbia in 1991–92. Professor Greenhalgh's study of the palace was based on his own observations and photographs taken before the most recent conflict, as well as earlier drawings, excavations, and written records.

To see the full exhibit, you can connect to the opening page at either of two Web locations:

```
http://www.ncsa.uiuc.edu/SDG/Experimental/split/
splitl.html or http://sunsite.unc.edu/expo/
palace.exhibit/intro.html
```

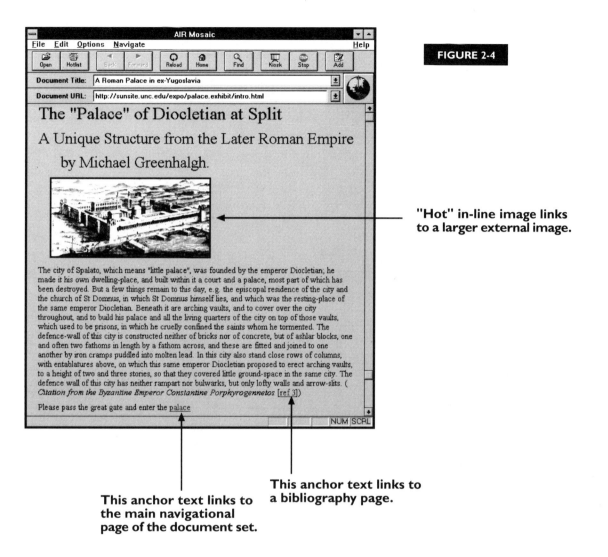

**FIGURE 2-4**

"Hot" in-line image links to a larger external image.

This anchor text links to the main navigational page of the document set.

This anchor text links to a bibliography page.

Figure 2-4 shows the opening page. Note that the opening page of a Web document is referred to by any of several terms, including *home page* and *welcome page.* Just below the headings at the top of this example is an *in-line image,* a graphics file that is loaded and displayed when you open the document. This particular image happens to be "hot," and when you click on it within the browser display, a larger version of the same picture is displayed: an *external image* that is loaded separately. (We'll discuss the difference between these types of image in chapter 6.) The image is a reproduction of a drawing by the master Baroque architect Johann Fischer von Erlach, representing the palace complex as it appeared in 1721.

In addition to the introductory text, notice that there are two anchor texts on this page. An *anchor* is hot text (or a hot graphic) that contains a hypertext link to another location. **[ref 3]** is one anchor text; if you click on this text in the browser, you jump to a page containing a bibliography of sources on the topic of this publication. The other anchor text is **palace.** Click on this text and you jump to the next topical page, which contains numerous additional anchors.

Figure 2-5 shows this next page, with the heading "Welcome to the Palace." This is an artfully designed navigational page, from which you

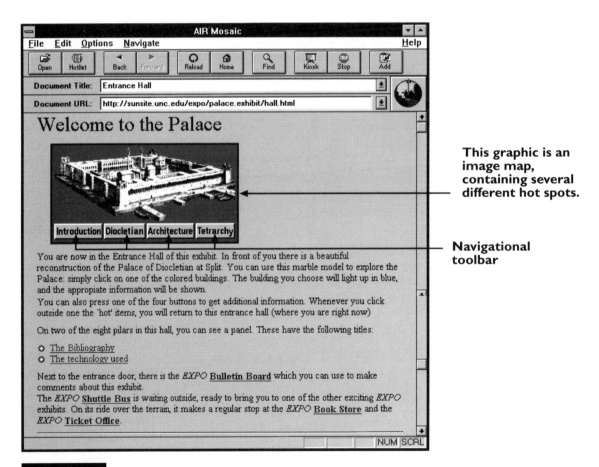

**FIGURE 2-5**

**How to Publish on the Internet**

can move to any of the main subtopics in the document. The graphic at the top, again representing the palace, is an *image map* that contains several hot spots. Depending on which part of the image you click on, you can connect to a topic page that discusses the corresponding section of the palace complex. At the base of the graphic is a toolbar with four rectangular buttons. Clicking on any of these buttons takes you to a corresponding subtopic:

- **Introduction:** A detailed introduction to the palace, discussing its origins, its name, and its original purposes
- **Diocletian:** A discussion of the emperor and his passion for building
- **Architecture:** A discussion of the architectural features, including comparisons with other contemporary Roman structures
- **Tetrarchy:** A discussion of the political system through which Diocletian ruled

Because this screen is meant purely as a navigational page, the text mainly concerns instructions about how to move through the document. The various anchors in the text contain links to the bibliography page, to a page discussing the graphic technology used by Greenhalgh and Van Hoesel, and to several locations external to this document. (In the case of this Web location, *The Palace of Diocletian at Split* is one exhibit in a collection of others that have been assembled as a collaborative project.) All in all, the interactive design is excellent, for users have the opportunity to choose which topic to jump to next, in the form of more anchor texts and hot graphics, throughout the *Palace* exhibit.

In sum, *The Palace of Diocletian at Split* makes intelligent use of hypertext and graphics within a fascinating set of documents. This Internet publication is a fine example of a project that was undertaken for professional reasons (it's a good learning tool), but it also clearly reflects the personal interest of its creator. Professor Greenhalgh's love for his subject is evident throughout this publication.

### Fractured Hypertales

Now we're going to take an even greater leap, not just across time and geographic space but across mindsets as well. From the left-brain-dominant explorations of New Guinean art and late Roman architecture, we move to a right-brain-dominant work of whimsical fantasy.

Todd Tibbetts, an on-line designer for Free Range Media, Inc., creates what he calls *Fractured Hypertales*—tales told through hypermedia.

They're composed of text and pictures, but that doesn't quite describe them. You might think of a hypertale as a story that begins as if it were a page in a book, but when you get to the bottom of the page, you have a choice about where to go next. Hypertales are, in other words, *interactive* stories.

Let's look at one called "Sleeping Humptylocks and the Three Beanstalks." If you're familiar with the Euro-American tradition of children's stories you'll recognize that this title is a "fractured" composite of several popular tales. Even before you begin, you make a choice: between the English- and Spanish-language versions. "Humptylocks" is located at `http://www.well.com/Community/WholeEarth/tt.home/` `HUMPTYLOCKS/hi.html`.

Figure 2-6 shows the first screen of the Humptylocks narrative. Notice that to move on to the next page of the story, you click on one of the text options at the bottom of the screen. Depending on the choice, the story then takes a narrative line corresponding to the new location depicted on the next screen: outside one of the three windows or outside the door. If you choose Exit thru door, you bring up the screen shown in figure 2-7.

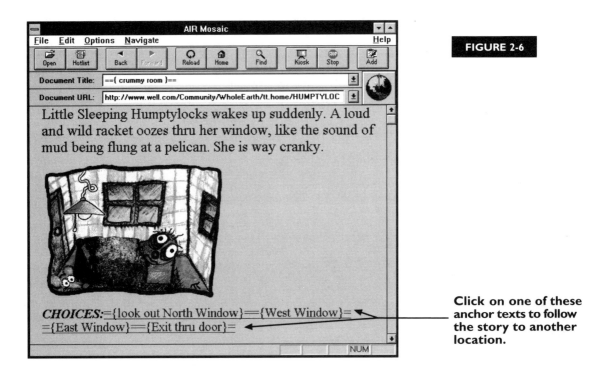

**FIGURE 2-6**

Click on one of these anchor texts to follow the story to another location.

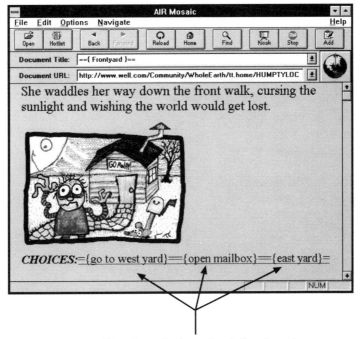

**Further choices for following the story in different directions.**

**FIGURE 2-7**

Again you have the option of continuing the story in any of several different directions. This multiple-choice option continues throughout the hypertale, thus giving you plenty of opportunities to try out varying narrative paths until you finally reach the end. A lot of things about the hypertales are fun: the wit and whimsy of the stories, the oddball narrative and comical illustrations, and—most of all—the chance to explore the variety of twists and turns you yourself can choose to give the story.

## SPRY City

Next stop is *SPRY City,* a service-oriented set of documents contained at the Web site of SPRY Inc. SPRY's Web site exists primarily for the commercial purposes of this Seattle-based software company. However, as a service to their customers and for the benefit of anyone who cruises the World Wide Web, SPRY has included several pages containing links to numerous other Web sites. From the *SPRY City* pages, you can get instant access to information about museums, travel, computers and computing, educational resources, business, government, and sporting goods.

*SPRY City* is located at `http://www.spry.com/sp_city/sp_city.html`.

The large graphic on the *SPRY City* welcome page is an image map—actually two rectangular image maps constructed as navigational toolbars. Click on any of the seven labeled images (Art Museum, Travel Agent, Com-

**FIGURE 2-8**

SPRY City's image map graphic links to many information resources.

Click on the Computer Store, for example, for a list of links to dozens of Web sites featuring computer information, services, and products.

puter Store, etc.), and you jump immediately to a page listing information resources in the category you've chosen. Each item in this list represents a direct link to the resource. Thus, if you are viewing the screen shown in figure 2-8 on your browser and you click on the Computer Store image, you jump to a screen that looks like figure 2-9:

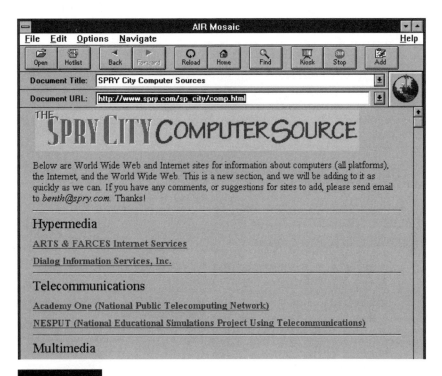

**FIGURE 2-9**

And from here, if you click on ART & FARCES Internet Services, for example, you jump to the Web site of ART & FARCES Internet Services. The *SPRY City Computer Source* page lists a wide range of services and information resources, from Internet tools to archives of graphics files.

Other categories of resources listed in *SPRY City* are arranged by the categories that appear in the image map on the welcome page:

- Art Museum: Exhibits from, and information about, a number of museums around the world, plus connections to Web sites featuring humor and comics, literature, film, and other areas of creative work.
- Travel Agent: Information about cities and regions you might be planning to visit.

- School House: Information about education and science; Web sites for various colleges, universities, and libraries and their programs.
- Business Center: Business information and resources, including stock market quotes, legal resources, and some corporate Web sites.
- City Hall: A link to the Web site of the White House in Washington, D.C., plus connections to the U.S. Small Business Administration's Web site, the Web sites of Her Majesty's Treasury (United Kingdom) and the Singapore Ministry of Education, plus various other national and international government sites.
- Sporting Goods: Information, equipment, and resources for a variety of sports and recreational activities, from mountain climbing to horse racing and from juggling to aviation.

*SPRY City* joins a growing trend of Web resource guides that help to organize some of the vast contents existing on the Internet.


## Some Additional Points of Interest

We can't show you everything—what do you expect on a threepenny tour?—but we do want to mention a few more Web projects we think are particularly interesting:

- Project Gutenberg is a long-term, collaborative effort as ambitious as its name. Contributors from a number of universities are endeavoring to publish as many great literary classics as their energy and resources will support. Access locations are in flux as we write, but try connecting through O'Reilly and Associates' Global Network Navigator (GNN) at `http://gnn.com/gnn/wic/lit.07.html`.
- MARVEL (U.S. Library of Congress) stands for Machine-Assisted Realization of the Virtual Electronic Library. The name doesn't even begin to describe the scope of services and information brought to you by the biggest library in the western hemisphere. Connect to it at `gopher://marvel.loc.gov`.
- CancerNet, the Web site of the National Cancer Institute (NCI)'s Information Center, offers medically accurate and up-to-date information about many forms of cancer. You can browse NCI's Physician Data Query system and read fact sheets on cancer-related topics. This Web site offers access to a particularly valuable set of informational materials on breast cancer. Its connecting point is `http://biomed.nus.sg/Cancer/welcome.html`.
- *Centre de Données Astronomiques de Strasbourg* (CDS), the Strasbourg Astronomical Data Center in France, offers a Web site dedicated to the

collection and distribution of astronomical data. Via the CDS Web site, you can gain access to SIMBAD, the world-reference database for the identification of astronomical objects, and various other astronomy information. You can read the contents in French, English, German, Spanish, or Italian. The CDS home page is at `http://cdsweb.u-strasbg.fr/CDS.html`.

## SOME COMMERCIAL USES OF THE WORLD WIDE WEB

The business community, by and large, remained unenthusiastic about the Internet until the value of utilizing World Wide Web technology became apparent. 1994 was the year that saw companies large and small begin jumping onto the Web in increasing numbers. Their eagerness to carve out a space on the Web has spawned yet another sub-industry of the computer world, companies that specialize in creating Web sites and providing server facilities.

We're going to take a close look at what three companies are doing with their dedicated Web sites, and then mention several additional interesting examples. We admit that our choices for this survey are arbitrary; there are so many examples that, as they say, you could write a book about it.

## SPRY Inc.

SPRY is a software company that specializes in Internet applications and services. The company uses its Web site to market its software, which it is equipped to do directly over the Internet, and to provide support services for its products. SPRY also posts announcements about employment opportunities, as well as press releases and other corporate news. The *SPRY City* pages, as we mentioned earlier, are a courtesy feature that serves as a directory to hundreds of other locations on the World Wide Web. You can find SPRY's Web site at `http://www.spry.com`.

SPRY's welcome page (figure 2-10) packs a lot of connecting points onto one screen. The banner graphic at the top contains image-mapped hot spots that link to the company's major product lines, Internet In A Box, AIR Series 3.0, and AIR Mosaic Express. The "What's New" section, which is updated frequently, connects to current corporate announcements and press releases. Farther down the page, a navigational graphic contains links to general information about the company, the *SPRY City* listings, and product support information.

---

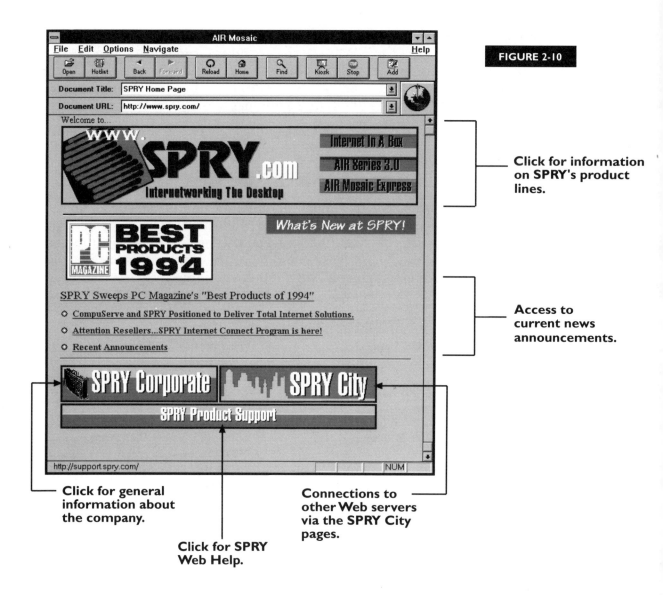

FIGURE 2-10

Click for information on SPRY's product lines.

Access to current news announcements.

Click for general information about the company.

Click for SPRY Web Help.

Connections to other Web servers via the SPRY City pages.

If you click on the SPRY Product Support graphic while viewing this page in your browser, you open a page that looks like figure 2-11. The SPRY Web Help page is an on-line help system that you access over the Internet. To get specific information, you can click on one of the hot graphics or text lines in the middle of the screen, or you can instead activate a topic search by entering a keyword in a text box lower on the page.

As you might expect of an Internet software company, SPRY makes excellent use of Web technology to market and support its products.

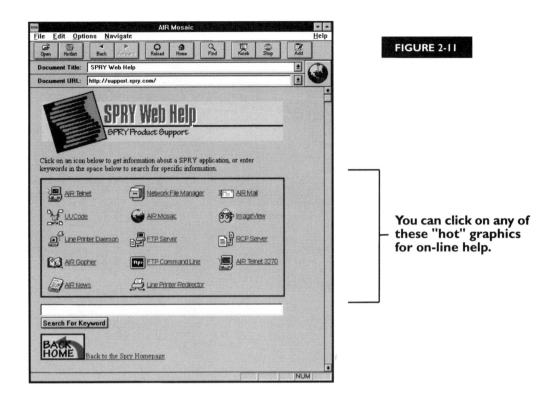

FIGURE 2-11

You can click on any of these "hot" graphics for on-line help.

## Dealernet: The Virtual Showroom

DealerNet® is what we might call a virtual consortium of auto dealerships. It is a network of auto dealers that began as the Web site of one actual auto dealership in suburban Seattle and expanded to include dealers elsewhere in the United States. DealerNet is located at `http://www.dealernet.com`.

The opening page (figure 2-12) gives a brief introduction to DealerNet, plus access to the various products and services offered. The large graphic is an image map, and the smaller images within it link to pages describing the products and services. If you click on the Dealers image, for example, you bring up information about the individual dealers who are represented in DealerNet. Notice that one of the product lines includes boats and recreational vehicles—DealerNet is not only about cars.

Other links take you to information about parts and accessories (some of which are available via an on-line order form), as well as "related services" (loans and insurance). The AutoWorld topic contains information about the automobile industry, its past and future.

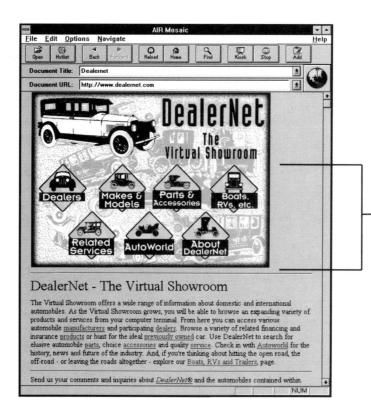

FIGURE 2-12

Small graphics link to subtopics describing products and services.

If you click on the Makes & Models image while viewing this page in your browser, you open a screen that looks like figure 2-13. At the time of this writing, DealerNet is only beginning to develop, and the familiar manufacturer symbols shown in figure 2-13 represent only a few of the lines likely to be represented. In any case, if you click on the Volvo symbol, you see a screen like that shown in figure 2-14, presented by Rood Nissan/Volvo of Lynnwood, Washington.

From this screen, you can specify Volvo models from either the 850 Series or the 900 Series for a closer look. Related screens contain photos of the car models, manufacturer's suggested list price, warranty information, and other data. Rood Nissan/Volvo adds a series of map graphics that show where the dealership is geographically located—in the world, in the United States, and in the Seattle area.

DealerNet's innovative Web site provides a good example of how to publish a commercial message on the Internet. The message is different

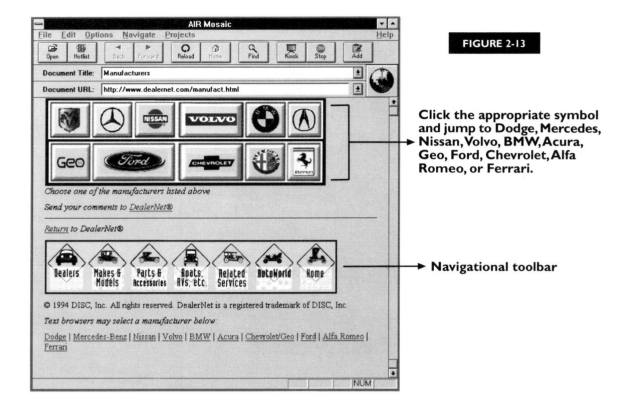

FIGURE 2-13

Click the appropriate symbol and jump to Dodge, Mercedes, Nissan, Volvo, BMW, Acura, Geo, Ford, Chevrolet, Alfa Romeo, or Ferrari.

Navigational toolbar

from conventional advertisements. It is designed to give the reader a fair amount of information about the various companies' products—but only as much information as the reader wishes to see. By placing their content on the Internet in a tasteful, unobtrusive way, the businesses participating in DealerNet mean to show their respect for the Net's special culture, which derives from its noncommercial origins and the sensitivity of many users about commercialism on the Net (more on this in chapter 3).

## Free Range Media, Inc.

Free Range Media, Inc., is an Internet publishing company whose major focus is on creating Web sites for commercial and noncommercial customers. Not surprisingly, the company has its own Web site, located at `http://www.freerange.com`. (See figure 2-15.)

Free Range uses its Web site for the usual business functions—demonstrating and marketing its products and services, posting press

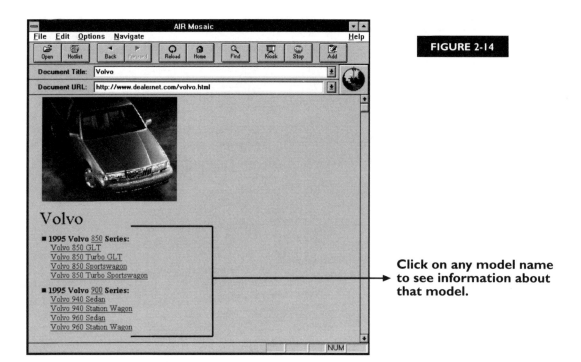

FIGURE 2-14

Click on any model name to see information about that model.

releases and other company announcements, and advertising job openings—but the site also serves other purposes. Its "WWW Adventures" page (shown in figure 2-16) links to several sections that provide general- or special-interest services to Web users.

The "500 Channels" section, like *SPRY City,* offers readers a directory of other interesting Web sites, in this case arranged alphabetically rather than by subject categories. The "Open Mike" section serves as a forum for readers to post comments and carry on discussions.

Two other sections make Free Range's Web site particularly interesting. "Arts & Crafts," under development as of this writing, will be an outlet for craftspeople to exhibit some of their work, beginning with an origami exhibit ("Live to fold, fold to live!"). "Stories and Tales" is a showcase for hypermedia artists who make use of HTML in creative works that blend text, graphics, sound, and video presentations. Some of the current links in this section are to the "Fractured Hypertales" described earlier in this chapter.

Thus, Free Range Media uses its Web site as a kind of hybrid, supplementing its commercial presentation by devoting some of its server space to creative work and Internet community activities.

FIGURE 2-15

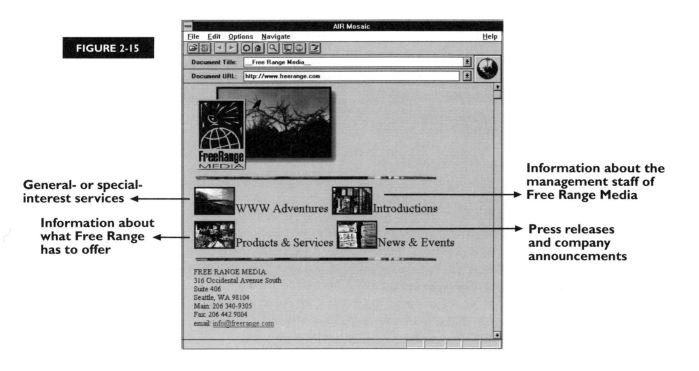

General- or special-interest services ←

Information about what Free Range has to offer ←

Information about the management staff of Free Range Media →

Press releases and company announcements →

FIGURE 2-16

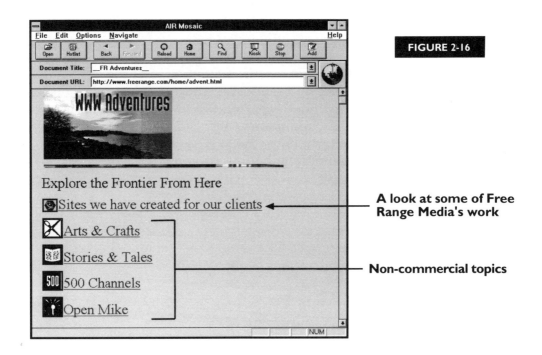

A look at some of Free Range Media's work

Non-commercial topics

## A Few More Examples

Again, we want to mention a handful of additional Web sites, drawn arbitrarily from the wide world of the World Wide Web:

- *Time* magazine on-line. At `http://pathfinder.com`, you can gain access to the venerable newsmagazine's on-line services. There's a daily headline news listing, for example, in addition to *TIME World Wide,* both of which offer up-to-date (and sometimes up-to-the-hour) news stories as they break.
- Online BookStore (OBS), at `http://marketplace.com/0/obs/obshome.html`, markets both electronic books and conventionally printed books. OBS is also involved in electronic publishing and offers consulting and training on Internet publishing.
- DeLorme Mapping, at `http://www.delorme.com`, is a map publisher, as well as a producer of mapping software and databases. DeLorme's samples of electronic maps are worth checking out, particularly the series of maps focusing on recent news events.
- Mountain Travel*Sobek, the Adventure Company, accessible through GNN at `http://gnn.com/gnn/bus/sobek/index.html`, is a travel firm specializing in outdoor experiences. Want to find out about opportunities for trekking in Nepal, or river rafting on the Zambesi? Check out the offerings of Mountain Travel*Sobek.

## HOME PORT

We've reached the end of our threepenny tour of the World Wide Web as we began it, on an exotic note. Bet you never thought you could travel around the world without experiencing jet lag. We've shown you some of the ways institutions, companies, and individuals have made creative use of the hypermedia technology the Web is based on. We hope you've found in this little tour something that inspires you to create your own materials.

# 3  The World Wide Web:

## Size, Popularity, and Potential

Companies and individuals are breaking new ground every day, discovering ever more creative ways to present their messages on the Web. And yet, the potential for combining graphics, text, sound, and video is still in its infancy. Where is it all going?

## THE MASS OF THE MEDIUM

In 1994, Matthew Gray, a student at the Massachusetts Institute of Technology (MIT), began measuring the size and growth of the Web. He used the World Wide Web Wanderer, a tool he designed, as well as other methods of tracking, counting, and estimating. His conclusion: "Wow, the Web is BIG!"

Now, this isn't a very precise statistic, as Mr. Gray would be quick to acknowledge. He and others have supplemented this evaluation with a variety of more concrete statistics, published at the MIT Web site and elsewhere on the Net. They have measured the traffic on the Web (in number of bytes transferred over a specified period of time), counted the number of Web sites, and estimated the number of Internet users.

The results clearly point to a tremendous and continually accelerating growth. Consider, for example, the following data coming out of Gray's research, bearing in mind that the Web was born in 1990:

- In June 1993, there were approximately 130 Web sites in operation around the world. By October 1994, Gray had compiled a list of more than 4,000—and was struggling to keep up with the numbers. By the end of 1994, his count of the total was as high as 12,000 Web sites.

❏ By September 1994, as much traffic was flowing on the Web every 15 minutes as the total traffic in the year 1992.

If you're interested in seeing the latest available data, we recommend that you look it up on the Net. Matthew Gray periodically updates his statistics and posts them at `http://www.netgen.com/info/growth.html`.

---

### How big is BIG?

Do you like really big numbers? Here are some, from Matthew Gray's data on World Wide Web traffic in 1994:

❏ 10 gigabytes (that is, 10 billion bytes) total for one day in May
❏ 13 gigabytes over the course of a six-hour period in September
❏ 50 gigabytes total for one day in November

How much is 50 gigabytes? We know in theory what that number means, but we cannot conceive of that many *anythings* in our physical reality. Here is what the number looks like written out in all its many-ciphered glory: 50,000,000,000.

Do you like arcane calculations? If you start counting aloud by 100s and don't stop until you reach 50,000,000,000, we predict you will be counting for 11½ years. This assumes, of course, that you count steadily while you're eating, drinking, sleeping, and sucking throat lozenges.

---

Bytes of data are pretty abstract. You might well ask, How many *people* are we talking about?

That's much harder to count. It's possible to tally the number of "hits" (connections) to a given Web site, but it's not possible—at least, not yet possible—to know precisely how many individuals are making such hits throughout the intricate Web network. Educated guesses, however, are always being made. By the third quarter of 1994, one set of figures commonly used to estimate the user base of the entire Internet (including the Web) was 20 to 30 million people with a growth rate of 10% to 20% per month. An even more tantalizing figure, for those of us who love big numbers, was offered as a projection in 1993 by Vinton Cerf, President of the Internet Society. In testimony before the U.S. House of Representatives,

Committee on Science, Space and Technology, on March 23, 1993, Cerf predicted 100 million Internet users in the foreseeable future.

These figures have been widely debated, as there is no Nielson rating or its equivalent for the Internet. However, there can be no doubt that the real numbers are in the tens of millions and growing. As the more user-friendly browsers and other graphical applications spread, the proportion of Internet users who are specifically dialing in to the World Wide Web increases.

Whatever the actual size of the Web at this moment, the growth of this very young medium has been phenomenal. In 1995, it seems that everyone is jumping on the bandwidth-wagon. Internet access is now available through CompuServe, America Online, Delphi, and other commercial on-line services. IBM and Microsoft are bundling graphical Internet software into their new operating systems. Internet access is also possible from your Macintosh and through NeXt. This means that more and more people are acquiring the means to a graphical Internet connection—it's definitely not just for UNIX users any more! So if you're still wondering how big your potential publishing audience is, it is, in Matthew Gray's well-chosen word, BIG.

## CONTENT GROWTH VS. AUDIENCE GROWTH: WHO'S TUNING IN TO WHAT?

Along with the growth in the Web audience and traffic, there has of course been an equal growth in content materials and interactive applications. The explosion in number of Web sites tells us that more and more materials are being posted. The result is that, while the Web audience is burgeoning, the competition for that audience is heating up as well.

There's so much to see, so much to experience, that no two Internet-cruising experiences today are likely to be the same. The only time there's a heavy concentration of viewers on one site is when the site is so strikingly unusual, or the sponsor so large, that it's hard to miss. Thus long before the advent of those much-ballyhooed 500 television channels, the World Wide Web is giving its audiences a staggering array of choices.

Should this discourage you? No, but there is a lesson to be learned if you are going to publish successfully on the Web. You've got to contour your presentation so that it's finished, focused, and located at a Web site that's accessible to your ideal audience.

## INFORMATION COMMUNITIES

The key to reaching your ideal audience is in the concept of the *information community*. As amazing as the Internet is, it's important to keep in mind that it is only a platform—a delivery system—just as broadcast and print are platforms. The power of the mass media lies in the existence of information communities. The TV audience watching Monday night football and the readership of the *New York Times* are large groups of people who are drawn into communities by the medium of their preference. So too with the potential of the Internet and the World Wide Web: communities are developing around types of information that bind people in shared purposes.

Take, for example, World Cup USA '94. This monumental soccer tournament was both a sports event and an electronic event. As national teams from around the world vied for the title, a huge, global audience watched and listened in stadiums, on radio, and on television. And did you know that many fans also followed the games via the Internet? There was a Web site for the World Cup, offering an up-to-the-minute reporting service on the games. The World Cup Web site was a model of instantaneous reportage, covering all games that were being played at the moment, whether in Los Angeles, Chicago, or any other venue. Current statistics enriched the coverage, and richly colored graphics gave life to the display.

FIGURE 3-1

**The global community brought together by the World Cup USA '94 included the players, of course, as well as the fans who saw the games first-hand....**

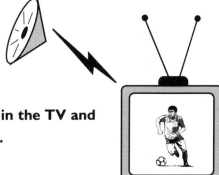

**...tens of millions in the TV and radio audiences....**

**...and thousands of Internet users checking the scores from the World Cup USA '94 Web site.**

Here was an enormous global community, hundreds of millions strong, with their collective attention focused on one series of events. They were "gathered together" not by being all in the same place (although, to be sure, the individual stadiums where the games were played were filled); by far the larger number were gathered *electronically*—in front of television sets, radios, and computer screens.

We'll have a lot more to say about information communities in Part Two. Hold this thought for now: Information communities are the future of Internet communication.

## CONTENT AND COMPETITION

Today, private businesses and public companies are drawn onto the World Wide Web by the potential for immediate and direct transactions.

A number of business models have been implemented for the Net. In chapter 2, we saw how DealerNet emerged as a creative way for car dealers to attract customers, and software companies such as SPRY offer sales and technical service from their Web sites. Two more examples are the Home Shopping Network, which has purchased Internet Shopping Network, and Warner Books, the publisher of this book, which has taken to the Web as a way of adapting its content to the cutting edge and attracting customers. Hundreds of companies are scrambling for creative ways of getting onto the Web and turning their Web sites into new revenue streams.

### Commercial Use of the Internet: A Sensitive Issue

There is a controversy within the broad Internet community about the use of this powerful platform for commercial purposes. Some may even object to the fact that we're discussing commercial publishing on the Net. The fact is, however, that commercial organizations have a right to be on the Net.

That having been said, it is important for every commercial organization to bear in mind the Internet's unique environment. If you use the Internet as a marketing medium, you should be prepared to respect the Net's special culture. Your potential audience consists of people who consider the Internet to be *theirs*. They are on the Net because they want to be a part of the information exchange, and many of them are aware that the Net had its origins in public, not commercial, institutions. Some Net users may not wish to see commercially oriented content at all and will resent it if it pops up on their screens. Advertisers and sponsoring agents must be sensitive to this special environment or risk audience backlash.

This doesn't mean the Net is off-limits to advertising, solicitation, and other commercial activities. Indeed, a growing number of Net users are finding the commercial information—and liking it. Commercial information needs to be offered to the Internet audience in a way that is tasteful, engaging, and unintrusive. If you want people to see your information, put out the welcome mat and ask them in, but don't go knocking on their doors. "In your face" advertising does not belong on the Net.

This point has been emphasized by some important players in the mass-media markets. Internet etiquette has been discussed in *Advertising Age,* the *Wall Street Journal,* and other business-oriented publications. Steve Case, of America Online, has suggested that "advertising" as we know it in the conventional media sense may not be the right model for commercial messages on the Internet. Case and many others believe there is a place for marketing on the Net, but its forms and messages need to be carefully designed to suit the unique culture of the Net and the Web. Little by little, a code of correct practices is growing up for marketing over the Net. It's a positive step toward realizing the full benefit of the Internet for everybody's profit.

## EXPRESSING YOURSELF THROUGH THE WEB

What if your publishing goals are noncommercial? Can you achieve them on the Web?

Absolutely.

Although the Web is a great medium for commercial publication, remember that it was originally conceived as a not-for-profit means for exchanging scientific information, and a wide-ranging excursion on the Web today will reveal a truly "world-wide" scope of topics and interests.

Somewhere in there, there's the perfect place for your material. Whether it's intelligent discourse or creative foolishness; whether your interests lie in gardening, model trains, theology, mythology, astrology, epidemiology, or . . . you name it—we think you get the picture. Your ability to profit by publishing on the World Wide Net is as great as your imagination.

The key to unlocking the possibilities lies in understanding the nature of the Web, learning how to prepare your content, and planning your strategy for reaching out to and maintaining the right information community. These are the topics we'll explore in Part Two.

# PART TWO

# PUBLISHING ON THE WORLD WIDE WEB

If you've read Part One of this book, you've had a chance to learn the basic facts about the Internet and the World Wide Web. You've also taken a glance at what several existing Web sites look like. Now it's time to get to work.

Part Two provides all you need to know to produce attractive, well-crafted documents and put them out on the Web. Think of this section as a primer on Web publishing. You'll learn how to format your text, how to use hypertext codes to structure your documents for interactive use, and how to add graphics. You'll also learn some of the elements of style, structure, and etiquette. And finally, you'll read about ways of reaching your optimum audience by working with the concept of information communities.

## HARDWARE AND SOFTWARE REQUIREMENTS

To publish on the World Wide Web, you'll need a computer with network access and the appropriate software.

### Computer and Network Access

You can use almost any good-quality personal computer or work-station that runs its programs on a recent version of the Windows, UNIX, Macintosh, or OS/2 platform. Any of these operating sytems can be configured with the appropriate software to communicate with Web servers. As with all other aspects of computing, the better your equipment, the faster and more efficient will be your Net connections—but this doesn't mean you need to pawn your furniture to buy a new computer. An IBM-compatible personal computer with an 80386 coprocessor or better, or a Macintosh of similar power, will do the job.

As for connecting hardware, there are two basic routes to the Internet. If you work for an organization whose network is connected to the Internet, great; you don't need a modem, although you may have to contact your system administrator about setting up an Internet account. Once that's done, you're connected via your institutional network.

If you're going to be cruising the Internet solo—that is, without benefit of an institutional network connection—you'll need to connect via a modem and telephone line to a service provider. We strongly recommend a high-speed modem, one that runs at 14,400 baud or faster. Although you can use a slower modem, you'll be able to transfer files over the World Wide Web with much greater alacrity if you use a higher-speed modem. Prices have been steadily declining in recent years, so a new modem won't cost you an arm and a leg; the investment will pay off by saving you time and frustration.

Even with a high-speed modem, you will find that access to large HTML files over a conventional analog telephone line is slow compared with using files on your own hard disk or a local area network (LAN). It's slow compared with access via most institutional lines, too. Something better is just on the horizon: fiber-optic networks and integrated services digital network (ISDN) lines which, when available, will substantially improve file transfer. By late 1994, ISDN lines were being marketed on a limited basis in a few regions of the United States. The technology will undoubtedly spread to meet the demand for Internet services, so if an ISDN line is not yet available to you, be patient; it will come soon. In the meantime, you can do well enough with a standard telephone line.

## Software

The software you need includes a word processor and a browser. Any standard word processor will work for creating hypertext documents, as long as the program is capable of saving files in text (ASCII) format. Also, any browser software that reads hypertext documents—this includes Mosaic, Netscape, Cello, WinWeb, MacWeb, Quadralay GHWIS, and others—will enable you to view your work as your Internet readers will eventually see it.

In addition, there are several products available that help to automate the process of building HTML (Hypertext Markup Language) into your documents. Add-on tools are now available for WordPerfect and Microsoft Word for Windows, for example. Besides these add-ons, there are complete products available that are specifically designed for creating HTML documents. Commercially available examples include HoTMetaL Pro and CyberLeaf. Other programs are available as freeware or shareware on the Internet. You can find a list by using your browser to go to

`http://www11.w3.org/hypertext/WWW/Tools.`

If you have one of these special software tools, you may find it helpful in creating hypertext documents, but if you don't have one, you will not be at a significant disadvantage.

## WHAT'S IN PART TWO

4. **HTML: Building Hypertext.** How to use the code language of hypertext for building the textual elements of Web documents.
5. **Anchors: Weaving the Web by Building Links.** How to create links to connect topics, both within a document and across documents.
6. **Illustration, Decoration, and Navigation: Using Graphics and Other Media.** How to use graphical images in your documents for illustrative, decorative, and navigational purposes.
7. **Style and Process: Maintaining Consistency in Your Documents.** How to maintain consistency and logic within your documents, and how to respect and perpetuate the special culture of the Internet.
8. **Information Communities: Reaching and Sustaining Your Audience.** How to identify the audience you want to attract to your Internet publications, and how to locate and position your content so that your ideal audience finds it.

Okay, are you ready? Let's get to work!

# 4

# HTML:

## Building Hypertext

In chapter 1, we discussed the nature of hypertext and its crucial function in building documents for the World Wide Web. In this chapter, we focus on HTML, the codes that mark text for conversion to hypertext. When you create a document containing HTML codes, you are in effect preparing it to comply with the Hypertext Transfer Protocol, or HTTP—the specific protocol that governs the transport of files over the Web. HTML code makes it possible for your documents to be displayed similarly across different platforms (Windows, UNIX, Macintosh, OS/2, etc.) wherever in the world your files travel.

As we said in chapter 1, you don't need to know how the transport protocol, HTTP, works; however, you do have to know how to use the markup language, HTML, to code your Web documents. This chapter describes how to use the basic codes for identifying and formatting text elements in a document. Subsequent chapters will discuss how to add *anchors,* which you use to link elements within and across documents, and *graphics,* which you use to illustrate, navigate, and add visual appeal.

## HTML: WHAT IT IS

HTML stands for *Hypertext Markup Language.* It is a set of codes that you insert to identify the different parts of your document, specify the appearance of text, and create links between related topics. For example, there is one set of codes for identifying your document's title, another for specifying italic or bold formatting, and another for formatting a numbered or bulleted list. And there are many others.

## HTML, unabridged

If you want to consult the complete specification for HTML, it is available on-line at http://info.cern.ch/hypertext/WWW/MarkUp/HTML.html. This "spec" lists the codes that comply with the standards of the International Standards Organization (ISO). That means the codes are recognized around the world so that, for example, if you designate text as a heading, it will be displayed as a heading by HTTP-compliant software everywhere. The spec was written by Tim Berners-Lee, the original developer of HTTP and the World Wide Web, together with Dan Connolly and Karen Olson Muldrow.

We recommend that you download this valuable resource from the Net and keep it available as a reference. The HTML spec is a work in progress that undergoes frequent revision, so having on-line access to it is better than having a hard-copy publication. You can, of course, print your own copy of the current version and update it as the on-line version changes.

For another valuable resource that is closely derived from the CERN spec referenced above, see http://www.ncsa.uiuc.edu/General/Internet/WWW/HTMLPrimer.html.

The two text samples in figure 4-1 illustrate a few of the codes that constitute HTML.

| Text without HTML codes | Text including HTML codes |
|---|---|
| Publishing Snazzy Stuff<br><br>Do you want to give your Web documents pizzazz? Do you want your audience to remember your content and be itching to return to your Web site? Then you need to master the art of using the Hypertext Markup Language (HTML). HTML will turn boring, everyday text into eye-catching, readable text that makes it easy for your audience to catch your message. | <html><head><br><title>Publishing Snazzy Stuff</title><br></head><br><body><br><h1>Publishing Snazzy Stuff</h1><br><p>Do you want to give your Internet documents <b>pizzazz?</b> Do you want your audience to remember your content and be itching to return to your Web site? Then you need to master the art of using the <i>Hypertext Markup Language (HTML).</i> HTML will turn boring, everyday text into eye-catching, readable text that makes it easy for your audience to catch your message.<br></body><br></html> |

FIGURE 4-1

Note that the text sample on the right shows markup codes, but not the visual effects of the codes. This is "raw" HTML text, as it looks while you are creating a document. To see how the codes affect the text, you have to view the finished document through a browser. Just by looking at the sample on the right in figure 4-1, however, you might be able to guess what some of the codes mean: <title> denotes the beginning of a document's title, <b> marks boldface text, and so on. We'll discuss the specific codes used in this illustration, as well as others, later in this chapter.

If you've ever worked with SGML, the *Standard General Markup Language* used for coding document files destined for print publication, you'll recognize the logic of HTML codes. HTML is in fact a subset of SGML codes, with its own *document type definition (DTD);* that is, by placing HTML codes in a document, you define that document as a hypertext document. The presence of HTML codes means the document can be transported over the Internet under the Hypertext Transport Protocol (HTTP), and read with a browser.

---

### HTML, HTTP, and the Web

HTML, the set of codes you use in creating hypertext documents, is the language of HTTP, the transfer protocol that moves hypertext files around the Web. As important as HTTP is, it is only one of the protocols supported by the World Wide Web project. The Web is a complex of protocols moving files of different sorts, containing different kinds of information. FTP (file transfer protocol) is another of the protocols. Separate additional protocols transport newsgroups, electronic mail (e-mail), and whois (a directory of people who have authority over any part of the Internet). All of these protocols, intertwined in a collaborative movement of files and information, are what make up that intricate phenomenon known as the World Wide Web.

---

As we mentioned in chapter 1, a Web server sends a document to its clients with HTML codes embedded in it. The browser translates these codes into interactive forms on the computer screen, with text and graphics, and sometimes sound and video images. Thus, the HTML codes tell the client software how to lay out and structure the document, and how to display the various elements within it—headings and body text, character formats, graphics, and other elements.

**The file name extension** .html (.htm). It's important for you to know that HTML files must be given file names with the extension .html or `.htm`. These extensions are comparable to some you may be familiar with from word processors, for example `.doc`, `.wpf`, `.txt`, or `.wps`, which are added to files automatically. If you are using special HTML software such as HoTMetaL Pro or CyberLeaf, the appropriate `.html` or `.htm` extension will also be added to your file names automatically. However, if you are creating the files with a non-HTML word processor, you have to be sure to add `.html` or `.htm` to an HTML file name manually the first time you save it.

Which do you use, `.html` or `.htm`? If you work with DOS, Windows, or any other operating system that restricts file extensions to three characters, use `.htm`; if you work with UNIX, Macintosh, OS/2 (HPFS format), or any other system that supports file extensions longer than three characters, use `.html`. These extensions tag the files so that HTML software will recognize them.

Examples:

| Operating system | File name |
|---|---|
| DOS, Windows (pre-Windows 95), OS/2 (FAT format) | `bouillab.htm` |
| Windows 95 | `bouillabaisse.htm` |
| UNIX, Macintosh, OS/2 (HPFS format) | `bouillabaisse.html` |

You'll notice that the file name used in the DOS, Windows, and OS/2 (FAT) example above conforms to the traditional eight-character limit (`bouillab`). If you're running a later version of OS/2 or Windows 95, you can give your file a name as long as you please (well, up to the new limits—256 characters for Windows 95; or 254 characters, including the extension, for OS/2). Under Windows 95, you still have to limit the extension to three characters. Thus, in Windows, you could name this file

---

**N O T E** File names are case-sensitive. This is because a great many Internet servers are based on UNIX, which treats file names with case sensitivity. You can type a file name in either upper or lower case, or you can mix the cases, but remember that if you do, you and everybody else who ever needs to type the file name must use the exact same upper- and lowercase pattern. It's easy to get mixed up if your cases are mixed, so it's generally wise to settle on one pattern— all lowercase or all uppercase—and be consistent.

french_bouillabaisse_in_a_pot.htm, if that suits your fancy; in OS/2, it would be french_bouillabaisse_in_a_pot.html.

## STARTING POINTS

So much for abstractions. Let's roll up our sleeves and begin.

### Software

Begin where? On your own computer, using a program you feel comfortable with. You can write HTML code using almost any standard text-editing program—Windows Notebook, Microsoft Word (for Windows, MS-DOS, or Macintosh), WordPerfect for Windows, AmiPro, or any other word-processing program that can save your document in text (ASCII) format. You just need to remember two things from the start: First, you do not use the usual formatting features of your word processor (character/font formats or attributes, paragraph or line formats), because these will be marked by special HTML codes; and second, when you finish, you must be sure to save the document as a text (ASCII) file and give it a file name with an .html or .htm extension.

### If You Have Special SGML or HTML Software

As we mentioned in the introduction to Part Two, you can use one of the relatively new software applications now available for creating HTML: CyberLeaf, HoTMetaL Pro, or any of the applications obtainable via the Internet. If your customary word processor is WordPerfect, you can use the SGML add-on called Intellitag. If you use Word for Windows, try Microsoft Internet Assistant. You might find that these editing programs lighten the task of applying the HTML codes.

There are some advantages to using a specific HTML-building software like HoTMetaL Pro or CyberLeaf. One is that you won't have to repair typographical errors within the code elements, because you command the software to insert the elements without your having to type them character by character. Another is that you can view images, tables, and other such features graphically as you build your documents.

You will notice that the instructions in the rest of this chapter are aimed at the person who uses a standard word processor. If you use special HTML software, you should still read along; some of what you read will not precisely match the steps you take, because your HTML-building software does a part of the work. However, it's a good idea for you to learn the basic HTML constructs that we explain here, for two reasons. First, as we show the codes, we also explain exactly what they mean and how you use the elements they create—elements that your HTML software also creates. You need to understand these elements and how they work in your documents. Second, the "raw" codes will exist in your HTML document as we describe them, whether you type them in manually or insert them. You will see them in your browser when you view the source code for your documents, and you will want to know exactly what the codes mean.

### If You Don't Have Special SGML or HTML Software

If you do not have a special SGML or HTML software tool, don't despair. Manually building the HTML documents you need for publishing on the Web is not at all hard. In fact, you might prefer the "hands-on" control you have by working with the codes manually. If your word processor supports macros, you can, of course, build in some of your own automating features by creating macros. And you don't have to learn (or buy!) another new software program.

## ANGLE BRACKETS, TAGS, AND SPACING

The first thing you need to understand are three crucial elements in the HTML code set: the use of *angle brackets, tags,* and *spacing.*

### Angle Brackets

In the raw, HTML code elements are *always* enclosed within the characters < and >. (We say "in the raw" because this is how you create the elements when you do it without using special HTML-building software, and this is how you see the elements when you view them in your browser's source code window.) These characters are conventionally known by at least three sets of names: angle brackets, "less than" and "greater than" signs, and single chevrons (single as opposed to double chevrons, which look like « and »). It doesn't matter what you call them, as long as you know that you must use them if you write HTML codes manually. In this book, whenever we have to refer to them by name—which shouldn't be very often—we'll call them angle brackets.

## Tags

Tags mark the beginning and (usually) the end of specially coded text elements—and even the beginning and end of the HTML document itself. At the very beginning of a document, you type an `<html>` start tag, and at the very end of the document, you type an `</html>` end tag.

Notice the difference between these two tag codes: the end tag contains a forward slash (/), but the start tag does not. This is true of all start/end tag pairs. You might think of the slash as the equivalent of the diagonal line in international signs prohibiting or canceling something. Instead of "No Smoking" or "End of 100km Speed Zone," a code containing the HTML slash might mean "End of Bold Format," as in `</b>`, or "End of HTML Document," as in `</html>`.

You use start/end tags with most of the specific codes. All text that falls between the start tag and the end tag is affected by the code you're using. For example, in the following line

```
<title>Publishing Snazzy Stuff</title>
```

the words "Publishing Snazzy Stuff," which fall between the start tag `<title>` and the end tag `</title>`, are the title and will be displayed as title text when the document is read with a browser.

The same principle applies when a set of tags is used to mark one phrase within a longer passage of text:

```
You need to master the art of using the <i>Hypertext
Markup Language (HTML).</i> HTML will turn boring, ev-
eryday text into eye-catching . . .
```

In this example, the phrase "Hypertext Markup Language (HTML)." which is affected by the tags `<i>` and `</i>`, will appear in italics *(italics)* when displayed by a browser. The rest of the text in these two lines will be displayed in regular (non-italic) type.

Not all of the HTML codes require both start and end tags. Those that do will be identified in the following discussion of the codes.

---

**N O T E** Start and end tags are also sometimes called *container codes,* because they contain information that will be acted upon by the browser or server.

---

## Spacing

You may have noticed, in the preceding examples, that HTML codes butt right up against the text they affect. It's important to pay attention to the spacing conventions when you type in the codes, because everything you type, including spaces, will be read by the browser and built into the screen display. In the title line `<title>Publishing Snazzy Stuff </title>`, for example, there is no space between the title codes and the title text. If you were to type a space after `<title>`, as in `<title> Publishing Snazzy Stuff</title>`, then the browser would add that space when it displays your document—and the title would not be flush left on the line (assuming that's where the browser ordinarily displays it).

Correspondingly, in places where you *want* a space, you have to make sure you type it in. Let's look again at the two sample lines we used earlier:

```
You need to master the art of using the <i>Hypertext
Markup Language (HTML).</i> HTML will turn boring, ev-
eryday text into eye-catching . . .
```

Notice that there is a space before the code `<i>` and again after `</i>`. If you were to leave those spaces out, your text would run together when it is displayed, as in:

```
. . . theHypertext . . .
```

In figure 4-1, you might also have noticed that some of the codes, for example `<head>` and `<body>`, start on new paragraph lines. Technically, it doesn't matter whether you start a code on a new paragraph line or not; browsers read only the text codes, not paragraph keystrokes. If you want to, you can run an entire document together, because the codes themselves tell the browser where to start new paragraphs. Thus, you could type the text in figure 4-1 like this:

```
<html><head><title>Publishing Snazzy Stuff</title></
head><body><p>Do you want to give your Internet
documents <b>pizzazz?</b> Do you want your audience to
remember your content and be itching to return to your
Web site? Then you need to master the art of using the
<i>Hypertext Markup Language (HTML).</i>. HTML will
turn boring, everyday text into eye-catching,
readable text that makes it easy for your audience to
catch your message.</body></html>
```

Obviously, typing your document like this will make it very hard to see its structure and even harder to visualize what the document will look like when viewed with a browser.

Typing certain code elements on new paragraph lines, therefore, is one way to help yourself see the layout of your document while you're creating it. Just as importantly, it means that you can more easily maintain and troubleshoot your document—and, of course, it also means that anyone else who needs to work with the document will have an easier time of it. We don't have any specific rules to offer about where to type in the paragraph lines; use your own visual sense about which elements should start new paragraphs and which should not. And bear in mind that you, and possibly others, will need to understand the layout clearly, both while the document is under construction and after it is completed.

If you've never worked with a markup code before, seeing it in your document may take some getting used to; your text will look strange and unnatural, and you may make a few typographical mistakes on your first attempts. But you'll soon get accustomed to it.

## THE BASIC HTML TEXT CODES

There are quite a number of codes for use in HTML documents. We're not going to discuss all of them in detail; as we've indicated, HTML is a living code system that undergoes frequent revision, and your best source of information for the complete code set will always be the on-line HTML specification (see sidebar "HTML, unabridged," earlier in this chapter). We'll concentrate on the codes that you're most likely to need for creating your Web documents.

We can break the HTML text codes down into three general types:

- Block codes
- Font codes
- List codes

Let's examine the most important specific codes within each of these type categories. Then we'll discuss one further type of code you'll probably find useful: comment tags.

## Block Codes

You use block codes to identify blocks of text that represent specific structural elements of your document, for example the title and the body text.

---

These codes work to separate the text elements they affect from other text elements, sending a signal to the browser to display the blocks as you intend them—as the title or the body text, that is.

The following illustration shows the main parts of an HTML document as it is viewed through a standard browser:

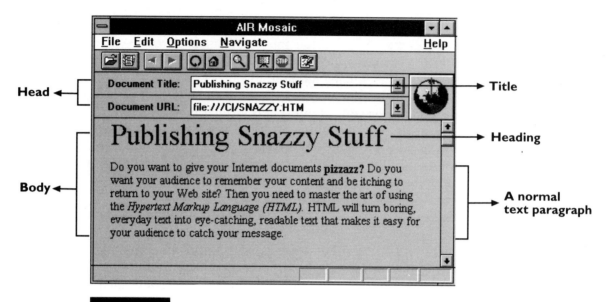

**FIGURE 4-2**

The block codes we're going to discuss are those identifying the HTML document itself; the head, title, and body of a document; addresses; headings, normal text paragraphs, and block quotation paragraphs; line breaks; and horizontal rule. Note that, in each pair of start/end tags, a slash (/) distinguishes the end tag.

| | |
|---|---|
| **\<html>** \</html> | **HTML tags.** \<html> marks the beginning of an HTML document, and \</html> marks the document's end. No text should precede \<html>, and no text should follow \</html>. These tags are required in every HTML document. |
| **\<head>** \</head> | **Head tags.** These tags mark the beginning and end of the head of a document. When viewed with a browser, the head will be displayed at the top of a document, separately from the document's body. The head generally contains the document's title, and it may automatically include other identifying information about the document, such as its URL (uniform resource locator). |

**&lt;title&gt;**
**&lt;/title&gt;**

**Title tags.** These mark the beginning and end of a document's title. There can be only one title for any document, and it must be contained within the document's head. The title cannot contain anchors, paragraph tags, or emphasis tags (such as bold or italic). When viewed with a browser, the title generally occupies the top line of the document's head.

The following example shows a title within the head of an HTML document.

*If you write this:*

```
<html><head>
<title>Sorcery Today</title>
</head>
```

*It will be displayed similar to this:*

| Sorcery Today |
|---|

**&lt;address&gt;**
**&lt;/address&gt;**

**Address tags.** These mark the beginning and end of an address element. The address element may be an actual address, such as the address of a document's author, or it may be only the author's name and title or affiliation. It ordinarily appears at the top or bottom of a document.

Here's an example.

*If you write this:*

```
<address>M. Mandrake<br>
Apprentice Sorcerer<br>
mandrake@witchery.com
</address>
```

*It will be displayed similar to this:*

M. Mandrake
Apprentice Sorcerer
mandrake@witchery.com

NOTE: The &lt;br&gt; code represents a line break. We'll discuss this code in a moment.

**&lt;body&gt;**
**&lt;/body&gt;**

**Body tags.** These mark the beginning and end of the body of an HTML document. The body contains all the information the document is designed to give, including hypertext links to subtopics and other documents. You can include within the body of a document virtually all HTML elements except those reserved for the document's head. Thus, you can include an address, anchors, blockquotes, font codes (boldface, italic), graphics, headings, and normal text paragraphs.

The following is a simple example.

*If you write this:*

```
<body>
<p>Contrary to what many today think,
sorcery did not die with the passing
of the Middle Ages. Of course, many
additional paragraphs would be
needed to prove this argument, but we
must stop here and add the end tags.
</body>
```

*It will be displayed similar to this:*

Contrary to what many today think, sorcery did not die with the passing of the Middle Ages. Of course, many additional paragraphs would be needed to prove this argument, but we must stop here and add the end tags.

NOTE: The &lt;p&gt; code represents a paragraph. We'll discuss this code in a moment.

| | |
|---|---|
| **\<h1\>...\</h1\>** | **Heading tags.** These mark the beginning and end of headings and subheadings. HTML |
| **\<h2\>...\</h2\>** | allows for as many as six levels of headings and subheadings in a document. The num- |
| **\<h3\>...\</h3\>** | bers in the code designate these levels in the obvious way: \<h1\> is the start tag for a |
| **\<h4\>...\</h4\>** | first-level heading, and \</h1\> is its end tag; \<h2\> and \</h2\> mark a second-level head- |
| **\<h5\>...\</h5\>** | ing, and so on. Note that \<h1\> and \</h1\> generally demark the heading that you will |
| **\<h6\>...\</h6\>** | want to use as the first heading in the body of your document—a title line, if you will, |

that is separate from the title that appears in the document's head.

You generally do not insert font codes in headings because the heading formats are determined by the client software that will display the document (the browser). Similarly, you don't need to use paragraph coding to add white space between the heading and the next line of text, as the line spacing will also be determined by the browser. Depending on how the browser is configured, the different heading levels will be distinguished by point size, boldface and/or italics, larger and smaller font sizes, indentation or lack of indentation, and perhaps other such typological qualities.

See the following example.

*If you write this:*

```
<h1>Four Modern Sorcerers</h1>
<p> This is the story of four modern-
day sorcerers, starting with M.
Mandrake.
<h2>M. Mandrake</h2>
<p>M. Mandrake was born in the
province of Capolubreanu, amid
```

*It will be displayed similar to this:*

**Four Modern Sorcerers**

This is the story of four modern-day sorcerers, starting with M. Mandrake.

**M. Mandrake**

M. Mandrake was born in the province of Capolubreanu, amid . . .

| | |
|---|---|
| **\<p\>** | **Paragraph tags.** The \<p\> tag marks the beginning of a normal text paragraph. Every |
| **\</p\>** | new paragraph must begin with a \<p\> tag. The \</p\> tag at the end of the paragraph, |
| (optional) | however, is optional. |

One reason for using the \</p\> end tag is that it makes the paragraph element a container code. This means that you can modify the appearance of a given paragraph to make it flush left, flush right, or centered. This is a new HTML feature that is not fully implemented as of this writing. For information about it, see chapter 11, "The Next Chapter."

As with headings, you don't add white space before or after a paragraph, since that will be done according to the configuration of the browser that reads your document. The same is true of first-line indentation; the browser configuration will determine whether or not paragraphs are indented, and by how much.

See the following example.

*If you write this:*

```
<p>No sensible persons would insert
HTML codes into their everyday
speech, but they sure are useful for
creating hypertext documents.</p>
```

*It will be displayed similar to this:*

No sensible persons would insert HTML codes into their everyday speech, but they sure are useful for creating hypertext documents.

**How to Publish on the Internet**

**&lt;br&gt;**  **Line break.** You use the line break code where you would use a line break keystroke or a newline character (↵) in word processing: when you want to start a new line without starting a new paragraph. Ordinarily, you insert a &lt;br&gt; code at the end of a line within a block of text that is already tagged as a normal paragraph. Lines of poetry often use breaks in this fashion, as in the following example from the *Rubaiyat of Omar Khayyam:*

| *If you write this:* | *It will be displayed similar to this:* |
|---|---|
| &lt;p&gt; Ah, my Belovéd, fill the Cup that clears&lt;br&gt;<br>Today of past Regrets and future Fears:&lt;br&gt;<br>Tomorrow?—Why, Tomorrow I may be&lt;br&gt;<br>Myself with Yesterday's Sev'n thousand Years.&lt;/p&gt; | Ah, my Belovéd, fill the Cup that clears<br>Today of past Regrets and future Fears:<br>Tomorrow?—Why, Tomorrow I may be<br>Myself with Yesterday's Sev'n thousand Years. |

—From *Rubaiyat of Omar Khayyam,* transl. Edward Fitzgerald (New York: Grosset & Dunlap, 1946)

**&lt;blockquote&gt;**  **Block quotation tags.** These tags set off a citation in a separate paragraph. As with
**&lt;/blockquote&gt;** normal paragraphs, the particular display of a blockquote paragraph will be determined by the browser configuration. Typically, it will be left-indented, and possibly also right-indented, and there will be some extra white space above and below the blockquote. See the following example.

| *If you write this:* | *It will be displayed similar to this:* |
|---|---|
| &lt;p&gt;Americans have always been ambivalent about egalitarianism. As Alexis de Tocqueville wrote more than 150 years ago:<br>&lt;blockquote&gt;An American is forever talking of the admirable equality which prevails in the United States: aloud, he makes it the boast of his country, but in secret, he deplores it for himself . . . &lt;/blockquote&gt; | Americans have always been ambivalent about egalitarianism. As Alexis de Tocqueville wrote more than 150 years ago:<br><br>An American is forever talking of the admirable equality which prevails in the United States: aloud, he makes it the boast of his country, but in secret, he deplores it for himself . . . |

—From Tocqueville, *Democracy in America,* ed. R. Hefner (New York: Mentor Books, 1963)

NOTE: If a blockquote comes in the middle of a normal paragraph, you do not need to use the &lt;p&gt; code to tag the continuation of the normal paragraph following the blockquote.

**&lt;hr&gt;**  **Horizontal rule.** This code represents a divider between two text elements—a line or bar, for example. You can use it to draw a distinct boundary between a heading and the text that follows, or between two headings. The particular style and look of a horizontal rule are determined by the browser configuration. The following example illustrates one possibility.

```
<h1>AKC Classifications of Dogs</h1>
<hr>
<h2>Sporting Dogs</h2>
<p>This category of dogs includes
pointers, retrievers, setters, and
spaniels.
```

**AKC Classifications of Dogs**

**Sporting Dogs**
This category of dogs includes pointers, retrievers, setters, and spaniels.

These are the main block codes, which you use to define the basic structural elements of an HTML document. We'll mention them again when we present some tips on using the basic HTML codes, later in this chapter. Let's move on now to the font codes.

## Font Codes

Font codes are codes that change the appearance of text characters. Generally, you use font codes within the body of your content to italicize characters; make them bold; change their color; or give them a fixed-width, or monospace, quality similar to typewriter characters.

When talking about font codes, it is useful to draw a distinction between *logical* and *physical* code types. Logical code types give the browser a general instruction about how to display characters; they mark text for emphasis, or as a title citation, or for special treatment of code samples. The logical types leave it up to the browser configuration as to exactly how the designated text will be displayed—whether to make the characters

### Should you use logical or physical code types?

In most circumstances, it's probably better to use a logical code type when you're specifying font formats. That way, you let your readers' browser configurations decide how to treat the text. This approach lends itself to greater compatibility across computer platforms. More importantly, the logical types are better suited to the numerous different ways users may be configuring their browsers. For example, a user might want to reserve italics for a particular purpose, such as quotations, and prefer to display emphasis in a different color. By using the logical type <em> for emphasis (instead of <i>), you allow the user the freedom to do this.

Of course, the decision is yours. You may have a good reason to prefer the more specific font designations produced by the physical code types, and if so, you can use them.

bold, italic, a different color, or distinct in some other way. In contrast, physical code types instruct the browser to format text specifically as bold-face, italics, or typewriter (monospace) font.

**Logical code types.** The following four codes mark text for general treatment. They tell the browser, in effect, "Give these characters special emphasis," or "Treat these characters as a title (of a book, newspaper, movie, play, etc.)," or "Format these characters in a way that tells the reader they represent literal computer code." When the text is read by a browser, the browser determines how to display the characters on the basis of how it is configured to treat them.

**\<em\>**
**\</em\>**

**Emphasis tags.** These tags mark the beginning and end of general emphasis format. Depending on the configuration of the browser, \<em\> might cause characters to be displayed in italics or, in some cases, a different color from the surrounding text. The following is an example.

*If you write this:*

```
Your Honor, I <em>most emphatically
</em> deny the charges.
```

*It will be displayed like this:*

Your Honor, I *most emphatically* deny the charges.

**\<strong\>**
**\</strong\>**

**Strong tags.** Similar in purpose to \<em\>, \<strong\> tags give typographical emphasis to the text characters affected. Most often, \<strong\> is rendered as bold; in all cases, it is treated differently from \<em\>. The following is an example.

*If you write this:*

```
<strong>Never, ever</strong>
attempt to dash across the freeway
during rush hour!
```

*It will be displayed like this:*

**Never, ever** attempt to dash across the freeway during rush hour!

**\<cite\>**
**\</cite\>**

**Citation tags.** You can use these tags to mark the title of a book, a play, a film, or anything else you are citing. \<cite\> is typically translated into italic format, but the specific character display is again up to the browser configuration. See the following example.

*If you write this:*

```
<cite>Gone with the Wind</cite> and
<cite>The Last of the Mohicans
</cite> are both book titles and
movie titles.
```

*It will be displayed like this:*

*Gone with the Wind* and *The Last of the Mohicans* are both book titles and movie titles.

**\<code\>**
**\</code\>**

**Code tags.** These tags designate text to be displayed in a font appropriate to lines of sample code, typically a monospace font. See the following example.

| *If you write this:* | *It will be displayed like this:* |
|---|---|
| To make contact with the Library of Congress, type the following: `<code>telnet locis.loc.gov</code>` | To make contact with the Library of Congress, type the following: `telnet locis.loc.gov` |

**Physical code types.** The following three codes mark text for specific treatment. They instruct the browser to format text as you prefer to designate the type face—bold, italic, or typewriter (monospace) font.

**\<b\>**
**\</b\>**

**Bold tags.** These tags mark text specifically for display in boldface, as in the following example.

| *If you write this:* | *It will be displayed like this:* |
|---|---|
| Some style guides require that all headings be displayed in bold type, for example `<b>Books by Women Authors</b>`. | Some style guides require that all headings be displayed in bold type, for example **Books by Women Authors**. |

**\<i\>**
**\</i\>**

**Italic tags.** These tags mark text specifically for display in italics, as in the following example.

| *If you write this:* | *It will be displayed like this:* |
|---|---|
| Many style guides require that book titles be displayed in italics, for example `<i>Pride and Prejudice</i>`. | Many style guides require that all book titles be displayed in italics, for example *Pride and Prejudice.* |

**\<tt\>**
**\</tt\>**

**Typewriter font tags.** These tags mark text specifically for display in a fixed-width, typewriter-style font (monospaced). Here's an example.

| *If you write this:* | *It will be displayed like this:* |
|---|---|
| In technical manuals, sample lines of computer code are often printed in a monospace font such as the following: `<tt>Input UserID$, Password$</tt>` | In technical manuals, sample lines of computer code are often printed in a monospace font such as the following: `Input UserID$, Password$` |

## List Codes

We've discussed the main block and font codes. Next we'll look at list codes. You use list codes to format listed text items. The three types of lists we'll cover in this section are:

▫ Unordered lists
▫ Ordered lists
▫ Definition lists

---

**\<ul\>. . .\</ul\>** **Unordered list.** The \<ul\> and \</ul\> tags mark the beginning and end of an unordered
**\<li\>** list. An unordered list contains items that are not numbered or given priority rankings. They may be marked by bullets or not, depending on how the browser is configured to read unordered lists. The \<ul\> start tag must be immediately followed by \<li\> and the first list item. The \<li\> code (for *list item*) marks the beginning of each item in the list.

The following example assumes the browser will add bullets to the items. Note that you do not use an end tag with the \<li\> code.

| *If you write this:* | *It will be displayed like this:* |
|---|---|
| ```<br><ul><br><li> Four and twenty blackbirds<br><li> Three little pigs<br><li> The pied piper of Hamelin<br></ul><br>``` | • Four and twenty blackbirds<br>• Three little pigs<br>• The pied piper of Hamelin |

**\<ol\>. . .\</ol\>** **Ordered list.** \<ol\> and \</ol\> mark the beginning and end of an ordered (numbered)
**\<li\>** list. The items in an ordered list are numbered to denote their sequence or rank. The \<ol\> start tag must be immediately followed by \<li\> and the first list item. As with unordered lists, \<li\> marks the beginning of each item in the list and, again, you do not use an end tag with the \<li\> code.

| *If you write this:* | *It will be displayed like this:* |
|---|---|
| ```<br><ol><br><li> Plug your computer in.<br><li> Turn it on.<br><li> Start your Internet software.<br></ol><br>``` | 1. Plug your computer in.<br>2. Turn it on.<br>3. Start your Internet software. |

**\<dl\>. . .\</dl\>** **Definition list.** \<dl\> and \</dl\> mark the beginning and end of a definition list. Defini-
**\<dt\>** tion lists are formatted in a way that is set up for defining terms. The specific format
**\<dd\>** depends on the browser configuration. The \<dl\> start tag must be immediately followed by \<dt\> and the first term. \<dt\> marks the beginning of each term in the list. Each

---

term must be immediately followed by the <dd> code, marking the beginning of each definition.

| *If you write this:* | *It will be displayed like this:* |
|---|---|
| ```<dl>``` | Dodgers |
| ```<dt>Dodgers<dd>L.A. baseball team.``` |   L.A. baseball team. |
| ```<dt>Brooklyn<dd>Former hometown of``` | Brooklyn |
| ```the Dodgers.``` |   Former hometown of the Dodgers. |
| ```</dl>``` | |

## Comments

There are times when you might want to add comments to your raw document but you don't want the comments to appear to your audience. Such comments can be used to flag information that may need to be checked or periodically updated. You can use comments as a way of reminding yourself what the purpose of some information is; or you can direct comments to others who might also work on your document, as a way of explaining something to them. A comment can be used as a signature identifying the person who adds material to a document, or for marking the date and time a piece of the document is changed.

<!--
-->

**Comment tags.** <!-- marks the beginning of a comment, and --> marks the comment's end. Notice that these tags are unlike all other start/end tags in that each of them has only one angle bracket, and the end tag has no slash. All text that you type between the two sets of double hyphens will be treated as a comment—that is, it will not be displayed by the browser.

| *If you write this:* | *It will be displayed like this:* |
|---|---|
| The most populous city in the world is Mexico City, and number two is Cairo. <!--Check population stats each time doc. is updated.--> Others in the top ten include Tokyo, . . . | The most populous city in the world is Mexico City, and number two is Cairo. Others in the top ten include Tokyo. . . . |

The ability to write comments into your hypertext document is an example of how publishing on the Internet is part publishing and part *software development.* Comments are an integral part of software development; they are an element that computer programmers routinely write into their code. You don't see them, but they are there—in the code underlying your word processor, your spreadsheet application, your electronic calendar, and everything else you use with your computer. You might think of comments as notes that the programmers write to themselves, or to other programmers; they point out what's going on in the code at specific points, and in doing so they are a necessary tool for maintenance, troubleshooting, and modifications to the way a program works. You too can use comments as you write hypertext documents.

## One More Example Document

Figure 4-3 shows a complete sample HTML document in its "raw" form. It doesn't contain all of the codes we've discussed, but it does have HTML,

```
<html><head>
<title>How to Purchase Our Products Over the Internet</title>
</head>
<body>
<h1>How to Purchase Our Products Over the Internet</h1>
<p>Do you long for a <em>simple</em> way to do your shopping? A way that
provides all the possibilities of a virtual department store? Then read
on.</p>
<h1>Our Simple Method</h1>
<p>Our method is the newest on the Internet. It leads you through room after
room of delightful products that you <em>see on your screen</em>. Each
product is presented with its price and delivery charge. You can pick out
the products you like, place your order, and expect delivery within two
days. <strong>Within two days!</strong> Can you believe it?
<h2>What Do We Have to Offer?</h2>
<p>We carry a full line of men's and women's clothing, plus cosmetics and
fragrances for the ladies and grooming accessories for the gents. We also
carry fashion accessories, hats, and <em>a whole lot more.</em>And quality?
Take it from one of our leading customers, who writes:
<blockquote>I've never seen better-quality stuff than what you folks sell
over the Internet. You can sure count on my business.
</blockquote> <!--We could use a few more testimonials like this-->
<p><strong>So be the first on your block to shop with us!</strong></p>
</body>
</html>
```

**FIGURE 4-3**

head, title, body, and blockquote tags; paragraph codes, both with and without end tags; first-level heading tags; emphasis and strong tags; and a comment. See if you can identify each code and the text affected by it. And see if you can visualize how this document might look when the browser interprets all the codes.

## TIPS FOR USING THE HTML TEXT CODES

As you work with the basic codes, you'll discover your own methods of using them. Don't be afraid to experiment while you're creating documents; you can afford to make mistakes while you're learning. Just be sure you save your document as a local file until you're certain it's ready for the world to see.

While you're still feeling your way through the wonders of HTML, here are a few tips that you might find helpful.

**Use heading levels sparingly.** HTML supports six levels of headings, but it's rarely a good idea to use them all. The "real estate" of a computer screen is limited, and it's easy to make the display too complicated. Remember that readers have to scroll down to follow a lengthy screen topic, and they will soon lose their sense of where a subtopic fits in the logical scheme of your presentation. Remember also that you're working with hypertext—and that means you have a great deal of flexibility in how you connect related topics. For most documents, three heading levels should be enough to organize the content effectively, and as you become experienced in using hypertext, you may even find three heading levels more than you need.

**When in doubt, use logical font code types.** If you're not sure whether to use <em> or <i>, <strong> or <b>, or another logical code type versus a physical type, go with the logical type. That means <em>, <strong>, <cite>, or <code>. Leave it up to your readers' browsers to apply the specific display font.

## WHAT'S NEXT?

Lab 1, the exercise that follows, gives you an opportunity to try out what you've just learned. You'll go through the steps of creating a simple HTML document, saving it as a local file, and viewing it with your browser. But note this: you're not just "going through the steps"—you're creating a real

This is a controversial question: Should you skip over a heading level when you're designing a document? For example, instead of using a level-3 heading (h3) immediately subordinate to a level-2 heading (h2), can you use a level-4 heading (h4), as in the following illustration?

# Heading ........................ (h1)

Text text text text text text text

## Heading ........................ (h2)

Text text text text text text text

### Heading ........................ (h4)

Text text text text text text

There are reasons why you might want to do this. You know that browsers are generally configured to display heading levels in increasingly smaller fonts, and for logical or design reasons you want to give particular emphasis to the difference between level-2 topics and those of the next level down. So you want to skip h3. Should you?

There are many who argue that you shouldn't. Skipping a heading level, they say, violates international Web standards and can confound the configuration scheme of browsers. Browsers are programmed to organize heading levels in logical patterns, and you should not try to impose your own logic under the guise of a design choice.

We don't feel strongly about this issue. We believe there might be some design considerations that warrant skipping a heading level. As for messing up the logic of the world's browsers, it isn't such a big issue. By using <h1> through <h6> tags, you are employing *logical* rather than *physical* code types, and all browsers are still free to display these types according to their particular configurations. (For information about logical and physical code types, see the discussion earlier in this chapter.)

If you are using an automated SGML/HTML-editing application, however, you may not have any choice. Some SGML/HTML editors automatically order headings in a nonbreaking sequence, and you may or may not be able to override the sequence.

HTML document that could be posted on a Web server! The same is true of subsequent labs. You'll be creating documents that are technically fit for posting.

By saving a document as a local file, of course, you're not posting it on the Internet. A local file means one that stays on your computer's hard disk. You can adapt the steps in lab 1 to create a document on your own choice of topic and post it on the Net if you want to. We think, however, that before you do this, you should save your lab document in a local directory and read further in this book. There you'll discover more ways of building HTML documents, including especially what you'll learn in the next chapter: how to add *anchors* that will make your documents truly interactive by linking topics, both within a document and from one document to another.

## Lab 1

# Creating and Viewing
# Your First HTML Document

There are two parts to this exercise. The first, Creating an HTML Document, requires a lot of steps, but they are all pretty easy. The second, Viewing Your HTML Document, consists of only one step—and it, too, is easy.

Note that this exercise is written for those who do not use an SGML editor or a special HTML-building application such as HoTMetaL Pro or CyberLeaf. If you do use such an application, feel free to try it out on this exercise. Instead of typing the codes and their angle brackets, < >, just insert the corresponding HTML element into your document.

### Creating an HTML Document

1. Open a text-editing program—for example Windows Notebook, Microsoft Word for Windows, WordPerfect for Windows, or any other word-processing program that can save your document in text (ASCII) format.

2. With your cursor at the beginning of a blank document, type:

   `<html>`

   This tag marks the beginning of an HTML document.

3. On the same line, and without adding a space, type:

   `<head>`

   This tag marks the beginning of the head portion of your document.

4. Press ENTER to start a new line, and then type:

   `<title>My First HTML Document</title>`

   This is an example of opening and closing tags. `<title>` marks the beginning of the title of your document; `My first HTML Document` is the title; and `</title>` marks the end of the title. Notice the addition of the slash (/) to mark the end of the title. When the finished document is viewed in a browser, the title will be displayed in a title bar.

5. Press ENTER to start another new line, and then type:

```
</head>
```

This is the closing code for the head of your document. The head contains the title code and the actual title (in this case, "My First HTML Document").

6. Press ENTER, and then type:

```
<body>
```

This tag marks the beginning of the body of your document.

7. Type:

```
<h1>The First of Much to Come</h1>
```

This line produces a first-level heading. Note that the codes follow a pattern like those for the title: <h1> and </h1> mark the beginning and the end of the heading.

8. Press ENTER, and then type:

```
<p>
```

This is the beginning code for a paragraph. Note that every paragraph needs this beginning tag. Note also that a paragraph does not need a closing tag at the end, especially if it is followed by another text paragraph.

9. Type a descriptive paragraph about yourself, including the words *creative* and *forceful.* For example:

```
I am a person of varying moods. Today I'm feeling very
creative. I believe I can communicate ideas in a force-
ful manner.
```

10. Move the cursor to the beginning of the word *creative* and insert:

```
<i>
```

11. Move the cursor to the end of *creative* and insert:

```
</i>
```

This will make "creative" appear in italics. Notice that these tags mirror what we've seen before, signaling the beginning and end of the italic formatting.

**12.** Repeat steps 10 and 11 with the word *forceful,* only substitute <b> and </b> for the formatting codes.

This will make "forceful" appear in boldface.

**13.** Move the cursor to the end of the paragraph and insert:

`</p>`

In this instance, we are using </p> to end the paragraph. We don't need to add this tag, but it will help us remember that the next tag we add is something other than another standard text paragraph.

**14.** Press ENTER, and then type:

`<h2>More to Come</h2>`

This creates a second-level heading, or subheading.

**15.** Press ENTER again, and then type the following:

`<p>Just you wait and see. If you thought the first paragraph was exciting, those that follow will have you clutching your armrest!</p>`

Note again that the </p> code at the end of this paragraph is optional.

**16.** Press ENTER, and then type:

`</body>`

**17.** Press ENTER once more, and then type:

`</html>`

The last two code elements, </body> and </html>, match their counterparts at the beginning of the document, closing the body of your text and signaling the end of an HTML document.

**18.** Save the document on your hard disk as text (ASCII), and then close the file. Give it the file name `first.html` (if your system supports four-character file extensions) or `first.htm` (if your system supports only three-character extensions).

## Viewing Your HTML Document

❑ Using your browser (or the one included in the software that came with this book), open the file `first.htm` (or `first.html`) that you just created.

If you are prompted to specify the type of file you are opening, it is a *local* file (that is, one that is stored on your computer's hard disk).

That's all! You should now be seeing the document on your screen, and it should look something like this:

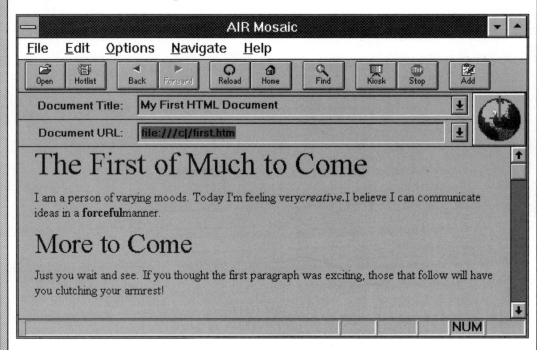

**Note:** Make sure to save all your lab documents for future reference in later chapters!

# 5 Anchors:

## Weaving the Web by Building Links

In the last chapter, we explored the basic HTML codes for identifying and formatting text elements in a document. Now, we'll discuss the codes that link pieces of information to each other. These are known as *anchor* codes.

Links are the crucial element in hypertext. They are what make possible the apparently seamless flow of connections around the World Wide Web. It is because of links between topics that a reader can jump from place to place within a document simply by pointing and clicking the mouse. And it is again because of links that a reader can jump to another document with just a click of the mouse. In fact, by using the anchor code that creates a link, you can in theory tie your document to any other point on the World Wide Web. This makes the Web not merely seamless, but indeed borderless. With the ability to form links to any other point, you can create connections along the information superhighway that make the "superhighway" image seem like a rather weak metaphor for what is happening; for what we're talking about is a global flow of communications across borders, continents, and oceans—all possible through the click of a mouse.

## THINKING ABOUT LINKING

When you create hypertext links, you are, in a sense, adding a third dimension to your content. Your content can be read on a computer screen from side to side and from top to bottom, like non-hypertext documents, but it can also be read from one "surface" to another. When you look at a computer screen, you of course see a flat, two-dimensional surface. But when you point with your mouse to a hypertext link and click on it, presto! You instantly find yourself in another location, as if you have hopped through the surface into another compartment of the document, or outside the document altogether.

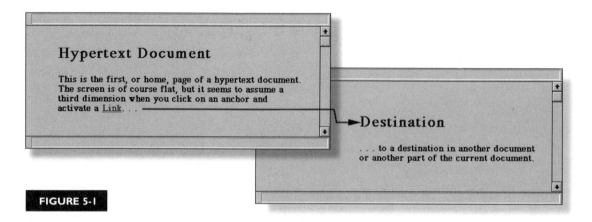

FIGURE 5-1

Hypertext is, in fact, not new. If you have used on-line help with software products, you are already familiar with hypertext; you've seen help screens with navigational jumps and definition jumps, and you probably don't even give a thought to the coding that underlies your ability to move so easily through the topics. For example, you may be using a word processor and suddenly need help with changing your margins. You open the help topic and search for topics about margins, see a title that fits, and click on it. Bingo—the topic appears on your screen. What made it do that? Hypertext.

The point is that something you may have taken for granted, as a given in the software world, is actually a rather remarkable technology. Hard to do?—not at all. You just have to learn a few details about using the anchor code, as well as a few tactical concepts that will help you make logical, effective links.

## Who's Driving This Document?

The whole point of hypertext is in providing an *interactive* context for your audience. Your readers can make choices about how to follow the progression of your content; they can jump to definitions or tangential topics that you build in; or they can check a cross-reference in another document and then return to the point in your document where they left off.

In an important sense, your reader becomes the "driver" of the document, deciding whether to steer through it in a linear fashion or veer off in this or that direction at any number of points along the route. You've given the reader the wheel—the ability to control the direction of his or her journey through your content.

You needn't worry about losing control over your material. It's still a document that reflects your ideas, knowledge, and creativity—and it's one that allows you to share your material with others in a way that's much more effective than a conventional publication. Not only will readers appreciate the opportunity to make logical choices as they read, but if your

---

### Interactive communication and learning

Interactive learning has interested educators and researchers for some time, and there is now a substantial body of research demonstrating the power of interactive communication in educational settings. At the Second International WWW Conference '94, "Mosaic and the Web," held in Chicago, more than 30 papers and posters were presented on the subject of education and the web. The topics ranged from "Designing a Server for a K-8 School," presented by Bonnie Thurber and Bob Davis, to "Uses of Mosaic in a University Setting," delivered by Judy Cossel Rice, Rosina Bignall, Dalinda Bond, and Phillip J. Windley. Other topics included language learning, frog dissection, C programming, and even publishing on the Web.

The studies generally concentrate on how interactive techniques affect the learning process. Control tests usually compare the results of students who learn through interactive methods with those who learn by conventional, largely passive, methods. The overwhelming evidence is that interactive methods are far superior.

One expert who has done a lot of thinking about the interactive delivery of information is John Houston, Director of Strategic Consulting for ModemMedia, an interactive advertising agency. According to Houston, the benefit of interactive learning over passive methods lies in *cognitive elaboration*. Cognitive elaboration occurs when a person must process information in an active manner. One example, from traditional learning methods, is writing down a passage from a book rather than simply reading it, as a way to study for an exam. Computerized learning methods build in a great deal of interactivity, requiring students to make choices and do exercises as they learn.

Whether your aim is educational or not, the principle of cognitive elaboration applies to your publications on the Internet. Interactive communication is bound to be more effective than conventional, one-way communication because it engages your readers, brings them into the logical process, and challenges them to make decisions about how to read your content.

---

document is effectively constructed and your points are well delivered, chances are they'll absorb the material more thoroughly than they would if they were reading a conventional publication. (See the accompanying sidebar.) Add graphics, and they'll absorb it even better. And sound—still better.

## How to Create a Link: Anchors and Destinations

To create a link, two elements are needed. On one end is the *anchor:* the spot in your document that serves as the jumping-off point to another location. On the other end is the *destination:* the point that the anchor connects to. These two elements require two different sets of codes.

**The anchor.** As with other HTML elements, you designate text as an anchor by enclosing it between a start tag and an end tag. (Note that graphics can also be used as anchors, but we'll leave that until chapter 6, where we discuss graphical elements. For now, we'll stick to anchors that are based on text elements.)

The basic tags for an anchor are:

```
<a>. . .</a>
```

This, however, is only the beginning of the information needed in the code for an anchor. The "a" in the tags identifies the text in between as an anchor, but it doesn't tell what the anchor is attached to. Additional information is needed, information that precisely locates the other end of the link—the destination to which your readers will jump when they click the anchor. That additional information goes into the anchor's start tag. Here's an example:

```
<a href="#george">
```

The href characters are what is called an *attribute.* That's a fancy word for an additional piece of coding needed to make the information more specific. You'll find that certain HTML codes besides the anchor code can also take attributes that add specific information to the base code. What's important for now is that you will use the href attribute in every anchor you create. The four characters href stand for *hypertext reference.*

The equal sign (=) is another piece of the anchor coding that you'll always use. What follows the equal sign, however, is a unique set of characters that will be different for every destination. This is known as the *identifier* of the attribute. In our example <a href="#george">, the characters george are the identifier. The identifier points to a precise location elsewhere in the document, a location that is marked by a destination code containing the same identifier—in this case, george. That location will be the point a reader jumps to when clicking on the anchor. Notice that, within the anchor code, a number sign (#) precedes the george characters, and both the number sign and the george characters are enclosed in quotation marks.

This is what the complete anchor, including its end tag, looks like in the context of some surrounding HTML text:

```
<a href="#george">George Harrison</a> was one of the
original lads from Liverpool who formed a musical group
that became a legend as the Beatles.
```

When this text is read by a browser, the name "George Harrison" will be displayed differently from the surrounding text; typically, it is a different color, or it is underlined, or both. This indicates to readers that if they click on "George Harrison," they will jump to another topic that's keyed to the anchor code. Figure 5-2 illustrates how the anchor we've just described might look when seen with a browser.

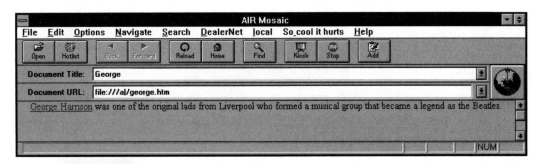

**FIGURE 5-2**

**The destination.** To define the destination of a link, you use the basic ⟨a⟩ and ⟨/a⟩ tags together with a different attribute: name. Again, you type in an equal sign (=) and follow it with the identifier contained in the anchor code. The following is the start tag for a destination that the anchor in the preceding example would jump to:

```
<a name=george>
```

Notice that the identifier in the destination code does *not* include a number sign. If you prefer, you can use quotation marks (as in the anchor code), in which case the destination tag would be ⟨a name="george"⟩.

This is how the complete destination anchor might look in the context of some surrounding HTML text:

```
<a name = george>George Harrison</a>, b. Liverpool, En-
gland, 1943; gained fame as a member of the rock band,
The Beatles.
```

## Putting Things Together: The "Beatles" Document

By now, you may have pieced together what it is that we're doing in our examples. We are working with a hypothetical document about the Beatles. Somewhere in this document we are including the sentence "George Harrison was one of the original lads from Liverpool who formed a musical group that became a legend as the Beatles." The name "George Harrison" is formatted as anchor text, and when our readers click on it while viewing the document with their browsers, they jump to another topic that contains information specifically about George Harrison.

We'll continue to work with this hypothetical document—and a couple of additional, related hypothetical documents—through the rest of this chapter.

### Protect yourself!

Beware the legal pitfalls inherent in publishing. If you plan to use materials that have been published previously, be sure to obtain permission from whoever owns the copyright to those materials. If you plan to use sound clips taken from recordings, do not forget that the recordings have been copyrighted and trademarked. You are not legally entitled to use any part of them without permission, and you can expect big trouble if you do. We are (perhaps blithely) describing a hypothetical Web site dedicated to Beatles lore, but we hasten to add the caveat that any material about the Beatles that has been previously published, recorded, filmed, or otherwise presented to the public—and probably much that has not been presented to the public—is likely to fall under copyright or trademark protection. You might have to pay a heavy fee to obtain permission for using such material.

We say this not to scare you away from a hot idea, but to caution you that, just as in traditional publishing, publishing on the Internet carries with it the responsibility to operate within the letter of the law. Book publishers and authors are required to secure permissions for the use of previously published materials, and they regularly do this. Obtaining permissions is usually not a prohibitive obstacle on the way to publishing a great piece of work, but it is always a necessary step.

**How to Publish on the Internet**

## Internal and External Links

When we work with anchors and destinations, we need to keep in mind a basic distinction between *internal* and *external* links. By *internal* links, we mean links that take place within one document. The example we used above, linking from the anchor `<a href = "#george">...</a>` to the destination `<a name = george>...</a>`, jumps the reader to another location within the same document, typically a related topic. A new screen appears with its own text and other content elements—perhaps including more anchors that link to still other screens—but the reader has not left the original file. This is an internal link.

By *external links*, we mean links that jump the reader to outside documents. By clicking on the anchor for an external link, the reader opens a different file. That "external" file is the destination described by the identifier in the anchor. To make such a link possible, the anchor must contain coding that defines the destination (that is, the external file) in terms of its precise, unique location, whether that location be within another directory of the same Web server or on a different Web server halfway around the world.

## INTERNAL LINKS

Internal links require both anchor tags and destination tags. If you've followed our discussion to this point in the chapter, these tags should already be familiar.

---

**`<a href="#`*`identifier`*`">`**
**`</a>`**

**Anchor tags.** These tags mark the beginning and end of an anchor. By clicking on this element in your document, the reader can jump to another location within the same document, usually a related topic.

In the example below, the identifier `george` is the text string that tells the reader's browser where to jump to. Between the start tag and the end tag is the string `George Harrison`. This is the anchor text—the text your readers can click on to jump to a related topic. Notice the quotation marks and the number sign (**#**); these are required.

***Example***
`<a href = "#george">George Harrison</a>`

**`<a name = `*`identifier`*`>`**
**`</a>`**

**Destination tags.** These tags mark the beginning and end of a destination, the point in your document to which the reader jumps. The identifier may or may not be enclosed in quotation marks (see note below). No number sign is used.

---

**Anchors**

In the following example, the text string george mirrors the identifier in the preceding start tag, telling the reader's browser that this is the place to jump to. George Harrison is the destination text—the text your readers will land on when they click on the anchor described in the preceding example.

***Example***

```
<a name=george>George Harrison</a>
```

---

> **N O T E**  In your destination tag, it's best to limit your identifier to one word, or to run two words together without a space between, as in, for example, georgeh. If you must use two words with a space between, then you must also enclose the entire identifier in quotation marks, as in "george h".

We've discussed this example enough that it should be pretty clear by now, but let's add one more word about the codes. The start tag for an anchor, as we've displayed it above, is `<a href="#identifier">`. Be aware that you do not literally type *identifier*; this is a generic term which, in this case, stands for a specific string of characters that are keyed to a destination within your document. Notice that the start tag for a destination is given above as `<a name=identifier>`; again, the generic term *identifier* stands for something specific—namely the same string of characters used in the anchor code. It is this identical pair of identifiers that link the anchor and the destination.

Note once more that, in the anchor code, you add a number sign (#) at the beginning of the identifier and enclose *#identifier* in quotation marks, as in our example, `"#george"`. You do not use a number sign in the destination code, and you do not need to use quotation marks unless the identifier contains a space.

**When to use internal links.**  Obviously, you use an internal link when you want to allow the reader to jump to another point within the same document. But, more specifically, there are any number of ways you might want to make use of internal links:

- You can create a table of contents (TOC) on the home page of your document, linking each topic or chapter listed in the TOC to the beginning of the actual topic or chapter.
- If your document contains a number of subtopics that relate to a main topic, you can link each of them to anchors within the main topic.

❑ If your document contains a glossary of technical terms, you can connect each term listed in the glossary to one or more anchors where that term occurs in the main text.

As you develop experience in creating hypertext documents, you'll discover more ways of putting this tool to work—and maybe you'll even invent some uses yourself.

**Lab exercise.** That's all there is to internal links. Before going on to the next section, we recommend that you turn now to the end of this chapter and work through lab 2, Creating Internal Links. That will give you an opportunity to try out what you've just learned.

## EXTERNAL LINKS

An internal link, as we've just seen, is very simple in concept: the reader clicks on the anchor text and jumps to a related topic in the same document. No muss, no fuss; no question about where in the wide world of the World Wide Web the destination is located. It's in another part of the document you're looking at. An external link, on the other hand, is a bit more complicated, because it takes the reader to another file—a document that is outside, or *external to,* the current document.

Here's what the codes for an external link look like:

---

**\<a href=** "*URL*"\>
\</a\>

**Anchor tags for an external link.** These tags mark the beginning and end of an anchor for a link to another document. By clicking on the anchor text, the reader opens the other document. In the start tag, *URL* stands for the location of the new document as defined by its uniform resource locator (URL), which comprises the destination document's path and file name including extension.

No destination tags are needed.

Two examples follow. In both, the anchor text is Ringo Starr. Clicking on this anchor tells the browser to retrieve and open the destination document whose file name is ringo.html. In the first example, this file is located on the same server, in the directory /persons. In the second example, the file is located in the directory /sixties on a different server named www.muzick.com.

***Examples***
```
<a href="persons/ringo.html"> Ringo Starr</a>
<a href="http://www.muzick.com/sixties/ringo.html">Ringo
Starr</a>
```

---

There are some new concepts here in these two anchors that we haven't explained yet, beginning with the concept of the uniform resource locator (URL). Let's turn to that now.

## Uniform Resource Locator (URL)

A URL is a string of characters that describes a file's specific and unique location on the Internet. Any file on the World Wide Web can be located by using its URL. To link your document to another document, your anchor code must identify the file and its location precisely so that the reader's browser can retrieve and open it. To tell the browser this information, you use a URL.

A full, or absolute, URL contains the following components:

- The transfer protocol (for Web services, this is `http`)
- The server name
- The directory path to the file
- The file name

The second of the two examples shown above contains a full URL. We can diagram it like this:

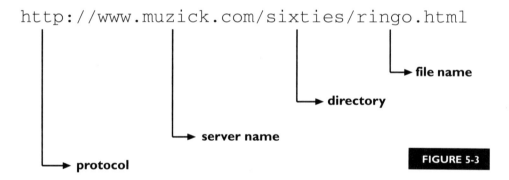

```
http://www.muzick.com/sixties/ringo.html
```
→ file name
→ directory
→ server name
→ protocol

FIGURE 5-3

Notice that you use the forward slash (/) as a path separator, and a colon plus a double forward slash to separate the protocol from the server name. Within an anchor's start tag, you enclose the entire URL in quotation marks:

```
<a href="http://www.muzick.com/sixties">
```

If you want to link to a specific location within the document, you add a destination identifier to the anchor code. (We'll show an example of this later, in the section "External Links to Internal Destinations.")

**How to Publish on the Internet**

When you include this information in an anchor, you're telling the reader's browser everything it needs to know to go out onto the Internet, find and retrieve the file you're linking to, and display the document on the reader's screen.

## The URL as an address

You can think of the uniform resource locator (URL) as the address of a file. Just as the postal service finds you at your mailing address, your Internet transport protocol finds a file at its URL address. The formats for writing the two types of address are different, and in fact it might seem as though you write a URL backward (compared with writing a postal address), but we can nevertheless draw analogies between the parts of each address. The transfer protocol (HTTP) can be compared to the country, or state, in a postal address; the domain name (in our example www.muzick.com) is like a city where many files reside; the directory path brings us closer in to our destination, just as a street name and number, and perhaps a building name or district designation (such as *VI. arrondissement* in Paris), help the postal carrier zero in on a postal destination; and finally, there is the file name itself, analogous to the individual addressee of a letter.

**Two rules about URLs.** Here are two rules of thumb you should keep in mind when working with URLs:

▫ Because UNIX systems treat path and file names as case-sensitive, you must also, regardless of the platform you are working on. Be aware, for example, that `ringo.html` is not the same as `RINGO.HTML`.
▫ Do not type any spaces within a URL.

**Absolute vs. Relative URLs.** The full URL code shown in figure 5-3 represents what is called an *Absolute URL*. It designates an absolute location for a file; that is, it specifies that the file resides on //X server, and its path through the directory system of that server is /Y/Z . . . , etc. An Absolute URL directs the reader's browser to retrieve the file from the specified server and path, and from nowhere else. This means that if the file is moved, its Absolute URL changes and must be respecified in order to locate the file. You specify an Absolute URL by including all of the information listed above: transfer protocol, server name, directory path, and file name (including extension).

A *Relative URL*, in contrast, designates a file location that is relative to the file containing the anchor. Generally, this means the two files are located at the same Web site—that is, on the hard disk of the same computer. You do not need to specify the name of the server, and you specify the path only to the extent that it is different from that of the file containing the anchor. Figure 5-4 illustrates a Relative URL, which you will recognize as the first example in our earlier discussion of the anchor codes:

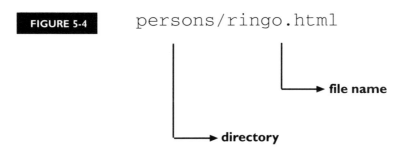

When a browser reads this Relative URL, it assumes that the destination file is on the same server. The browser further assumes that `persons` is a subdirectory one level below the server's root directory, and it looks for the file `ringo.html` in that subdirectory. If there is more than one level of subdirectories in the path, you need to separate them all by slashes, as in `popmusic/beatles/persons/ringo.html`.

---

**Slashes and backslashes**

If you use DOS or Windows, you are probably quite habituated to typing the backslash (\) as a separator within directory paths. UNIX systems, however, use the forward slash (/) as the separator. And because most Internet servers are currently based on UNIX, the forward slash is standard in Internet file-location syntax.

You can use single backslashes as path separators in a URL, and UNIX will translate them as forward slashes. Be aware, however, that you cannot use double backslashes to separate the protocol from the server name. Hence, the following examples:

**Can be used**   `http://www.server.com\dir\dir\filename.html`
                  `dir\dir\filename.html`

**Cannot be used** `http:\\www.server.com\dir\dir\filename.html`

You will recognize the first and third examples as Absolute URLs and the second as a Relative URL.

---

> **N O T E** As a shortcut in typing the path for a Relative URL, you can use the convention of two dots (..) to stand for a parent directory. If, for example, the path reads `../persons/ringo.html`, the destination file and the original file are in different subdirectories, but the two subdirectories are in the same parent directory. Remember that the two dots need to be repeated, together with the slash, for each step backward through subdirectories.

**If the destination file is on another drive.** It often happens that a server stores files on more than one hard disk drive. If the destination file is located on the same server but a different drive—say, drive `d:` instead of drive `c:`—then you simply insert the drive designator in front of the directory path, as in the following anchor:

```
<a href="d:/persons/ringo.html">Ringo Starr</a>
```

## Using Relative URLs

Relative URLs are useful when you work with a set of files that overlap or relate to each other in one or more respects, and you keep them together in the same Web site. Their contents cover too much territory to fit snugly into one document, and so you don't want to include them all in the same file.

If you link them by using Relative URLs, they always stay linked *relative to each other.* That means you can rename the Web site they are on, or even move it to a different server if you need to, without affecting the links established among the files.

As an example, let's return to our hypothetical article on the Beatles. Suppose the main topic on the Beatles turns out to be quite a large document: it discusses their beginnings, the development of their career, and ultimately their breakup; it tallies the sales of their records and lists their awards; it may include graphics that show the group in concert as well as sound clips of their songs (assuming we can acquire permission to use these materials!). It becomes obvious to us that biographies of the individual members need to be separate documents, especially since they all went off in different directions after the Beatles disbanded. So that's what we do: we create separate documents, one each for Paul McCartney, John Lennon, Ringo Starr, and George Harrison. And we key them in to the main document about the Beatles by building external links, using Relative URLs in the anchor codes.

We think you will find the use of Relative URLs an extremely serviceable tool for your World Wide Web publications.

---

## Using Absolute URLs

There may be times when you want to link your document to one on another Web server. You can do this, whether that other server is just across the street or halfway around the world. All you need to know is the exact name of the file, as well as its server name and directory path.

Again following our working example, let's now create a cross-reference from our document about the Beatles to another document about the Rolling Stones. Like the Beatles, the Stones started their career in England, brought it to America in the mid-1960s, and became a tremendous success around the world. There are any number of instances where the two groups' careers paralleled or overlapped with each other, and that's why we need to create links between our Beatles article and one about the Stones. In our hypothetical case, we have discovered a good piece on the Rolling Stones on a Web server named www.hardrock.com, and that's the file we want to link our document to.

We do it with an external link that contains an Absolute URL, such as the one in the start tag of the following anchor:

```
<a href="http://www.hardrock.com/groups/stones.
html">Rolling Stones</a>
```

This anchor, as you've probably already figured out, jumps the reader from the anchor text Rolling Stones to the file stones.html on the server www.hardrock.com.

Why an Absolute URL? Because the destination file is on a different server, you cannot link to it by using a URL that is relative to the file you're linking from. To link to a file on a different server, always use an Absolute URL.

Do you see where this is taking us? External links are a powerful tool. They give you the ability to connect your publications with others that exist on Web servers the world over. Let your imagination, and your growing familiarity with the World Wide Web, suggest all the ways you can make this tool work for your publications.

## EXTERNAL LINKS TO INTERNAL DESTINATIONS

So far, we've been talking about linking to an external document per se; that is, when the reader clicks on an anchor in the original document, the link opens a second document at its beginning (or home page). There is, however, a further variation on the theme of external links: an external link can also be set up to jump the reader to a particular location within a

**How to Publish on the Internet**

different document. Instead of opening the second document at its beginning, the link can open it to a specific topic or subtopic.

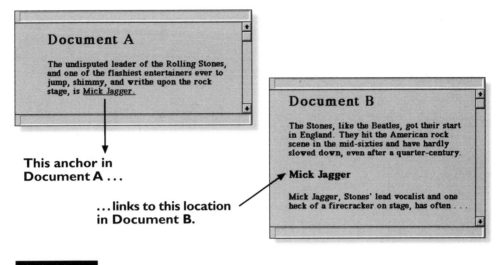

**FIGURE 5-5**

Here are the codes for external links to internal destinations:

---

**\<a href=**"*URL#identifier*"**>** | **Anchor tags: external link to an internal destination.** These tags mark the beginning and end of an anchor for a link to a specific destination within another document. By clicking the anchor text, the reader opens the other document to the location defined by the identifier. As before, *URL* stands for the location of the new document as defined by its uniform resource locator (URL).

*identifier* stands for the specific code that identifies the destination within the new document.

You need to complete this link by adding destination tags as described below.

Two examples follow. In the first, the anchor text is George Harrison. Clicking on this anchor tells the browser to retrieve and open the document beatles.html at the location marked by george. This file is located on the same server, in the directory /groups.

In the second example, the anchor text is Mick Jagger. Clicking on this anchor tells the browser to retrieve and open the document stones.html at the location marked by mick. This file is located on a different server named `www.hardrock.com` in the directory `/groups`.

***Examples***

`<a href = "groups/beatles.htm#george">George Harrison</a>`
`<a href = "http://www.hardrock.com/groups/stones.html#mick">Mick Jagger</a>`

**`<a name = `*`identifier`*`>`**      **Destination tags.** These tags mark the beginning and end of a destination. You insert these tags around the destination text in the document you want your readers to jump to. Notice that the tags are in the same format as the destination tags for internal links.

The two following examples mirror the start tag examples above. There is no general difference between a destination tag for a file on the same server and one on a different server.

***Example***

`<a name = george>George Harrison</a>`
`<a name = mick>Mick Jagger</a>`

## Using External Links to Internal Destinations

You use this type of link when you want to allow your reader to jump not just to a different document, but to a specific topic or subtopic within it. In many cases, the destination document may be a more broadly aimed discussion that is mostly unrelated to the content from which the reader has jumped. Your readers should not have to find their way through the structure of the larger document if you can send them right to the point they are interested in.

For an example, let's return to our "Beatles" article. Suppose we've previously created a document about "The Ed Sullivan Show," a popular variety program on network television during the 1950s and 1960s, and how this program showcased new musical talents. The Beatles were one of the biggest new talents Ed Sullivan, the show's producer and master of ceremonies, discovered. We want to link our article on the Beatles to the passage in the "Ed Sullivan Show" document that describes their appearance on that program, because it marked the Beatles' American debut. But we don't want to make our readers have to pick their way through the other topics in this broader document. So we use a link that takes them directly to the discussion of the Beatles' appearance. The anchor and destination for the link might look like this (assuming the two documents are located on the same server):

```
<a href="sullivan.html#beatles">The Ed Sullivan
Show</a>
<a name=beatles>The Beatles' American Debut</a>
```

Figure 5-6 illustrates how the link might look when viewed with a browser.

This anchor in
Document A . . .

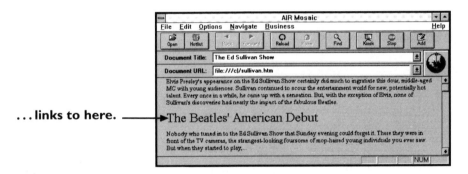

. . . links to here.

FIGURE 5-6

**Can you use an Absolute URL for a link to an internal destination?** The answer is "Yes, but . . ." The issue concerns whose document you're linking to. Generally, files located on a different server are somebody else's files. To link to a point inside another document, you have to be able to insert a destination code into it. If it's somebody else's document, you probably won't be able to do that—unless the "owner" of that document lets you change the HTML source code for it (or unless there is already a destination code in place at the location you want to link to). Assuming that's not the case, you will still be able to link to the document, but not to a specific point within it.

We suspect that external links to internal destinations are something you will primarily use between documents you store together at the same Web site. For these, you will be using Relative URLs in your anchors.

This is not to say that you won't ever be creating documents and locating them on different servers. You might. If you get involved in a large collaborative project, for example, you may be linking documents on your own server to those on somebody else's. An example of this is Project Gutenberg, the massive effort to assemble a giant Web site containing much of the world's great literature. The Project Gutenberg Web site is actually spread across several Web servers in different geographic locations.

But that's probably not something you'll be doing right off the bat. In the meantime, we think you'll find that you will rarely use an Absolute URL to create an external link to an internal destination.

**Lab exercise.** We've covered a lot of ground. Are you ready for another lab? Lab 3, Creating External Links, will give you an opportunity to apply the anchor codes we've just discussed. Turn to the end of this chapter and try it out.

## STRATEGIES OF LINKING

Anchors are the tools that make your hypertext documents work as hypertext documents. If you think about it, you can begin to see what anchors mean for the flow of information. You can create an anchor in Document A that links to Document B. You can create anchors in Document B that link to Documents C, D, and E. From those documents, further links can multiply until, in theory, all World Wide Web documents are linked directly or indirectly.

This is a tantalizing idea, the thought that all Web documents fit somehow into one gigantic logical relationship to each other, but it's obviously an abstraction and it has little to do with the practical matter of publishing your content in a coherent way. The point is that the possibilities for linking information are almost infinite. The challenge is to devise strategies that make the most sensible use of the possibilities.

Let's consider a few ways to apply the tools of linking. We can start by taking a *structural* approach, drawing analogies with some familiar forms in conventional publication. Later, we'll look at some models that are slightly more complex because they derive from a *functional* approach. (Bear in mind that these two categories, structural and functional, are never discrete; they often overlap, as structure sometimes defines function and function sometimes dictates the form of a document.)

## Using Links: Some Structural Models

There are any number of potential models for structuring hypertext documents. We're going to discuss four as examples:

- Hierarchical model
- Article model
- Brochure model
- Sequential/cyclical model

**Hierarchical model.** One of the simplest models for organizing information is a hierarchical structure, in which one main document contains anchors linking to other documents. These in turn might link to a third "tier" of documents, and so on. Taking our "Beatles" article, we might diagram this model as shown in figure 5-7.

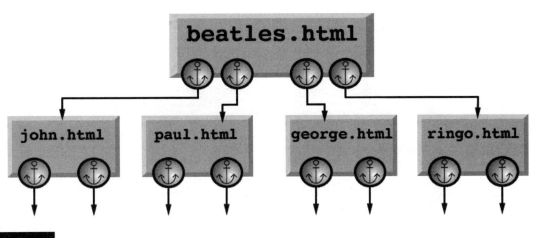

FIGURE 5-7

Structurally, this hierarchical model resembles what we see in organizational charts, in which the chief position of an organization is represented in one box at the top of the structure and layers of subordinate positions flow downward through the chart. In figure 5-7, the file beatles.html links, through anchors, to files containing information about the four members of the group: John Lennon, Paul McCartney, George Harrison, and Ringo Starr. We might imagine a further layer of links to subtopics such as Childhood, Career After the Beatles, Women in His Life, or Death (in the case of John Lennon). These subtopics could exist either within the four documents (as internal links) or in separate additional documents (as external links).

A structure like this, simple though it is, offers considerable opportunity for expanding a body of information and linking its pieces together in an interactive form. It may not be the right structure for your information, however. Let's consider some others.

**Article model.** Another relatively simple model is one based on the structure of conventionally published articles. In this model, let's assume only one document that focuses, from beginning to end, on one self-contained subject. For purposes of illustration, we'll say it's an article on ski slopes in the Pacific Northwest. What we're looking for is a way to construct certain elements of a conventional magazine article in hypertext form—sidebars, footnotes, and citations, for example.

Figure 5-8 shows a paragraph of text from the body of this hypothetical article.

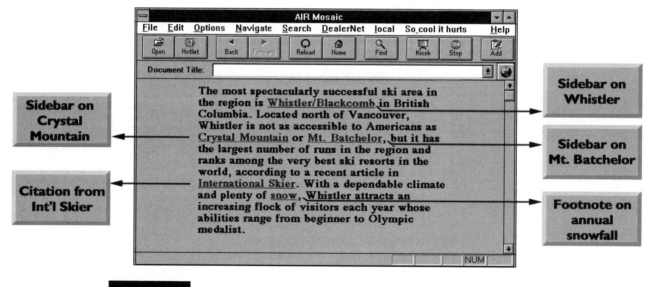

**FIGURE 5-8**

In this paragraph, anchors link the text strings **Whistler/Blackcomb, Crystal Mountain,** and **Mt. Batchelor** to sidebars that contain information on each of these ski areas: location, number of runs, length and difficulty of runs, typical opening and closing dates of the season, and other details. An anchor coded to ***International Skier*** links that text with a citation that contains the author and title of the article referred to, as well as the edition of the magazine *International Skier,* and perhaps the page numbers where the referenced article can be found. Finally, the word **snow** contains an anchor to a footnote giving statistics on the annual snowfall at Whistler/Blackcomb.

**Brochure model.** Still another hypertext possibility is a document structured like a folding brochure. Conventionally published brochures come in different sizes and shapes; bi-fold and tri-fold models are probably the most frequent, but it's not unusual to see four, six, and even more folds designed into a brochure.

The example we'll use is a tri-fold brochure. Let's say you're designing it for an organization as a way of circulating information about its products, services, or charitable purposes. You want a document that mimics the front flap, back flap, spine flap, and three inside panels of a printed tri-fold brochure. Figure 5-9 illustrates the model in both its printed and hypertext forms. The hypertext model is set up with subtopics that contain the kinds of information you would find on the separate panels of the printed brochure. The home page of the hypertext brochure, for example, might contain what would appear on the brochure's front flap—the title and other brief descriptive information, plus an eye-catching graphic—but it will also contain anchors that link to the other "panels." One anchor, for example, will link to the main body of the document; you might want to signal it with the anchor text **What We Have to Offer.** Another anchor on the home page might be called **Summary,** linking to a bulleted list, or some other representation, of the points contained in the body of your document—and analogous, loosely speaking, to either the first or the third inside panel of a printed, tri-fold brochure. Still another anchor on the home page might consist of the text **Contacts,** linking the reader to a screen with the kind of information you would expect to find on the back fold of the printed brochure: the address of your organization, the names of its officers, e-mail address(es), and so on.

Thus the document we are creating is not the exact equivalent of a printed brochure, but it is structurally modeled after a brochure. The example we described in the preceding paragraph happens also to be functionally similar to a printed brochure, but it doesn't need to be; the hypertext subtopics corresponding to the brochure's flaps could serve any reasonable functions related to the document's overall purpose. We've seen how many different uses the printed brochures can serve; the hyper-

## Printed Brochure

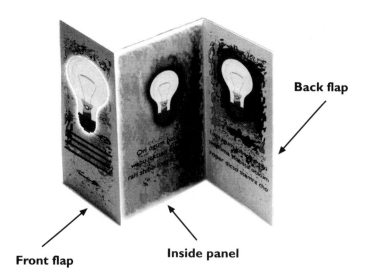

Back flap

Front flap

Inside panel

## Hypertext Brochure

Home page, mimicking the
front flap of a brochure, with
anchors linking to other
brochure-like pages

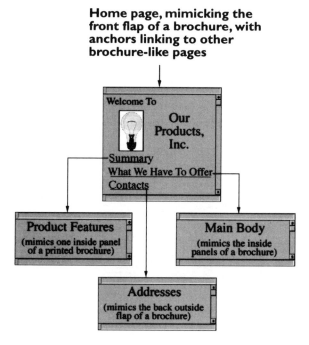

**FIGURE 5-9**

**100**

**How to Publish on the Internet**

text brochure is capable of even more uses because of the functional flexibility inherent in its structure.

**Sequential/cyclical model.** This structural model is perhaps a bit more abstract than the three we've just discussed, but it's another useful, and very logical, way to put a hypertext document together. The sequential/cyclical model gives us a good framework for delivering information of an instructional nature, and it has many other potential uses as well.

What we mean by *sequential/cyclical* is a sequence that, when followed through to its completion, leads back to the original point. Let's say, for example, you're writing a set of instructions for a beginning skier who is approaching the slopes for the first time. You want to get the skier to the lift, up the mountain, and back down to where he or she started from. The skier must follow a *sequence* of steps, but end up in a position from which the same steps can be repeated—hence the overall *cyclical* pattern of the instructions.

The simplest set of instructions might be diagrammed as in figure 5-10:

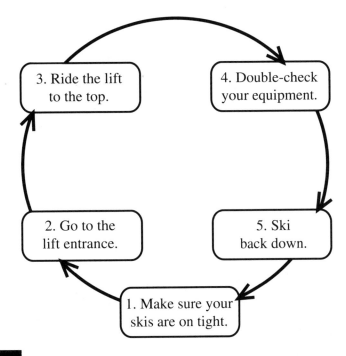

**FIGURE 5-10**

Remember, we're dealing in abstract terms for the moment; figure 5-10 is a logical diagram of the instructions' sequence.

In practical terms, you can set up the instructions in hypertext with a series of topics starting with Step 1, "Make sure your skis are on tight." Step 1 includes an anchor that links to Step 2, and so on. The links lead the reader through a cycle of instructions, returning again to Step 1 for another trip to the top of the slope.

Well, that's a start. However, even the beginning skier will recognize that these instructions are simplistic, so let's think about making them more detailed by including some substeps within each main step. You can, of course, simply list out a set of sub-instructions for each step. But suppose you want to get a bit fancier. Beginning with the logical sequence cycle we've already developed, you can build one or more *subcycles* into the logical pattern. Each subcycle represents a detour from the main sequence of instructions but leads back to the main path once again.

Figure 5-11, for example, focuses in on Step 4, "Double-check your equipment." The figure illustrates one possible way of breaking Step 4 into four sub-instructions: checking boots, skis and bindings, poles, and goggles. And then, having passed through that specific sequence, the next thing to do is to move on to Step 5.

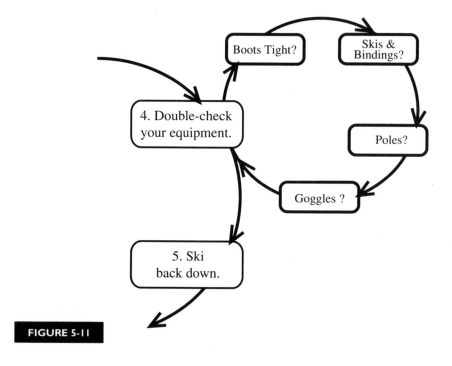

**FIGURE 5-11**

**How to Publish on the Internet**

As in the simpler cycle, you set up this sequence of steps (substeps) by creating links. Notice, however, that there are two anchors in (main) Step 4. One of them links to the substep "Boots tight?", and the other links directly to Step 5, "Ski back down." The reader can choose not to follow the substeps and take the direct path to Step 5. If the reader decides to read the sub-instructions, he or she can click the anchor that leads to "Boots tight?", go from there to "Skis and bindings?" and so on, until the anchor in the final substep, "Goggles?", takes the reader back to a "mirror" of Step 4.

What does this mean? The mirror of Step 4 is a separate screen with the same information contained in the original Step 4, but with only one anchor—the one that links directly to Step 5. Having stepped through the sub-instructions for Step 4, the reader does not have the option of repeating the subcycle.

Even this example remains simplistic, but it begins to show some of the complexity you can design into your topical structures. We recommended that you think your designs through carefully when you set out to create your documents for publication. Sketch out a diagram and draw in the links from topic to topic. Consider whether a new topic needs a separate document (and requires an external link) or just a heading within the document that contains the anchor linking to it (an internal link).

**Other structural models.** The four models we've just discussed hardly scratch the surface of the possibilities open to you. Consider the following additional ideas, and try to visualize or diagram them as hypertext documents:

- A story in which you give your readers the choice of a happy ending or a sad ending.
- A story based on a structural idea first proposed by the great Argentine writer Jorge Luis Borges, the "garden of forking paths": at each plot point, the reader chooses between two or more different alternative subsequences—she kisses him, she doesn't; the man picks up the wallet that's lying on the ground, or he doesn't; the escaping bank robber stops for the railroad crossing, or s/he floors the accelerator and tries to beat the oncoming train; and so on.
- A recipe for baking a cake, with choices along the way about making it a layer cake or loaf cake, big enough for a wedding reception or just the right size for a family of four, using sugar or honey as sweetener, adding raisins or chocolate chips, and other variable options.
- An imaginary conversation that includes Karl Marx, Groucho Marx, and

yourself, and that branches off onto a number of topics depending on the contributors' individual comments.

That's enough ideas about structural models. You will come up with many of your own. Let's turn now to some functional models of linking hypertext documents.

## Using Links: Some Functional Models

You may have noticed that some of the structural models we've been discussing have functional implications. We mentioned, for example, that the brochure model can be used for different purposes. A document meant for marketing can be modeled after an advertising brochure, with various types of marketing information strategically linked to the home page: types of product available, store locations or mail-order information, and so on. A document containing information about a library can also be modeled after a brochure, with the home page (designed like a brochure's front flap) containing links to a "flap" that lists the days and hours each branch of the library is open, another "flap" that summarizes the library's services and lending policies, and still another that lists telephone extensions for the library's specialized departments.

In these examples we've focused on structural features, but we've already begun to see those features—based on links—in strategic terms. That is, we are using links to perform specific functions. We want our document to convey various types of information about our company and our product line; or we want our document to tell users all about our library services; or we want it to serve as a tutorial on skiing.

When we talk about the functional aspects of hypertext documents, we begin to enter a more complex dimension of document design. As the opportunities for creating interactive features increase, the number and types of links we need in a document may increase, as well. The payoff for this increased complexity is a greater potential for flexibility in our documents.

And it's probably true that when you first think about creating a hypertext document, you don't say to yourself, "I want a document that looks or acts like an article, or a brochure, or a sequential/cyclical whatchamacallit." You probably say, "I want a document that effectively advertises my company's products, or instructs beginning skiers how to get up and down the slopes" or something along those lines. Sooner or later, you may think in terms of structural models, but what you really need is something that achieves your purpose. To achieve your functional aims, you might need to refer to more than one structural model as you construct your document. "Form follows function"—a controversial argument in the aesthetics of architecture—would seem to be less controversial in the design of hypertext publications.

Let's consider three examples of functional linking models in some greater detail. They are:

- Feedback form model
- Catalog model
- Technical manual/Help file model

**Feedback form.** An example of simple functionality is a standard feedback form. Let's say you are posting on the Web the Beatles documents we discussed earlier in this chapter. Aside from the general purpose of circulating information about the Beatles, you want readers to send you

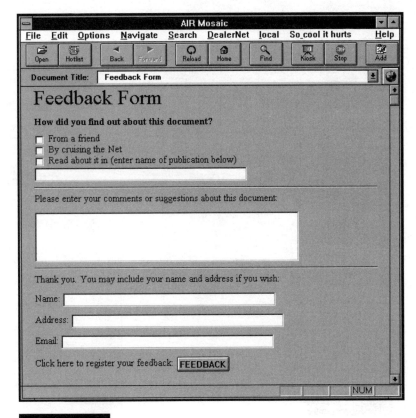

**FIGURE 5-12**

comments about the content and suggestions for improvements or additions to it. You can attach a simple feedback form, anchored to the home page of `beatles.html`. When readers click on a button labeled "Comments", they open a form that may have questions like those in figure 5-12.

The button on the bottom of this form, labeled "Feedback", can be coded so that when the reader clicks on it, the data entered on the feedback form is submitted to your Web site so you can read it. This is a more advanced HTML feature which we'll discuss in Part 3.

**Catalog model.** Another model is based on that old American institution, the mail-order catalog. This model is so familiar it requires no conceptual introduction. Let's start right off by imagining a clothing catalog.

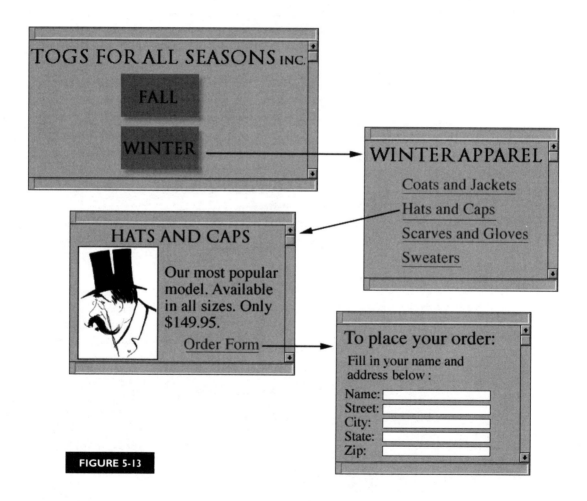

FIGURE 5-13

**How to Publish on the Internet**

Our electronic clothing catalog might have a slick home page, reminiscent of the glossy covers of traditional mail-order catalogs. Down the left margin of the home page, there might be four anchors that link respectively to Spring, Summer, Fall, and Winter fashions. (Remember that graphic images can also be coded as anchors, which would be entirely appropriate in this case.) When the reader clicks on, say, the Winter anchor, another screen appears with more graphical anchors that link to subsections featuring Coats and Jackets, Hats and Caps, Scarves and Gloves, Boots, Sweaters, and so on. Each of these subsections contains illustrative graphics and descriptions of the various products available. And each product-description screen contains an anchor linking to an order form.

**Technical manual/Help file model.** A more complicated model is one that is functionally based on a technical manual. This is an instructional type of document set in its basic conception, although what the instructional function leads us to can have other uses, as we shall see.

A set of documents based on this model might start with a title page that is linked to a table of contents (TOC) or list of topics and subtopics. Each item in the TOC/list of topics is anchor text; by clicking on it, the reader jumps to the first page of that topic or subtopic. At the end of a topic are further anchors that link to the next topic, the preceding topic, and perhaps the TOC. Within the body of a topic, you can add additional anchors that serve as cross-references to material explained in other topics. Finally, you can add an index that comprises a list of words and phrases; each word or phrase is coded as an anchor that links to the pertinent location in the document. Figure 5-14 illustrates this model.

Figure 5-14 illustrates a document designed for functioning as a manual on woodworking. The TOC page contains anchors linking to the various chapters. Notice that Chapter 4, on Cabinetry, contains a cross-reference to the subtopic "Sanding" in Chapter 2, on Basic Techniques.

You can see that this model bears some resemblance to an on-line help file in its hypertext navigation from topic to topic. However, it also resembles a printed manual, especially if you set it up in chapter format. The reader can choose whether to read the document in chapter-by-chapter sequence or jump around by using the index and cross-references.

So far, we're talking about one relatively complex document containing a lot of internal links. Carrying this model one step further, you might create a multi-document technical encyclopedia comprising numerous "volumes" (individual documents). Each "volume" might be on a separate

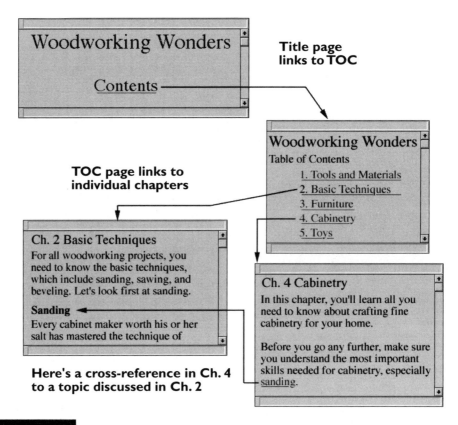

**FIGURE 5-14**

topic, with all the internal links from TOC to chapters or topics, and with internal cross-references. But you can also build in *external* links as cross-references, construct an index that covers the entire set of documents, and add an overall table of contents as well. In fact, if you want to take this model to its ultimate logic, you could call your Web site a "technical library," with the home page linking to a list of volumes in the library's collection.

**Technical manual as a structural model.** At the beginning of this section, we mentioned that the structural and functional categories often overlap. The technical manual model is a case in point. The structure that is apparent in this model—a TOC, separate but interrelated chapters, topics, or volumes, cross-references, and an index—can be applied to other kinds of

**How to Publish on the Internet**

documents. As examples, imagine applying this structure to documents such as:

- An electronic film magazine, with a feature article and sections on current reviews of American films and foreign films, recent festivals, and new video releases. And graphics, of course!
- A baseball report, monthly during the major-league season and perhaps once or twice during the off-season, with summaries of the past month, notable trends, quotable quotes, and cross-references to statistics from a database of baseball stats.
- An encyclopedia of music theory, with separate documents on Pre-Baroque, Baroque, Classical, Romantic, Post-Romantic, and Modern forms. (Sound clips, anybody?)
- A library of guides on dog ownership with separate volumes on choosing and caring for the perfect family dog, obedience training, health care and nutrition, and the history of dogs.

You fill in the rest of the list.


## NEXT UP

If you haven't yet turned to the labs for this chapter, you might want to do so now. Besides labs 2 and 3, which we've mentioned, labs 4 and 5 are also related to the topics we've been discussing. These labs walk you through some basic exercises in creating anchors and links. They will help you get the general idea of how to go about working with these essential and powerful hypertext tools. Remember to save the lab documents you create for future reference.

Then it's on to the next chapter, where you will learn how to spice up your documents by adding graphics.

## Lab 2

# Creating Internal Links

This is an exercise in applying anchor codes to create links within a document. Be sure to refer back to lab 1 if you aren't sure how to type in the basic HTML code elements. If you use special HTML-building software, just insert the corresponding HTML elements instead of typing the codes and their angle brackets < >.

### Creating Internal Links

1. Open your text-editing program—for example Windows Notebook, Microsoft Word for Windows, WordPerfect for Windows, or any other word-processing program that can save your document in text (ASCII) format.

2. Create a new HTML document by typing in the <html>, <head>, and <title> start tags.

   If you're in doubt about how to type these in, refer back to steps 2–4 of lab 1.

3. Type a title for your document (for example, My Second HTML Document), and add the </title> end tag.

4. As in Steps 5–6 of lab 1, add the end tag </head> and the start tag <body>.

5. Now type a first-level heading, for example An Exercise in Linking, between the tags <h1> and </h1>.

6. Type two, three, or four paragraphs of text—any text you like, as long as it contains the following:
   - A <p> tag at the beginning of each paragraph
   - Enough total lines to more than fill one screen with text (even if you have to type gibberish to make this much text)
   - This text somewhere in the first paragraph: The Beatles
   - This text somewhere in the second paragraph: Ringo Starr

7. Go to the occurrence of "The Beatles" in your first paragraph, and add anchor codes to this text, as, for example, in the following:

   `<a href="#beatles">The Beatles</a>`

**How to Publish on the Internet**

8. Do similarly with the occurrence of "Ringo Starr" in your second paragraph, as, for example, in the following:

`<a href = "#ringo">Starr</a>`

9. Following your final paragraph, press ENTER to start a new line, and type a level-2 heading such as the following:

`<h2>The Beatles: Four Lads from Liverpool</h2>`

10. Now add destination tags to this heading so that it looks like the following example:

`<h2><a name = beatles>The Beatles: Four Lads from Liverpool</a></h2>`

Notice that the destination tags are inserted between the heading tags and the heading text; the heading tags remain on the outside to ensure that the entire text string is treated as a heading.

11. Press ENTER, type <p>, and then type one or two additional paragraphs of text that contain, somewhere within them, the following link destination:

`<a name = ringo>Ringo, the drummer</a>`

Be sure you type <p> at the beginning of each paragraph.

12. Complete this document with the following steps:
    - Add the </body> and </html> tags at the bottom of the document.
    - Save the document on your hard disk as text (ASCII), giving it the file name `second.html` (if your system supports four-character file extensions) or `second.htm` (if your system supports only three-character extensions).
    - Close the file.

### Testing Your Links

1. Using your browser (or the one included in the software that came with this book), open the file `second.html` (or `second.htm`) that you just created. If you are prompted to specify the type of file you are opening, it is a local file (that is, one that is stored on your computer's hard disk).

2. In the first paragraph of the body, find the text "The Beatles," and click on it. This should jump you to the heading "The Beatles: Four Lads from Liverpool."

**3.** In the second paragraph of the body, find the text "Ringo Starr," and click on it. This should jump you to the text "Ringo, the drummer."

**How did you do?** If your links are not performing as expected, exit your browser and reopen the document in its original form. Check all anchor and destination codes, and fix them as needed. Then save the file, close it, and test it again with the browser.

# Lab 3

## Creating External Links

This is an exercise in applying anchor codes to create links from one document to another. To test this exercise, you will need to have completed the document created in lab 2. Be sure to refer back to labs 1 and 2 if you aren't sure how to type in the basic code elements. If you use special HTML-building software, just insert the corresponding HTML elements instead of typing the codes and their angle brackets < >.

### Creating External Links

1. Open your text-editing program—for example Windows Notebook, Microsoft Word for Windows, WordPerfect for Windows, or any other word-processing program that can save your document in text (ASCII) format.

2. Create a new HTML document, typing in the <html>, <head>, and <title> start tags. If you're in doubt about how to type these in, refer back to Steps 2–4 of lab 1.

3. Type a title for your document (for example, My Third HTML Document), and add the </title> end tag.

4. As in steps 5–6 of lab 1, add the end tag </head> and the start tag <body>.

5. Now type a first-level heading, for example Another Exercise in Linking, between the tags <h1> and </h1>.

6. Type one or two paragraphs of text—any text you like, as long as it contains the following:
   - A <p> tag at the beginning of each paragraph
   - This text somewhere in the first paragraph: first linking exercise
   - This text somewhere in the first or second paragraph: The Beatles

7. Go to the occurrence of "first linking exercise" in your first paragraph, and add to this text anchor codes containing a relative URL, so that the text looks like this:

```
<a href="second.html">first linking exercise</a>
```

**Note:** If the document you created in lab 2 has only the three-character extension `.htm`, then type the identifier as `"second.htm"`.

8. Go to the occurrence of "The Beatles" in your text, and add anchor codes with an internal identifier, so that the text looks like this:

```
<a href="second.html#beatles">The Beatles</a>
```

9. Complete this document with the following steps:
   - Add the `</body>` and `</html>` tags at the bottom of the document.
   - Save the document on your hard disk, *in the same directory where you saved second.htm(l)*.
     Be sure to save this document as text (ASCII). Give it the file name `third.html` (if your system supports four-character file extensions) or `third.htm` (if your system supports only three-character extensions).
   - Close the file.

### Testing Your Links

1. Using your browser, open the file `third.html` (or `third.htm`) that you just created. If you are prompted to specify the type of file you are opening, it is a local file (that is, one that is stored on your computer's hard disk).

2. Find the text "first linking exercise," and click on it. This should open your document `second.htm(l)` at its beginning.

3. Reopen `third.html` (or `third.htm`), find the text "The Beatles," and click on it. This should now open `second.htm(l)` to the heading "The Beatles: Four Lads from Liverpool."

**How did you do?** If your links are not performing as expected, exit your browser and reopen your new document in its original form. Check the anchor codes, and fix them as needed. Then save the file, close it, and test it again with the browser.

# Lab 4

## Creating an Electronic Brochure

In this exercise, you design and construct an HTML document modeled after the structure of a bi-fold brochure. Let's say you're working for a company that manufactures and sells widgets. You have a great product, and you want your audience on the World Wide Web to know about it. It's your job to design an electronic "brochure" that will get your company's message across.

If you use special HTML-building software, just insert the corresponding HTML elements instead of typing the codes and their angle brackets < >.

**Note:** Wherever you see an instruction for using the file extension .htm, you should use .html if your operating system supports four-character extensions.

### Creating an Electronic Brochure

1. Create a new HTML document by typing in the <html>, <head>, and <title> start tags.
2. Type a title for your document (for example, World's Best Widgets), and add the </title> end tag.
3. Add the end tag </head> and the start tag <body>.
4. Now design your home page as if it were the front flap of a brochure:
   - Type a first-level heading, for example, World's Best Widgets, between the tags <h1> and </h1>.
   - Press ENTER, type a <p> tag, and then type a line or so of text that will attract your audience to the contents of your brochure, for example: Have you spent half your life looking for the widget that's right for you? Well, look no further! We've got jut what you need!
   - Press ENTER and then type a second-level heading containing an anchor, for example the following:

   <h2><a href="qual.htm">World's Best Widgets: Quality at a reasonable price</a></h2>

   This anchor will link to the first "inside" flap of your brochure.

□ Repeat the preceding substep, changing the heading/anchor text and the identifier, as in the following example:

```
<h2><a href="descrip.htm">Meet The Widget</a><h2>
```

This anchor will link to the second inside flap.

□ And now add one more heading/anchor, such as the following:

```
<h2><a href="contact.htm">Marketing Information</a>
</h2>
```

This anchor will link to the "back" flap, containing marketing info.

You won't be adding a graphic to this page because we haven't discussed how to add graphics yet, but you might just want to think about what kind of graphic you'd like to add, and where you would put it on this home page.

**5.** Complete this document by adding the `</body>` and `</html>` tags, and then save it on your hard disk as a text (ASCII) file with the file name `widgets.htm`.

**6.** Now create a new document that will serve as your first inside flap. Give it a title like `World's Best Widgets: Quality at a Reasonable Price`, and make the first element in the document's body a level-one heading like the following:

```
<h1>Quality at a Reasonable Price</h1>
```

**7.** Press ENTER to start a new line, and then type in an unordered list of qualities that summarize how great your widgets are, using the `<ul>` and `<li>` codes, as in the following example:

```
<ul>
<li>100 percent effective in the industry's toughest
tests
<li>3-year unconditional guarantee
<li>Highest rating by the leading technical journal
<li>Lowest unit cost on the market
</ul>
```

**8.** Below the list, add anchors that link back to the home page and to the second inside flap:

```
<p><a href="widgets.htm">Home Page</a>
<p><a href="descrip.htm">Meet the Widget</a>
```

9. Complete this document by adding the `</body>` and `</html>` tags, and then save it on your hard disk as a text (ASCII) file with the file name `qual.htm`.

10. Create another document that will serve as your second inside flap. Give it a title like `Meet the Widget`, and make the first element in the document's body a level-one heading like the following:

    `<h1>Meet the Widget</h1>`

11. Type in the body of this document, using text elements that are already familiar to you: `<p>` tags, `<h2>` and `</h2>` tags, and so on. This is your chance to tell the world all about your unbeatable widgets, so give it your best!

12. Below the text, add anchors that link back to the home page and to the back flap:

    `<p><a href="widgets.htm">Home Page</a>`
    `<p><a href="contact.htm">Marketing Information</a>`

13. Complete this document by adding the `</body>` and `</html>` tags, and then save it on your hard disk as a text (ASCII) file with the file name `descrip.htm`.

14. Create the final document, which will serve as the back flap of your brochure. Give it the title `Widgets: Marketing Information`, and make the first element in the document's body a level-one heading like the following:

    `<h1>How to Order the World's Best Widgets</h1>`

15. Type a `<p>` tag, followed by a brief line such as:

    `To talk to one of our knowledgeable sales representatives, call us at 1-800-555-4567 today, or write to us at:`

16. Press ENTER, and add an address, using the `<address>`, `</address>`, and `<br>` tags, for example:

    `<address>World's Best Widgets, Inc.<br>`
    `11 Industrial Parkway<br>`
    `Pleasanton, NJ 07999`
    `</address>`

17. Below the address, add an anchor that links back to the home page:

    `<p><a href="widgets.htm">Home Page</a>`

**18.** Complete this document by adding the `</body>` and `</html>` tags, and then save it on your hard disk as a text (ASCII) file with the file name `contact.htm`.

**Note:** Be sure you save all documents in the same directory.

### Testing Your Brochure

**1.** Using your browser, open the file `widgets.htm` (or `widgets.html`) that you just created. If you are prompted to specify the type of file you are opening, it is a local file (that is, one that is stored on your computer's hard disk).

**2.** Read through the brochure, testing all links.

**How did you do?** If your links are not performing as expected, exit your browser and reopen the four documents you've just created in their original form. Check the anchor codes, and fix them as needed. Then save the files, close them, and test them again with the browser.

**How to Publish on the Internet**

# Lab 5

## Planning Linked Documents

This exercise is different from labs 1–4. We're not going to lead you step by step through a specific task; instead, we're going to ask you to consider carefully how you would put together an HTML document or two of your own choosing. In a way, we're asking you now to be an architect, rather than a carpenter; instead of building a structure, you're going to design one. Of course, once you've designed it, you may want to go ahead and build it. We won't stop you.

There are two parts to this exercise. Part A approaches the design task from a structural perspective, Part B from a functional angle. You may do either or both parts.

### A. Designing from a Structural Approach

1. Look around your home or your office, and pick up a printed publication of some sort. It can be a Sunday newspaper, a magazine, a book, or the *Encyclopædia Britannica*—it's up to you; just make sure it's something of, say, 25 pages or more.

2. Carefully analyze the publication's structure, and ask yourself how you might design a hypertext equivalent to it. Following are some specific questions you might ask:

   ▫ What is the first thing you see when you pick up the publication, and how might you design that first impression into a home page for your hypertext document?

   ▫ Does the publication have a table of contents? If so, how might you create a hypertext version of its TOC, with access to the TOC from the home page and access from the TOC to the sections, chapters, or volumes that would contain the document's content?

   ▫ Page through the publication, looking for specific structural elements. Does it have different sections that are laid out in different ways? cross-references? footnotes? sidebars? citations or other source references? ads, commercial or classified? How would you reproduce these features in hypertext?

   ▫ Does it have an index?

3. Plan your hypertext document, or set of documents, on the basis of how you answer the questions in Step 2. If it helps, take pencil and paper and diagram the structures. You might, for example, draw a freehand sketch—or a computer graphic—that illustrates the links comprising your hypothetical document set.

## B. Designing from a Functional Approach

We're going to state this task simply, but we acknowledge that it might be a complex exercise. Think of a function you might like a Web document to fulfill, and design a set of linked documents that would suit the purpose. The function could be:

- Instructional, as in a "how-to" guide or technical manual
- Informational, as in a newsletter or product announcement
- Entertaining, as in a collection of jokes or regional folk tales
- Any other function you think could be effectively fulfilled by circulating your content on the Web

Go to—you're on your way!

# 6 Illustration, Decoration, and Navigation:

## Using Graphics and Other Media

Anchors and links, which we discussed in chapter 5, give World Wide Web documents their structural flexibility and much of their interactive quality. *Graphics* give them their visual pizzazz.

What's the first thing that catches your eye when you open a Web document? Probably it's the title, heading, or introductory words at the top of the page, displayed in large, bold letters. You may have noticed that some of these initial headings are plain and others are attractively contained within a banner. Banners often contain vivid colors and a logo that stamps, or *brands,* the document in such a way that you instantly recognize the particular Web site. What is a banner, in hypertext terms? A graphic that is applied to give an initial heading visual appeal.

Or maybe your eye is caught by a picture on the screen. You may then discover that the picture turns out to be an anchor for a link to another screen. In any case, graphic art can immediately distinguish the look and feel of a Web document.

Take a look at figure 6-1 as an example. This is the home page of the Web site for Free Range Media. The banner heading is a combination of the company's logo and a picture of an open-air scene suggesting the "free range" of the company's name. Below the banner are four picture graphics that serve as anchors connecting to the topics "WWW Adventures," "Introductions," "Products & Services," and "News & Events."

Graphics can spice up a document, but even more importantly, they can be used to illustrate in ways that text alone cannot. And they can also be used as tools for helping your readers navigate around your Web site (the four anchor graphics in figure 6-1 being a case in point).

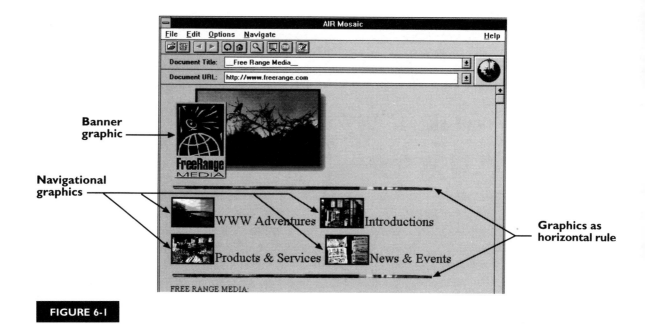

**Banner graphic**

**Navigational graphics**

**Graphics as horizontal rule**

FIGURE 6-1

In this chapter, we'll explore the use of graphics in hypertext documents. We'll explain the codes, show how to use them, and discuss strategies for employing graphics as illustrative, decorative, and navigational features within your documents. We'll also discuss video and sound—two additional features that have already begun to show their futuristic qualities on the World Wide Web.

## The Graphics Revolution on the World Wide Web

In its earliest incarnation, the World Wide Web existed without graphics. Text browsers, such as Lynx, were able to read HTML documents and allow their users to jump by way of links. It was clearly a better way to exploit the evolving file-transfer technologies of the Internet, introducing the structural flexibility and interactivity that we now associate with the Web.

In early 1993, however, a new development hit the Web with a tremendous impact: the release of a browser capable of delivering not just text, but *formatted* text and graphics—and ultimately sound and video as well. The new browser was named Mosaic.

Technologically, it was a short step from the World Wide Web standard as originally developed at CERN to the debut of Mosaic. According to Chris Wilson, the primary developer of Mosaic for Windows, all of the hypertext capabilities existed in the Web project but had not yet been fully exploited when the team at NCSA began its work. NCSA's first step was to find a way to implement rich text, so that the visually flat text transported on the Net could be formatted and structured effectively. Mosaic proved capable of interpreting rich text so as to produce bold and italic lettering, and a variety of font types and sizes. Not only does rich text relieve the monotony of Internet documents, but it greatly improves readability by making headings stand out and giving other specially formatted blocks of text their characteristic visual qualities.

Secondly, Mosaic made possible the use of graphical images. The engineers at NCSA were uniquely responsible for implementing the use of in-line images in Web documents. This, of course, is what gives Web publications their immediate visual appeal when viewed with a graphical browser such as Mosaic, and it is exactly what has attracted so many millions of new Internet aficionados in the short time since the first release of Mosaic.

No one foresaw the extent of the impact this would have on the computing world, not even the visionaries at NCSA. They knew they had achieved something of a breakthrough, but they didn't realize just how popular Mosaic would be until NCSA put its alpha release out on the server and, in Chris Wilson's words, "we started seeing hundreds and hundreds of downloads of it per day."

And the rest, as they say, is history.

---

Mosaic was developed within the National Center for Supercomputer Applications (NCSA) by a team led by Mark Andreesen. Another member of the NCSA team, Chris Wilson, led the effort to apply Mosaic in the Windows format, which is now the most popular client platform. In this highly sophisticated, user-friendly form, Mosaic set a level of standards that has quickly and dramatically changed the perceptions of people around the world about the nature of the Internet as a communications platform. Mosaic and other new browsers that have followed in its wake have revolutionized the look of the World Wide Web. Its specialized protocol, HTTP, now transports not just hyper*text,* but hyper*media.*

## GRAPHICS CODES AND GRAPHICS FILES

Here's the good news about adding graphics to your documents: There's only one basic code to learn—the Image (<img>) tag. Here's even better

---

news: You don't use a start tag and an end tag—one tag takes care of everything. You do need to know about four attributes that are used with the <img> tag—src (source), alt (for text alternative), align (for text alignment), and ismap (image mapping). Add a uniform resource locator (URL) code to indicate the name and location of the graphic file, and you've got the information needed to code a graphical image into a document.

### Image? What Image?

A graphical image is always contained in its own, separate file. You may be familiar with bitmaps (.bmp files), Tag Image File Format or TIFF (.tif) files, and other files created by various graphics applications. If you're using a word processor to write a conventional document, you can insert such graphics files into your document and they will be printed as graphical images.

The World Wide Web supports a growing number of graphics file types. GIF, or Graphics Interchange Format (.gif), and JPEG (.jpg) files have become the common standards. (JPEG stands for the Joint Photographic Experts Group, which developed the JPEG standard.) At the time of this writing, most of the available browsers support only GIF files as inline images; however, changes in browser capabilities are occurring rapidly, and we suspect that by the second half of 1995, JPEG files will also be commonly supported. It's likely that TIFF, Microsoft Paintbrush (.pcx), and perhaps other graphics file formats will follow before long.

You can use an existing graphics file, as long as it is of a type that the Web supports, or you can create one. To create one, use a graphics application software package that allows you the option of saving files in a format (for example, GIF) supported by the Web. There are a number of graphics packages available, both commercially and as shareware, that provide this capability.

So how do you insert a GIF, JPEG, or other graphics file into an HTML document? You don't, exactly; the graphics file exists separately from your HTML file. What you do is to insert a *pointer* within your HTML file—a code that "points to" the location of the graphics file. That code is an <img> tag, together with its attributes and the URL for the graphics file. The reader's browser interprets this code as an instruction to find and retrieve the graphics file, and display it in the document at the place where you've inserted the <img> tag.

**How to Publish on the Internet**

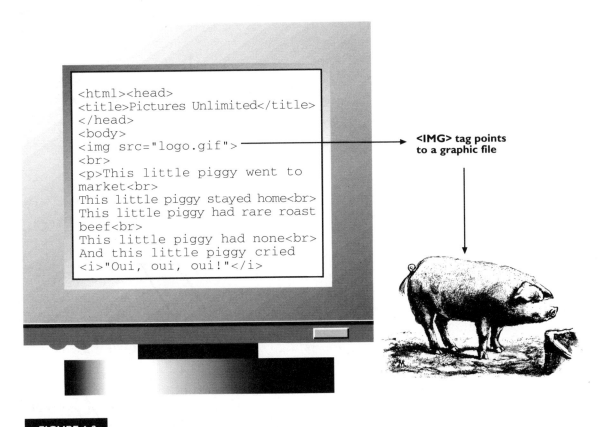

```
<html><head>
<title>Pictures Unlimited</title>
</head>
<body>
<img src="logo.gif">
<br>
<p>This little piggy went to
market<br>
This little piggy stayed home<br>
This little piggy had rare roast
beef<br>
This little piggy had none<br>
And this little piggy cried
<i>"Oui, oui, oui!"</i>
```

**<IMG> tag points
to a graphic file**

**FIGURE 6-2**

## The Image (<IMG>) Tag and Its Attributes

To add a graphic to your document, you use the <img> tag, together with one or more attributes and a URL. You must always use the src attribute, and you should also use the alt attribute. Here's what the tag looks like:

**<img src="*URL*"**
**alt="*text*">**     **Image tag with src and alt attributes.** This tag marks the place in a document where a graphic will be displayed. The src attribute signals that the name and location of the source file for the graphic will follow the = sign. *URL* stands for the location of the graphic file; this can be a Relative or an Absolute URL. The attribute alt instructs the browser to display the specified text if the browser cannot display the graphic. *text* stands for the text alternative that you specify.

Two examples follow. The first uses a Relative URL, the second an Absolute URL. Both specify that, if a browser cannot display the graphic, it displays the text alternative, "bird", instead.

***Code Examples***

*→ relative*

```
<img src="bird.gif" alt="bird">  →
<img src="http://www.birds.com/bird.gif" alt="bird">
```

*→ absolute.*

***Viewed Results***

**Graphic    Text**

bird

**Why use the `alt` attribute?** Because some browsers might be unable to display the graphic. There are three possible reasons why this might be true of a given browser:

- The browser is a *text-only* browser and cannot display graphics. Earlier browsers, for example Lynx, are only capable of reading text.
- The browser might be capable of displaying graphics, but the user has the in-line image switch turned off to minimize the time it takes for downloading files.
- An error has occurred—for example, the browser cannot find the graphics file, or the user's system is low on memory.

In any of these cases, your document needs to contain something that the user's browser can display instead of the graphic image. In the example above, if the text alternative "bird" is specified in the image tag, then the user will see the text "bird" and infer that what he or she is missing is a picture of a bird. Such text, no matter how descriptive, hardly compensates for a zippy graphic, but it's better than nothing.

The `alt` attribute is especially important if you're using the graphic as an anchor. If users cannot see the picture that represents the topic the link goes to, they need to see a textual description of the topic.

**The `align` and `ismap` attributes.** The `align` and `ismap` attributes are optional, but they both have their value. Note that we shall only describe `ismap` briefly here and devote more detail to it in Part Three of this book.

---

**align = top**
**align = middle**
**align = bottom**

`align` **attribute.** This attribute specifies the alignment of text relative to a graphic when text follows on the same line as the graphic. `top`, `middle`, and `bottom` are the three alternatives. The examples below illustrate. (Note that these examples use a Relative URL.)

```
<img src="square.gif" alt="square" align="top">
```
⊡ Square

```
<img src="square.gif" alt="square" align="middle">
```
⊡ Square

```
<img src="square.gif" alt="square" align="bottom">
```
⊡ Square

**ismap**    ismap **attribute.** This attribute allows image mapping—the ability to include multiple anchor destinations within one graphic, based on pixel coordinates. This means that a mouse click on one area of the graphic jumps to one topic and a mouse click on another area jumps to a different topic. Image mapping is an advanced HTML technique that requires you to write a map file for your Web server. We'll explain image mapping in chapter 9.

## File Formats, File Size, and Downloading Time: Some Rules of Thumb

GIF and JPEG files enable a browser to display them in relatively small file formats. This makes them suitable for the World Wide Web because users need to be able to download files from the Internet quickly. If you've worked with graphics files, you know that they can be very large, as measured in bytes. Unlike with candy bars, larger byte sizes do not necessarily yield more satisfaction. In fact, the larger the file size, the slower the download time. Certain other graphics file formats, such as TIFF, can produce an image that amounts to several megabytes of file size, which is guaranteed to try the patience of any Internet user. As additional file formats come to be supported by the Web, more and more choices will be available, and it will pay to keep in mind the need to minimize file size.

Besides file format, other factors are important in determining file size: complexity of the image, number of colors, and display size. Each of these factors correlates positively with file size: the more complex the image, the more bytes in the file; the greater the number of colors in an image, the more bytes; and the larger the image when displayed, again the more bytes. As we've suggested, however, these positive correlations have negative impacts on the speed of file transfer. The point is to minimize file size, no matter what the format. Some of the ways to do this are obvious, and some are not:

- Keep the display size to the minimum that's consistent with your screen design and the purpose of the graphic.
- Use a simple color scale, such as the conventional 16-color Windows palette; if you absolutely need more colors, go to a 256-color scale, but

avoid the much larger color scales that are available. (See also the note below.) Remember that a very small image with millions of colors can produce more bytes than a much larger image with only 16 colors.

- If you really need millions of colors for, say, a Monet reproduction, then you should create an *external image* and link to it from the location within your document. (See the discussion of external files in the next section.)
- Keep in mind that gray-scale is not black and white, and can result in a file as large as a color image.

> **N O T E**  To ensure consistent display quality, it's important that you use the same color palette for all in-line graphics within a document. When a browser opens a document, it "reads" the palette of the first in-line graphic, and that is the palette the browser uses to display all subsequent graphics. If any subsequent graphic contains colors that are not in the initial palette, its colors will not be displayed accurately.

## External Files: Images, Sound, and Video

So far, we've been discussing *in-line images*—images that are displayed within the HTML document itself. In-line images are loaded and displayed when you open an HTML document. *External images,* in contrast, are separate; they are not automatically loaded and displayed on your screen together with the text of the document you've loaded. They are, however, represented within the document by anchors that are associated with either text or in-line graphics. For example, you may see a small in-line image in a document that is actually a GIF file which loads automatically; this image, however, is also an anchor, and when you click on it, a larger JPEG file is loaded into your document. It may take a few seconds or so to load that image, and then what you see may be the same picture you saw a moment earlier—in the in-line image, that is—but on a substantially larger scale.

Technically, external images are not displayed by your browser; they are displayed in a different program, one that your browser calls as it loads the file for the external image. Your browser configuration determines which applications can be called; if your browser is not configured to read a specific graphics application, then you will not be able to view external images that have been created by that application (unless, of course, they have been converted to a format your browser can read).

Click on a GIF file displayed as an in-line graphic . . .

. . . and a larger, external graphic is loaded from a JPEG file.

Lorem ipsum dolor sit amet, consectetuer adipiscing elit, sed diam nonummy nibh euismod tincidunt ut laoreet dolore magna aliquam erat volutpat. Lorem ipsum dolor sit amet, elit, sed tincidun aliquam

**FIGURE 6-3**

**Illustration, Decoration, and Navigation**

**Including external files with an HTML document.** External images, as we've said, come from separate files; therefore, you link to an external image from within an HTML document as you would to a separate document—through an anchor. You create an anchor that specifies a URL as the destination, just as if you were creating an external text link. Thus, the code for an anchor built into the in-line graphic pictured in figure 6-3, linking to a file containing an external image, might look like the following:

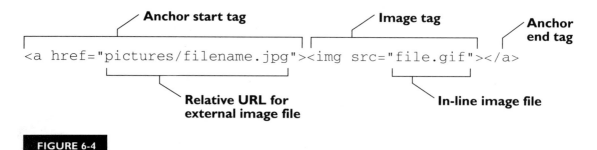

Anchor start tag    Image tag    Anchor end tag

```
<a href="pictures/filename.jpg"><img src="file.gif"></a>
```

Relative URL for external image file    In-line image file

FIGURE 6-4

Notice that the anchor code in this example contains an Absolute URL. As with the external links discussed in chapter 5, you must use an Absolute URL if the external graphics file is located at a different Web site.

**Sound and video files.** Sound and video are external files. When you load an HTML document, you will see placeholder images that function similarly to the in-line GIF-file image described two paragraphs above. That is, when you click on a placeholder image, your browser loads the sound or video file and then plays it.

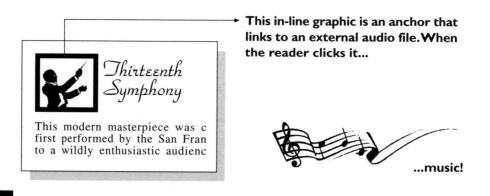

This in-line graphic is an anchor that links to an external audio file. When the reader clicks it...

*Thirteenth Symphony*

This modern masterpiece was c first performed by the San Fran to a wildly enthusiastic audienc

...music!

FIGURE 6-5

You include a sound or video file in an HTML document in the same way that you include a file containing an external image: by creating an anchor that links to the external file by specifying its URL as destination. If your readers' browsers support the file type, they will be able to hear the sound or see the video by clicking on the text or in-line graphic that contains the anchor.

At this time in the development of file-transfer technology, we must issue a caveat about the use of sound and video files. You can include sound and video in an HTML document by linking them as external files. However, you must beware that both sound files and video files tend to be extremely large. Let's modify that: sound files are extremely large, and video files can be humongous. It's not uncommon for a sound file to take five or ten minutes for downloading—and then only fifteen seconds to play back! The rule of thumb: use sound or video files only if you cannot think of another way to communicate the content effectively, and then keep them to a bare minimum in size. Even better advice might be not to use them at all until the technology improves to the point where files can be transported and downloaded efficiently. That time is coming.

## USING GRAPHICS: FUNCTIONS AND STRATAGEMS

As we mentioned earlier there are three main purposes to which you can put graphics in a hypertext document. You can use graphics to illustrate a point, to embellish or decorate the document, and to serve navigational purposes.

### Graphics for Illustration

Using graphics for illustration is so obvious that we don't need to persuade you why you might want to do it. If you've seen some of the better Web sites where graphic images are employed with great illustrative effect, you already understand how they fit into the environment of hypertext.

You can illustrate Web documents in every way you can think of illustrating printed documents. You can simply show a picture of something you are also describing in text, or you can show a picture of something you cannot adequately describe in words. Want to show off your company's latest necktie designs? illustrate the difference between a cutter and a sloop? make it perfectly clear to your reader what a dado is? Use graphics. For any conventional or unconventional illustrative purpose, you can employ the Web's capability of delivering graphical images.

**FIGURE 6-6**

Charts and graphs are another form of illustration. If your document discusses economic trends, baseball records, sales results, public-opinion surveys, demographic data, travel mileage between here and there and everywhere else, or any other subject that involves statistics, you can include charts and graphs of many different types.

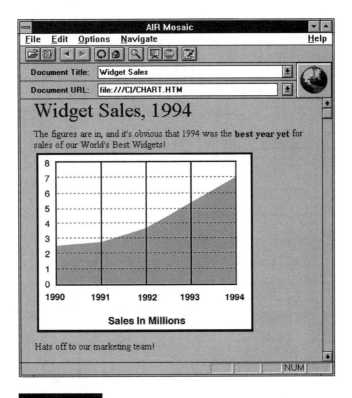

**FIGURE 6-7**

Still another way to use graphics is to convert your own photos for inclusion in an HTML document. If you think about it, you can probably come up with a hundred different purposes for doing something like this, from assembling a hypermedia family album to offering your classic Morgan M4 sports car for sale over the Internet.

You can scan your photos electronically and convert them to GIF files. Or you can convert already existing disk copies of photos to GIF format. A growing number of photo developing companies now offer to print your roll of film on a floppy disk, and many of them throw in the display software for free. Remember, however, that if you intend to use your photos in an HTML document, you still have to convert the file to a format that is supported by the Web protocol.

On a grander scale, one of the more interesting recent Web sites featured an exhibit of photographs taken by Ansel Adams to help the University of California celebrate its centennial in 1968. Together, the photos represented a portrait of the numerous UC branches during a time when that great university was not only celebrating an anniversary but also embroiled in the student movements of the sixties. If you're interested in seeing this exhibit, you can open the Web site's home page at `http://bookweb.cwis.uci.edu:8042/AdamsHome.html`

One can also find a growing number of Web sites that use graphic reproductions of art works. Many of them, including the on-line Andy Warhol Museum and *Le WebLouvre,* function as virtual museum exhibits. There are also some commercial Web sites growing up around the subject of art, for example that of the Medium for Global Access, Inc. (MGA). MGA's Web site offers works by a number of artists for sale over the Net and includes small graphical reproductions of the works offered.

Here are several interesting Web sites that focus on art:

- The Andy Warhol Museum, at `http://fridge.antaire.com:80/warhol/`
- *Le WebLouvre,* in two locations: European location at `http://mistral.enst.fr/`; North American location at `http://sunsite.unc.edu/louvre/`
- French Painting in the Eighteenth Century, from *Le Musée virtuèl,* at `http://dmf.culture.fr/`
- Horror, Fantasy, and the Grotesque in Art, at `http://www.ugcs.caltech.edu/~werdna/grotesque/grotesque.html`
- Japanese paintings from the *Ukiyo-e* style (17–19 c.), at `ftp://ftp.uwtc.washington.edu/pub/Japanese/Pictures/Ukiyo-e/`
- MGA Presents Access Art, at `http://www.mgainc.com/Art/HomePage.html`

⚠️ Once again, the subject of permissions rears its head. If you publish graphical reproductions of art works, be careful about securing the necessary permissions. This might be easy if you are the Webmaster of the Louvre's Web site, but it can be tricky if you or your organization does not own the original art works.

We are now knee-deep in complex graphics, and it's time to mention once more the issue of file size and transfer time. Art reproductions almost invariably create big files—sometimes upward of 200Kb. If your aim is to display GIF or JPEG representations of art works, you have no choice but to publish complex graphics that will cost your readers a great number of download minutes. In this case, the best rules of thumb are to understand your audience and give them images that are worth waiting for. If

**How to Publish on the Internet**

you dazzle them with great electronic reproductions, they shouldn't mind the download time.

### . . . But is it art?

There's been a lot of talk in recent years about who should be able to gain electronic access to works of art. Should all of us be able, at least in theory, to install giant, high-resolution monitors and display an electronic image of the Mona Lisa in our living rooms? Or should the rights to such electronic display be limited and sold at a high price to those who can afford to be electronic art collectors?

We're not taking a position on this debate, but we do want to add a comment about the nature of what you see when you see an electronic image, in the hope that the issue of rights can be kept in perspective. We do not consider an electronic image of the Mona Lisa to be art. It is an *image* of a piece of art, an *illustration* of a work of art—just as a mass-produced photo in an art textbook is merely an illustration. The original painting itself is not just pixels of color arranged on wood in an attractive pattern; it is the specific colors of Da Vinci's palette, it is the physical textures of the paint, it is the specific size and dimensions that Da Vinci chose for the portrait, it is the spirit of the artist himself that was given personally to the original work, and it is the history and timelessness of that piece of wood with those colors and textures.

Such qualities cannot be transmitted electronically. What can be transmitted, however, is an image that can represent a great work of art. Viewers who have not seen the actual work can get an idea of it, and those who have seen the original can be reminded of what the real work looks like.

## Graphics for Decoration, Embellishment, and Design

Illustrating a point and presenting information visually are not the only good reasons for using graphics. A quick cruise through some Web sites will reveal how the creative use of graphics can enhance the overall look and feel of a document. Graphics should become a part of any design for a document or (especially) a Web site that contains a number of interrelated documents. Indeed, using graphics in your document designs can fulfill an important function, that of *branding* your Web site: identifying your content as *your* content.

Why brand your documents? To give them a distinctive look and feel. Web documents would all look pretty much the same if we relied on text elements for design. Moreover, we wouldn't be able to influence their appearance much, because the text elements are all interpreted by the configurations of users' browsers. If you want your readers to be aware of your Web site; if you want them to experience a certain look and feel that you give your documents, use graphics in your design.

If you visit CommerceNet, for example, you immediately become aware that you are in a specific place on the World Wide Web. CommerceNet documents are laid out according to a consistent design, with eye-catching yellow bars that link to subtopics and banners that have a uniform appearance.

We advise you to put some time and careful thought into deciding how you want your documents to look, and resolve to keep your design consistent. Do you want to impress readers with your elegance, your flamboyance, your understated classiness? Do muted shades suit your style, or would neon tones work better? A bold banner around your heading, or just text characters?

There are a number of specific ways to use graphics for branding. Let's look first at banner graphics.

**Banner graphics.** Banner graphics are commonly used in Web sites, and for good reason: they are the first thing a reader sees after opening a Web document. We might compare the banner that we see in figure 6-8, containing a picture and stylized text, to the flag, or nameplate, of a newspaper—that topmost element on the first page of a newspaper which carries the name of the paper. Just as the flag of a well-known newspaper, such as the *New York Times,* will have a characteristic look because of its font and layout, the banner of this Web document announces its content in a visually specific fashion.

You create a banner graphic by designing it with a graphics software application and saving it in a format supported by the Web (such as GIF). Then you place it in your document by inserting an image code with the source attribute pointing to the file. The code for the banner graphic that appears in figure 6-8, for example, is:

```
<img src = "advent.gif">
```

in which advent.gif is the name of the graphics file. This is a Relative URL pointing to a GIF file that is located in the same directory as the document file. If the file were located in a different directory on the same server, for example a directory named graphics, the code would be:

```
<img src = "graphics/advent.gif">
```

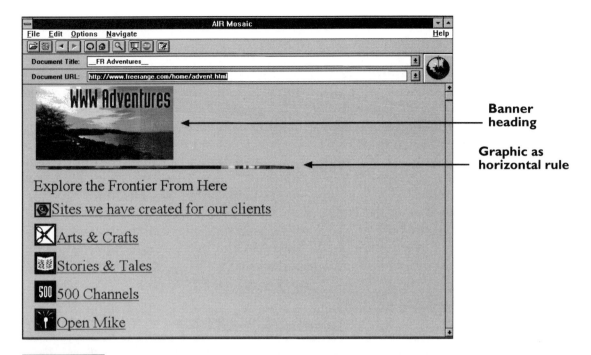

**Banner heading**

**Graphic as horizontal rule**

**FIGURE 6-8**

**Graphical embellishments.** Another way to put your imprint on your documents is by embellishing standard HTML elements such as horizontal rules and bullets. Actually, you do not embellish the HTML elements; you replace them with graphics.

In figure 6-8, the line dividing the banner from what follows below it is a stylized, very narrow graphic from a GIF file. Because the vertical dimension of this graphic is so small, the GIF file is relatively small and it costs little in download time. Crank up your imagination, and you might come up with a great idea for a graphic to use for dividers throughout your document—a snake, say, for a document about reptiles; a fishing rod, for a document about fishing. If you use the same graphic in place of the horizontal rule throughout your document, you'll have dividers that match your subject matter and add up to relatively few bytes.

You can also substitute a small graphic for standard HTML bullets in bulleted lists. Again, plumb your imagination for the right image—little pumpkins for a document about Halloween; basketballs; pine cones; machine nuts; you name it. Just keep the image tiny so that it's consistent with the size of the text it appears with. Tininess also means keeping the download time minimal.

**Customized font display.** One final issue of graphical design and embellishment concerns customized fonts. For normal text display, as we've pointed out, you generally leave the choice of fonts up to your readers' browser configurations. However, there may be elements in your document that require special fonts or that would at least be enhanced by the use of special fonts. If you are showing examples of calligraphy, for example, you do not want to leave the font choice up to the browser. If you want to include words or characters from languages based on different alphabets—Arabic or Hebrew words, for example, or Japanese Kanji characters—the best way to do this is to create those characters as graphical images. Save them in a GIF file, or in another format supported by the Web, and reference them in your document with <img> codes.

---

**Recycle those graphics**

Most browsers support file caching. This means that once a user has loaded a file for display, the browser reserves some memory to store that file temporarily as soon as the user opens another file. Cached files are more readily available to the browser than files that haven't been loaded. Therefore, a cached file can be reopened quickly, because the browser doesn't have to retrieve it again over the networks.

This is important for graphics files. Once a graphic is loaded into memory, it can be used again and again without the download time it costs initially. Thus, a document can reuse a graphic, no matter where or how many times it recurs, without slowing the viewer down significantly.

If you've decided to use graphical embellishments, you can save your readers a lot of time by reusing the same graphic for all horizontal rules within a document, and again by using just one graphic for all bullets. Whenever the browser encounters either of these graphical elements, it pulls the common file from memory and displays it without having to retrieve it over the Net.

---

## Graphics for Navigation

So far, the uses of graphics that we've discussed are not at all revolutionary in the world of publishing. Illustrative and decorative graphics in HTML documents necessitate some new methods of application, but in their general appearance and function, they are not different from the traditional graphics we see in books and other printed publications. However, the third usage of graphics, for navigational purposes, is unique to hypermedia documents.

When we talk about using graphics for navigation, we're talking about something that is qualitatively different: it's about using graphics as an *interface* between the reader and the information you are presenting. It's about adding buttons that function as if they were a part of your software: when the reader clicks on a button, he or she initiates an action—specifically, a jump to another location or the opening of a different document.

This is, of course, another way of restating the nature of hypertext and hypermedia, only now we are clearly not talking about text. We're talking about graphic images, in all sorts of designs, that can be made "hyper." Navigational graphics, as the name implies, are for moving around in hypermedia.

Let's use an example that should have a familiar ring to it. Figure 6-9 shows a navigational graphic in our hypothetical Beatles document. By clicking on the "George" button, the reader jumps to the topic "George Harrison," elsewhere in the document:

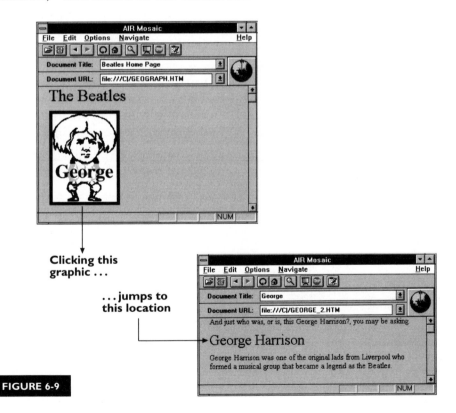

**Clicking this graphic . . .**

**. . . jumps to this location**

**FIGURE 6-9**

**How do they work?** Navigational graphics work the way anchors work. In fact, navigational graphics *are* anchors; their code consists of an image tag enclosed within anchor tags, as in the following example:

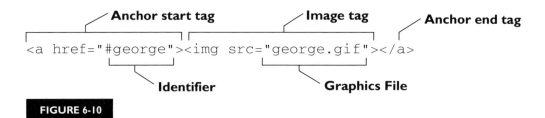

**FIGURE 6-10**

This is the source code for the anchored navigational graphic shown in figure 6-9. Notice that it is similar to the code in figure 6-4, in which we illustrated the code for linking to an external image. Notice, however, that the anchor in figure 6-10 points not to a graphics file, but to a destination within an HTML document—the same document; this is in fact the exact same anchor code, containing the same identifier, that we used back in chapter 5 when we discussed internal links. What's different is that now we are using an in-line graphics file (`george.gif`) in place of the anchor text (`George Harrison`) as the object the reader clicks on to jump to the destination.

As before, the destination must be marked by a pair of destination tags—in the current example, `<a name=george>` and `</a>`.

By changing the way the identifier is coded in the start tag, we can make this an external link. Again, as with hyper*text* links, we use an external link if the destination is located in a different directory or on a different server:

```
<a href="persons/george.html"><img src=
"george.gif"></a>
<a href="http://www.muzick.com/sixties/
george.html"><img src="george.gif"></a>
```

The first of these examples links to the file `george.html` located on the same server, the second links to a file by the same name but located on the server `www.muzick.com`. Because they both point to a file, and not a specific location within a document, no tags are needed to mark the destination.

**Directional graphics.** One of the simpler types of navigational graphics is *directional graphics*. There's nothing obscure about the meaning of the

**How to Publish on the Internet**

term; it refers to arrow graphics that, when clicked on, move the reader forward or backward in a document. Conventionally, a right arrow means "Click here to move to the next topic," and a left arrow means "Click here to move to the previous topic." You can also use an up arrow to refer to a broader topic or, alternatively, to a location one level higher in the document's organizational structure. Down arrows are not so common in HTML documents, but they can be used to move to a more specific, or more detailed, topic.

FIGURE 6-11

You create a directional graphic as you do any navigational graphic, by enclosing the image code within anchor tags. The <img> tag specifies the URL of the file containing the arrow graphic. As before, the anchor code contains an identifier pointing to the specific location that the arrow jumps to (the destination). A specific destination is marked by destination tags; if the destination is a file to be opened at its beginning, no destination tags are needed.

Don't be afraid to use your imagination when you create directional graphics; you are not required to use conventional arrows. If your document is about archery, you might want to use graphics depicting literal (rather than symbolic) arrows, feathers and all; if the topic is Native American lore, you could use arrowhead images. And you can go still farther afield. If your document is about bird watching, you might want to use directional graphics that display a bird's foot pointing in the appropriate direction, or the neck and head of a crane with the beak as pointer. If it's about hunting dogs, how about a German Shorthaired Pointer in the appropriate pose? Just keep the graphic small and reasonably simple, so that the size of the file stays within manageable limits.

FIGURE 6-12

**Modular graphics.** Modular graphics are composed of multiple button-like elements that represent anchors for several related links. As their name suggests, modular graphics fit several components together into an overall graphic. Each component has its separate function.

To see an example of a modular graphic, look again at the set of directional arrows shown in figure 6-11. Modular graphics can be used for topical navigation as well as directional. That is, instead of buttons that jump in a specific direction to a contiguous screen, the buttons can be links to topics elsewhere within your document—or in an entirely different document, even one located on another Web server.

The simple way to create modular graphics is to construct several individual graphical buttons, store them in the same directory location, and code them into your document side by side in one row. The following code is an example, using graphics files named `mod_1.gif, mod_2.gif,` and `mod_3.gif` to point to three graphical modules displayed together. They are linked, respectively, to destination files named `modlink1.html, modlink2.html,` and `modlink3.html`. (The code wraps at the end of the line; there should be no space where the line breaks in this illustration.)

```
<a href="modlinkl.html"><img src="mod_1.gif></a>
<a href="modlink2.html">
<img src="mod_2.gif"></a><a href="modlink3.html">
<img src="mod_3.gif"></a>
```

That's the simple, if boring, way to do it. Make sure there are no spaces between the ending and beginning angle brackets >< where they butt up against each other; that will ensure no spaces between the graphical modules when they are displayed by a browser.

A more elegant way to create modular graphics is to construct an image map, which entails building the separate components into one overall graphics file. If you refer back to figure 2-5 in chapter 2, you'll see an illustration of an image map. Creating an image map involves working with programs and scripts located on the Web server, and to discuss the topic here would be to get a bit ahead of ourselves. We'll come back to this in Part Three, where we discuss server scripting for image maps and other more advanced HTML and HTTP codes.

## AND FINALLY . . .

It's time for another lab. Turn to lab 6, Adding Navigational Graphics, to practice one aspect of what you've just learned about adding graphics to your HTML documents. Then we'll continue with chapter 7, where we'll step back from the nuts and bolts of HTML and discuss some principles and strategies of creating consistently good documents.

# Lab 6

## Adding Navigational Graphics to a Document

In this exercise, you add a navigational graphic to an existing document. We suggest that you add the graphic to `third.htm(l)`, the document you created in lab 3, and link the graphic to `second.htm(l)`, the document you created in lab 2.

**Note:** Wherever you see an instruction for using the file extension `.htm`, you should use `.html` if your operating system supports four-character extensions.

### Adding Navigational Graphics

1. Make sure you still have the two files `second.htm(l)` and `third.htm(l)` which you created in labs 2 and 3.
2. Using your text-editing program (or your HTML-building application), open the document `third.htm` and find the paragraph containing the text "The Beatles."
3. At the end of this paragraph, press ENTER.
4. Type the following anchor and image codes (or insert the appropriate elements and type in the identifier and the destination):

   `<a href="second.htm"><img src="beatles.gif"></a>`

   Make sure you type a space between `<a` and `href`, and again between `img` and `src`. These should be the only spaces on this line.
5. Check the document to make sure it contains all the necessary HTML codes, and save it under a new name, for example `fourth.htm`, and then close the document.
   - Save the document in text-only format.
   - Save the document on your hard disk, *in the same directory where you saved* `second.htm`.
6. Open a graphics application that offers you the option of saving a file in GIF format, and create a small graphic that you will use as an anchor.

Keep the graphic relatively simple, but feel free to design into it whatever suits your fancy. We suggest that you include in the graphic something (it can be text) to signal that this graphic will serve to open a document with text about the Beatles.

7. Complete the graphic and save it, *in the same directory as* `fourth.htm`, as a GIF file with the name `beatles.gif`. Then close the file.

8. Using your browser, open `fourth.htm`, and find the graphic in it that you've just created.

   If the graphic does not appear as you expect it to, exit your browser and check your previous work, both the `fourth.htm` source file and the `beatles.gif` graphic. Check also to make sure both of these files are stored in the same directory. When you feel confident that you've corrected all problems, reopen `fourth.htm` in your browser.

9. Click on the new graphic.

   This should open your document `second.htm(l)` at its beginning.

**How did you do?** If your links are not performing as expected, exit your browser and reopen the `fourth.htm` source file. Check the anchor codes, and fix them as needed. Then save the file, close it, and test it again with the browser.

**Note:** Remember to save your lab documents for future reference.

# 7 Style and Process:

## Maintaining Consistency in Your Documents

E ach of us has our own style of doing things—of speaking, riding a bicycle, crossing our legs. Certainly, we all have our own style of expressing our ideas. In publishing there is a vital place for originality and even quirkiness; however, when we create something for an audience beyond ourselves, there is also a need for standards of coherence, consistency, ease of use, and appropriateness of presentation.

In a way, these issues are an extension of branding, which we discussed in the previous chapter. Just as you consciously apply graphics to your document to give it a distinctive visual quality, you need to pay attention to the broader qualities of style that color the overall imprint your document makes on readers. For your readers' impressions of your material will be influenced by how your document looks and "feels," as well as by the logic and tone of its presentation. Some particular issues that call for care and planning are:

❑ How your document is designed and laid out overall, in terms of both visual appeal and usability
❑ Consistent standards for critical graphical and text elements
❑ Etiquette at the Web site: making your readers feel at home—and meeting their expectations

The need for stylistic consistency is all the more important if you are working on a large or long-term project, or if you are working with other people on the same project. In cases like these, a clear *sense* of style will not be enough; you need detailed, agreed-upon standards that map out the significant issues of style and process that will guide you through the project. You need, in other words, a set of specifications that will govern your operating procedures, from the planning stage to testing and release. This project "spec" will serve as both a reference source and a record of ongoing decisions about design, style, and process.

Finally, you must test your document before releasing it. Testing a hypermedia document means treating it not only as a piece of soon-to-be-published writing, but also as a piece of software.

Thus, you need to ensure consistency of style to produce quality documents and quality projects; you need a clearly articulated set of procedural guidelines to produce consistency of style; and you need to test your work to verify its quality.

---

## Write it down

We strongly recommend that you prepare a written style guide or project specification. That way, you don't have to rely on anybody's less-than-perfect memory about what "we" decided to do last month if "that" issue came up. Don't worry about perfection or definitiveness; just work out all the issues you can foresee, write up your "spec," and be prepared to treat it as a living document. Use this chapter as a set of guidelines, but even if you resolve all the issues we're laying out for you, you will no doubt run into more that still need to be resolved. And every time a new issue arises, be sure you record your decision about it and add it to your spec.

---

## THE BIG PICTURE: GENERAL ISSUES

Overall goals and procedures are an excellent place to start. You would not likely begin a project if you didn't have an idea—even if it's a vague idea—of what you hope to accomplish by doing it. Would you simply nail a few pieces of wood together and see what it turns out to be, or would you set out to build a birdhouse? So too with a publishing project. Figure out what you want to do, and begin it not by just diving in and writing HTML codes, but by planning the overall project. Think it through, sketch it out, discuss it with your teammates, talk it over with a friend while walking through a park, explain it to your spouse.

It's true that many a project has begun with nothing more than a hunch or a whim and then developed its own purpose and structure. Many more, however, have foundered for lack of motivation and direction. If you make the effort to plan your publishing project and give some careful thought to it, you might find that what started as a vague idea becomes a clear vision. In addition, you stand a good chance of preventing mistakes that would otherwise arise from lack of foresight. Not all mistakes, mind you—for it's nearly impossible to think of everything ahead of time, especially in an enterprise as new as World Wide Web publishing. But that's all the more reason for planning as much as you can at the outset.

## Project Goals and Other Beginning Points

First things first. Clarify your concept, and other issues will begin to fall into place. Think about the size and complexity of your project, figure out your personnel needs (if any, besides yourself), and start planning a schedule.

**Clarify your concept.** Let's say you have a great idea: you want to create a Web site around the theme of cooking. What does that mean? Food, of course, that's important. But what kinds of food? And there's a lot of other important stuff associated with food. What about cooking utensils, ovens and grills, and is gas really better than electricity? And do you need a full-blown food processor or will a Mouli mill do it, and where can you get the freshest vegetables, the choicest cuts of beef, and . . . hold it! Slow down a minute. Do you really want to have topics about all these things? What is this Web site all about, once again?

Okay, you think it through for a while and decide that what you really mean to do is to publish recipes for the twenty-five best meals you've ever cooked. You can name them, or at least narrow the choices down; and lo and behold, once you list them out, they suggest several identifiable categories. That savory secret your grandmother had for roasting the Thanksgiving turkey: that suggests a category about festive meals for family gatherings. Those special dumplings your Hungarian landlady showed you how to make while you were working your way through college, and the cold rotini salad you stumbled upon when you were out of olives and had to use capers instead: these two recipes sound like the start of a category you could call "Pastas, Dumplings, Potstickers, and Other Scrumptious Starches."

Eventually you realize there is plenty of material in your twenty-five best meals, and you can scrap the other topics. (Maybe you can just shelve them for now and keep them for a later project.) Good work! Sounds like a plan—or the beginning of a plan. And the topic of an introductory statement in your spec.

**Do you have a central motif?** At this point, you may or may not have a central motif in mind. A *motif,* as distinguished from a *concept,* is a theme or an image that runs through a work of music, art, or literature. (In music, it's a recurring musical theme or phrase, like the "Mimi" motif in *La Bohème.*) But if you do have a motif in mind, it would be a good idea to articulate it now, as best you can, so that it can inform your choices of graphics, layout, and perhaps terminology as you develop the project.

For example, suppose your ten best recipes are not really *your* ten best recipes; they are recipes you learned from various other good cooks—your grandmother, your Hungarian landlady, the foreign student who lived with your family one year while you were growing up, and so on. And each of these people had a characteristic saying related to cooking, such as "There's no such thing as too much sex or too much garlic," or "To prepare the perfect partridge, first let it fly through the hot kitchen." Bingo— you have a motif! You can place one saying at the top of each recipe, or include it in a brief introduction giving credit to the person who first showed you how to cook the dish you're about to describe.

**FIGURE 7-1**

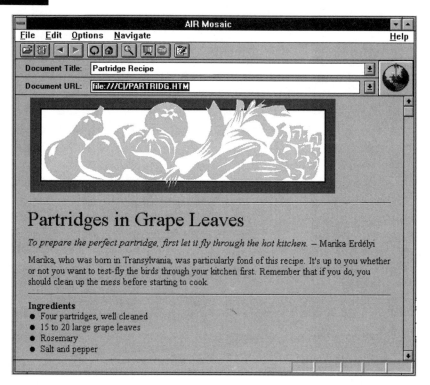

**How to Publish on the Internet**

Of course, your motif does not have to be verbal. It can be a specific graphical image, such as a mixing bowl and wooden spoon. Or it can be an ambient visual quality that conveys the sense, for example, of dining in a Mediterranean courtyard with grapevines and checkered tablecloths. It can be whatever your imagination tells you it should be.

The point is that if you have a central motif, you have a starting point for many specific design or editorial decisions that will pose themselves while you are developing the project. If you don't have one, don't lose sleep trying to think of one. Maybe a motif will occur to you while the project is under way. And maybe you don't need one at all.

**Personnel and scheduling.** Think about the scope of the project you are about to undertake. Can you do it by yourself, or do you need help? Think realistically about the time it will require. If you can do it by yourself, how long it will take? If you have a collaborator or an assistant, how long will it take? What role will this collaborator play—that of equal partner? research assistant? HTML builder? graphic designer?

Or will the project require a team of people—project manager, writer(s), HTML builder(s), editor(s), graphic designer(s), and proofreader(s)? If you've published materials in other media, you are aware that the process can be complex, time-consuming, and costly. Do not make the mistake of expecting HTML publishing to be free of these concerns.

And if you have worked solo on other types of projects, such as putting together a newsletter, a chapbook of your poetry, or a family cookbook, you know that the work does not do itself. It takes time, energy, and self-discipline.

In either case, it's a good idea to plan out your schedule before plunging into the project. Perhaps, because you've never published an HTML project, you won't be able to do more now than draw up a broad and approximate schedule, but try to assess your objectives and the work involved. Be honest and realistic, and be sure to include ramp-up time for everyone who has never worked on this sort of project before. Set milestone dates, and be prepared to adjust them if they prove too ambitious (or not ambitious enough!).

All these cautionary words are not meant to scare you off. An ounce of realism in the beginning can save a ton of frustration down the road (to coin a cliché). You don't want to assume, without thinking about it, that the project will take a week and then, two months later, find yourself trying to outline the third of eleven chapters. At this point, you might be tempted to abandon the whole exercise and take up tree farming instead. If, on the other hand, you've planned your project out and made reasonable "guesstimates" about the schedule, you will be in much better shape for reaching your milestones.

## Overall Structure and Design

Does your project entail building one document or multiple documents? What purpose will this document, or these documents, serve—instructional? commercial? entertainment?—and what does this suggest about possible structural models and frameworks? Who is your likely audience, and what kinds of overall design considerations should you take into account in order to serve their needs?

Your answers to these questions will give you a start toward building the foundations of your project, whether it be a single document or a more ambitious Web site.

**Structure and function redux.** This is the point at which you will want to think carefully about the structural and functional issues we raised in chapter 5 when discussing anchors and links. What kind of document, or set of documents, do you want to build? What is their purpose, and what structural HTML models are useful in designing them?

As we said then, you can start with either a structural or a functional approach. If you have a pretty good idea of how you want your Web site to operate, you can go ahead and plan its structure, addressing as many of the following issues as you now can:

▫ Home page: What information will it contain? What will this page look like—the cover page of a brochure? The title page of a book? Something else?
▫ How many topics should be linked to the home page (second-"layer" topics)? What should they be?
▫ Should these topics in your second "layer" be constructed within the main document (and addressed through internal links) or as separate documents (connected through external links)?
**Hint:** Size and complexity of these topics will give you a clue about whether they should be contained within the same document or in separate documents.
▫ How do you foresee the rest of the project's structure developing?

If it isn't clear at this point that you have a workable structural model, then back up one step and approach it from a functional perspective. Ask yourself again what you want this Web site to accomplish. When you are satisfied that you have the right answer, sketch out an overall design for your topics. Consider whether any of the structural models you know about will suit your purposes. Maybe you need to combine features from two or more structural models; maybe you need to come up with your own. In any case, clarifying your purpose will get you going in the right direction.

**Accessibility for text-only browsers.** In chapter 6, we discussed the use of the `alt` attribute with the `<img>` tag for navigational and illustrative graphics. Providing such alternative text for non-graphical browsers such as Lynx is a matter of courtesy and etiquette (and we'll mention it again in the context of etiquette, later in this chapter).

If your document or Web site is going to be heavy on graphics, there is another way of accommodating text-only browsers that you might consider. You could create alternative topics and sections that are entirely text-based, and link these sections to your home page. In effect, you would be offering your readers two "tracks" to your presentation. They can choose at the beginning which track to follow. In addition to readers with text-only browsers, this approach also accommodates those who have graphical browsers but choose to minimize downloading time by turning off their in-line image switch.

Providing two tracks requires a fair amount of extra work, so you should not commit yourself to it unless you feel strongly about serving those text-only readers. Think about who your audience is likely to be and what they are likely to expect from your site. You may just prefer to use the `alt` attribute and not build a complete text-only track. If you include text alternatives for all anchors and essential illustrative graphics, text-only browsers can at least navigate your documents and readers can follow your content adequately.

Of course, if graphical images are going to be the centerpiece of your documents—for example, if your Web site is a photo gallery or a cartoon series—then it doesn't make much sense to provide text alternatives at all. In this case, you simply have to forgo attempting to reach that part of the Internet audience that doesn't have graphical browsers.

## Write That Spec

However you decide the fundamental issues of overall structure and design, make sure your written spec conveys your vision of the project. This will give your collaborators something to refer to as they attempt to carry out your vision. They won't have to come running to you with questions about every little procedure, and you won't have to be constantly saying, "No, no, that's not what I had in mind."

And even if you are working alone, sometimes just having a clear "vision" statement to refer back to can help you stay on track as your project gathers its own momentum.

### Lab Exercise

Before going on to the next section, we recommend that you turn now to the end of this chapter and work through lab 7, Designing a Web Site. This is an exercise that you can try either by yourself or with a collaborative team. Gather the gang together in a conference room or around your dining-room table, bring out some snacks and your favorite beverage, and get involved in a little constructive fun.

## THE NITTY GRITTY: SPECIFIC DESIGN, EDITORIAL, AND PROCEDURAL ISSUES

Once you have the bigger issues of overall goals and structure mapped out, it's a good idea to think through some of the more specific issues and to include them in your written spec. Every serious publishing project employs an editorial style guide, whether it be the *Chicago Manual of Style* or an in-house style sheet, as well as a guide to design rules.

You might very well decide not to draw up your own editorial style guide and instead use a well-established resource such as the *Chicago Manual*. For design and procedural issues, however, you will need to think carefully at the beginning of your project about a number of nitty-gritty procedural matters. Unless you have a clear understanding about how you handle these issues, you will probably find yourself or your co-workers interrupting the creative process many times just to make decisions about how to design this type of page or what size that banner graphic should be.

We recommend that you decide at the outset which stylistic and design issues are important. Establish guidelines about them, and include the guidelines in your project specification. You need not take up every minute question at this time. But it will pay off in the long run if you can set standards for those issues that you believe are most likely to come up repeatedly in your project.

As your project moves forward and new issues of style crop up, be prepared to note them down, together with the decisions you make about resolving them. Add them to your spec so that when similar issues arise you can refer back to decisions already made. If your project is a large one and you have a sizable team of people working on it, it would be an excellent idea to appoint one person to be responsible for updating the spec.

The following three subsections discuss some design, editorial, and procedural/housekeeping issues that you might want to consider while you draw up your project spec.

## Design Specifications

You may be surprised when you discover how many seemingly small issues arise when you are designing and developing a document set for publication, whether it be for a conventional medium or the World Wide Web. From deciding on a "house style" down to what size special bullet graphics should be, having clear design specifications will help smooth your progress through many of these issues.

**House design style.** A house style is a set of specifications that are applicable to every document you or your company expects to produce. It can include standardized choices for a wide variety of text or graphic elements, from the size and theme of your banner graphics to the color and size of graphical bullets for bulleted lists.

Obviously, a house design style is closely related to branding. If you apply a distinctive house style, your documents will carry an imprint that readily identifies them to Internet users as yours. Naturally, you want that look and feel to be attractive and appropriate to your message. Brash, modest, assertive, simple—you can develop a house design style to express the character of your Web site.

You may want to start with a few general elements of house design— basic colors and banner graphics that will brand your Web site, layout of your home page, size and look of your navigational graphics and toolbar. You can always make additions and modifications to the house style down the road.

On the other hand, you may want to hold off on decisions about a house design style until you have some experience in developing and completing document sets. This might be the wiser choice if you are just starting out, do not have definite plans about future projects, and have no clear picture of how you want your documents to be identified. Or perhaps you do have a clear picture of future projects, but they will be so disparate that you don't want them to resemble each other in any way. Perhaps you are not building them for yourself but for a variety of other individuals or organizations. In this case, too, it would not make sense to establish a house design style.

**QuickTour.** How about providing easy access for your Web site in the form of QuickTour segments? A QuickTour is a page that outlines each of the topics in your document set and provides direct links to them.

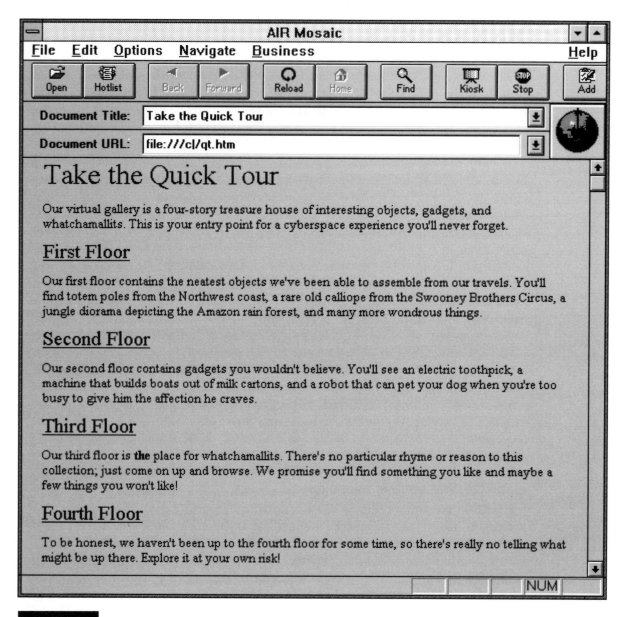

**FIGURE 7-2**

There are several ways you can make the QuickTour page readily accessible to your readers:

◻ If there are only a few main topics in your document—no more than, say, four or five—you can build the QuickTour onto your home page.
◻ If, on the other hand, you prefer to keep your home page "clean," you can construct the QuickTour as a separate page that is directly linked to your home page.
◻ You can use a QuickTour in place of a table of contents (TOC) if your TOC is relatively simple. If your TOC is longer or consists of multiple topic levels, on the other hand, you will want to keep it separate from the QuickTour but link them both to the home page.

If you decide to include a QuickTour page, build it into your design spec and spell out its contours.

**Heading levels.** Earlier, we discussed the question of keeping your heading levels in a non-breaking sequence. (See the sidebar "Should you jump heading levels?" in chapter 4.) You should decide which heading levels you are going to use and what degree of flexibility (if any) you are going to assume in following the standard progression from <h1> through <h6>.

Again, you may just want to make a preliminary decision about this issue until you have more experience working with HTML documents. Situations that arise while you're developing a document set may cause you to change your approach. If so, be sure to record your decision and build it into your spec.

In any case, you would be well advised *not* to design your own heading styles; that is, do not code them as bold or italic, and do not specify other physical characteristics, including white space before or after the heading. Use the logical types <h1>, <h2>, and so on, and leave the choice of fonts and spacing up to your readers' browsers. If you design your own styles into the headings, they may simply not look right in the screen environment of many browsers.

**Graphics: Colors.** You might want to refer back to our discussion in chapter 6 about graphics file sizes and your choice of color palettes. What we said there, in summary, is that the simpler your color scale, the smaller your file size; the smaller the file size, the less download time for your readers. And saving your readers download time is always a good idea.

Whatever your decision is about the number of colors you use in your graphics, bear in mind another rule we mentioned in chapter 6: do not mix color palettes within the same HTML file. Do not, for example, include one graphic based on one set of colors and another based on a different palette. The reason for this rule is that, typically, a browser will encounter the first graphic and load its palette; then the browser will display the image—and proceed to load the second image and display it on the basis of the first image's palette. The first graphic will look just fine, but the second one, based on a different palette, will not be interpreted correctly and may not look right.

**Graphics: image sizing and resolution.** Your spec should not attempt to be a graphics tutorial; graphics applications are separate and must be used in terms of their own procedures. However, working with any graphics application requires you to make judgments constantly about design issues. No matter which graphics application you use, you must be able to contour your images so that they suit your Web documents.

Size, resolution, and aspect ratio are all important for consistency and branding. In your design spec, you can stipulate the conditions of any graphical images you believe should have a consistent look. For example:

- You've decided to have a banner graphic on your home page that is $480 \times 30$ pixels. Do you also want banner graphics on the first pages of topic and subtopic sections? If so, should they be the same size, color, and design as your home-page banner?
- Your home page contains navigational graphics that link to four topics, and the first page of each of these four topics contains links to further subtopics. You might want to specify that all of the anchor graphics are square and of the same color, but that those linking from the four main topic pages to the subtopics be smaller.
- Will you include a navigational toolbar that provides direct links (a) back to the home page, (b) to other topics, (c) back to the previous topic, (d) to related documents, (e) elsewhere? What will this toolbar look like, and which locations will it appear in? You may, for example, decide to put the toolbar at the beginning of all major topics, but for subtopics, a "BACK" button or a "HOME PAGE" button might suffice.
- You're creating a document with a Halloween theme and have decided to use tiny pumpkins as bullets in bulleted lists. You need to include this decision in your design spec, of course, and you also need to stipulate the exact size of the pumpkin graphic to be used (for example, $15 \times 15$ pixels).

As for resolution, you will want to think carefully about the kinds of images you're publishing. You may want to specify different resolution levels for different kinds of images. If you have a map, for example, the resolution might not have to be so high. If you're showing images of art works, on the other hand, you may want to specify that those images be constructed in JPEG files, at very high resolution, with millions of colors so that the quality comes through (and download time be hanged).

**Image mapping and server scripting.** Two more sets of issues that you should consider while drawing up your design specifications have to do with image mapping and server scripting. In a nutshell, *image mapping* involves building multiple anchor destinations into one graphic, so that a mouse click on one area of the graphic jumps to one topic and a mouse click on another area jumps to a different topic. *Server scripting* has to do with programming a server for acting upon actions taken by clients, for example information a reader sends by by way of a feedback form.

Your design spec should include rules and guidelines about how to create and format image maps, as well as the coventions and language(s) your Web site uses for server scripting and input processing. We'll discuss these topics more fully in Part Three of this book.

## Editorial Style

In the beginning, it's probably a good idea to rely on an existing guide such as the *Chicago Manual of Style* for setting editorial standards. As you work your way through your first two or three projects, be sure to compile a list of individual issues as they come up, and include them in a working style sheet. Maybe after you've completed a number of projects, you'll be in a position to assemble a more comprehensive style guide based on the kinds of editorial questions that arise in your particular work. Maybe you will never feel a need for your own complete style guide; some more widely used standard, such as the *Chicago Manual,* will do just fine, as long as you supplement it with project-specific style sheets of two, three, four or so pages.

Even so, there are a few editorial matters that are specific to writing HTML documents, and you should address these even as you begin your first project. Write them up as a style sheet or as an "Editorial" section of your specifications, and make modifications as necessary during the course of your work.

Let's look at these issues.

**Make HTML titles self-explanatory.** The title of an HTML document should encapsulate the general content of the document or section it heads. This is important for at least two reasons. First, readers frequently search the Internet by title or subject matter. If your document has an accurate and explicit title, it can be found by someone running a search on that title or subject. Second, some browsers retrieve and display the title of a document before they retrieve the document itself, and readers often decide whether or not to continue loading the document on the basis of the title. If the title doesn't accurately tell them what is in the document, they might move on to something else; or they might resent the inaccuracy of the title once they see what is in the document.

Let's say you've completed a document in which you discuss the past twenty years' history of Southern Africa, through the monumental struggles that led to political independence for Namibia and majority rule in the Union of South Africa. It's an exciting topic, and your study is the culmination of years of research and months of preparing your work for World Wide Web publication. You're ready to post it on the Web, and you've decided to give it the title *Triumph At Last!*

In a sense, this is a wonderful and apt title, capturing in three words the emotions of those great political achievements. However, your title doesn't tell a reader browsing the Internet what the document is really about, and someone looking for a study of Southern Africa could easily pass it by. You would do much better with the title *Southern Africa: Freedom at Last* or something similarly descriptive, if less succinct.

And how about lengthy titles? Sometimes lengthy titles are necessary to capture the full sense of a document, but bear in mind that when a browser loads a title, there is a chance that the end of the title may run off into the scrolling region of the title display, whether it be in a search list or in the head of a browser screen. This might not deter some readers, but others may again pass it by if the part of the title they see does not appear to interest them. You would run this risk if the title of your Southern Africa piece is *Triumph at Last: The Past Twenty Years of Struggle, Pain, and Revolutionary Change in Southern Africa.* To avoid the problem a truncated title display might cause, turn that title around so that *Southern Africa* is up front, as in the second title line example in figure 7-3:

FIGURE 7-3

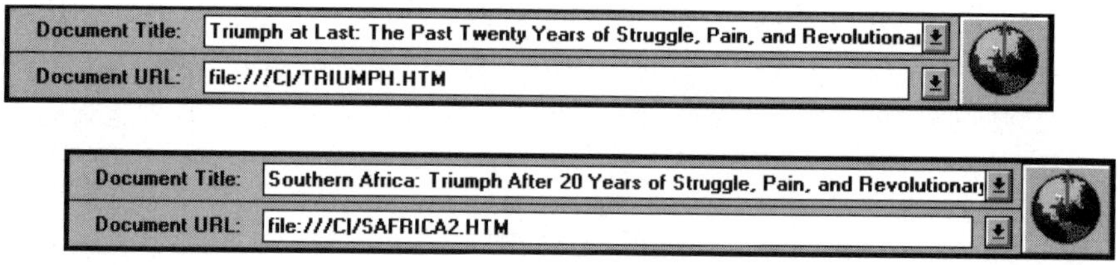

Document Title: Triumph at Last: The Past Twenty Years of Struggle, Pain, and Revolutionar ⬍
Document URL: file:///C|/TRIUMPH.HTM ⬍

Document Title: Southern Africa: Triumph After 20 Years of Struggle, Pain, and Revolutionar ⬍
Document URL: file:///C|/SAFRICA2.HTM ⬍

**How to Publish on the Internet**

In summary, the rules of thumb about document titles are:

- Make them explicit and accurate.
- Keep them as short as possible without losing descriptiveness.
- If you must write a lengthy title, put the most descriptive words up front.
- The title is no place for flippancy or obtuseness. If you want to attract an audience, let them know what is in your documents—don't make them have to guess. Save your sly wit for the content itself.

**Unsubtle text around anchors.** Anchors in your documents announce themselves. You can assume that when a reader sees text formatted as an anchor, he or she knows what to do with it. The browser displays it in a way that tells the reader it is an anchor—by underlining it or giving it a different color from normal text, or both; or by some other method that your reader recognizes. The same is true for anchor graphics: they are surrounded by a blue border or otherwise distinguished from ordinary graphics. You do not have to say "Click here for more information about ———" or anything similar. You should avoid such verbiage, for it is superfluous and unsubtle, and it adds unnecessary bytes to the size of your file.

**Sequence of heading levels.** The question of whether or not to maintain the linear sequence of heading levels <h1> through <h6> is one we've already discussed in the section "Design Specifications," earlier in this chapter and in greater detail in chapter 4. It is, of course, an editorial issue as much as it is a design issue, but we won't repeat here what we've said previously. Please refer back to our previous discussion of this.

**Paragraphing conventions for typing text in HTML source documents.** In chapter 4, we mentioned the need to separate elements in your HTML source documents by adding paragraphs. This point deserves to be repeated here. Structuring and designing a document so that it is easy to read within its coded format, as well as its viewed format, is a question of style. Obviously, it is the mark of a good style that your document reads well when viewed with a browser; similarly, good style dictates that the document be easy to follow in its code format. Lacking a clean style, your source documents will be harder to maintain and update, and if anyone other than their original author needs to work with them, it will not be a pleasant task.

Figure 7-4 shows an example of a good, clean source document style (on the left) and an example of a poor, hard to follow style (on the right):

| Good style | Bad style |
|---|---|
| ```html<br><html><head><br><title>Pictures Unlimited</title><br></head><br><body><br><img src = "logo.gif"><br><br><p>This little piggy went to<br>market<br><br>This little piggy stayed home<br><br>This little piggy had rare roast<br>beef<br><br>This little piggy had none<br><br>And this little piggy cried<br><i>"Oui, oui, oui!"</i> (it was a<br>French piggy)<br><br>All the way home.<br><br></body><br></html><br>``` | ```html<br><html><head><title>Pictures<br>Unlimited</title><br></head><body><img<br>src = "logo.gif"><br><p>This little<br>piggy went to market<br>This little<br>piggy stayed home<br>This little<br>piggy had rare roast beef<br>This<br>little piggy had none<br>And this<br>little piggy cried <i>"Oui, oui,<br>oui!"</i> (it was a French<br>piggy)<br>All the way home.<br></<br>body></html><br>``` |

FIGURE 7-4

## Procedural and Housekeeping Guidelines

When you undertake a publishing project of any substantial size, you quickly find a hundred small details that can add up to a huge housekeeping problem if they are not handled in an orderly fashion. These range from technical issues such as how you name files to logistical issues such as how one collaborator hands off work to another. And later, after a document is completed and posted on the Internet, you will discover that your work isn't over. At this point, you must turn your attention to maintaining your Web site.

As with other planning issues, it is hard to anticipate ahead of time all the questions that will arise. The following discussion represents a few of the most predictable procedural and housekeeping issues. You would do well to address them in the beginning, and write them into your project spec.

**File creation.** The more complex your document set, the more important it will be to decide upon conventions for naming files, size limits, and other file-related standards.

❑ **File-naming conventions.** You should impose a systematic file-naming standard so that, as multiple files accumulate, you can readily identify them by their names. If your document set is about farm animals, for example, you might name the files for your first-level topics `cows _000.html`, `pigs_000.html`, `ducks_000.html`, and so on. One level down, your subtopics might be `cows_100.html`, `cows_200.html`, `pigs_100.html`, `pigs_200.html`, and so on. Graphics files associated with these files might be given names and numbers that key to the topic levels:

| Topic/subtopic file | Graphics files |
| --- | --- |
| `cows_000.html` | `cows_001.gif, cows_002.gif,` `cows_003.gif...` |
| `cows_100.html` | `cows_101.gif, cows_102.gif,` `cows_103.gif...` |

These are, of course, only examples of one logical scheme for naming files. The point is to think carefully about how much information you need to code into each file name so that you can tell at a glance where the file fits into the structure of your document set.

▫ **File formats.** Which file formats do you plan to support? HTML, of course, and one or more conventional graphics formats such as GIF. But do you also plan to create any files in plain-text format (`.txt`) and include them in your files (to be displayed as text files)?

And if you are working with collaborators, it is crucial that you follow standard guidelines about the formats in which any non-HTML files are handed off. Will you support files in Microsoft Word? WordPerfect? Text only?

▫ **File sizes.** You might think about setting limits on the size of individual files you will create, especially graphics files and, if you plan to use them, sound or video files. Recall again the need to avoid overly large files to save your readers downloading time. You might, for example, start by setting a limit of 50K bytes on graphics files and 100K for sound files. If it proves impossible to provide materials you need within those limits, you can adjust them upward. But it is always a good rule of thumb to start by imposing some discipline on file size.

▫ **File linking.** We've discussed linking in numerous contexts, but we want to mention it one more time here. You may want to establish specific guidelines about what types of links you will and will not build into your documents. Will you link to files at other Web sites? Within your own documents, do you want to specify in advance which topics will link to each other? Do you want to set up links to definitions, notes, or other tangential topics?

- **File transfers.** Finally, if more than one person is working on your project, files will have to be passed between them. Planning for this becomes an issue, especially if you are working at different work sites. Do you transfer files over a shared server? Via FTP over the Internet? By floppy disk? Do all your collaborators know the method, and are they all equipped to use it?

**Storage.** Exactly where your files are to be stored is another issue that should be addressed in your project spec. Perhaps you are reserving space in one particular directory for all files; perhaps, on the other hand, you think it's wiser to create a multiple-directory/subdirectory structure. Whatever your approach, everyone who participates in the project needs to know where to put the files as they are created and where to find them as they need editing, illustrating, and tweaking. Don't forget to reserve space for every type of file you will be using, including:

- Text files (HTML and others)
- Graphics files
- Image-map files
- Server scripts

**File maintenance.** Okay, now we're looking ahead to that moment when you have released your project to the wide world of the World Wide Web. It will be thrilling, but before it happens, you should think about the day-to-day maintenance tasks of the site. Now is the best time, while you're writing up your procedural and housekeeping guidelines.

Most important, of course, is the question: Who? If you are the sole creator and "owner" of your Web site, then the answer is obvious. If you have collaborators, then you need to agree on who is responsible for such tasks as:

- Updating content
- Gathering feedback
- Replying to readers' queries, suggestions, and gripes
- Fixing bugs

And so on. Maybe you will agree to divide the tasks up. If your Web site is a forum for new literature, for example, perhaps one person will be responsible for collecting new poems and adding them to the site, and another will be responsible for adding short stories. In any case, it is a good idea to establish consensus on the maintenance tasks before you find yourself immersed in them.

## Lab Exercise

Do you hear the school bell? It's time for another lab. Turn to the end of this chapter and work through lab 7½. Why do we number it 7½? You'll have to read it to find out.

## ETIQUETTE

Have you noticed how often *etiquette,* a noun that has connotations of white gloves and tea parties, is spoken of in discussions about the Internet? Have you ever asked yourself why?

*Etiquette,* of course, refers to the forms, manners, and customs commonly practiced and expected in social or professional circumstances. When you enter someone's home as a guest, you expect to be welcomed cordially. Your host or hostess takes your coat, invites you in, and tries to make you feel comfortable. You may be offered a refreshment and a place to sit. People introduce themselves and you are encouraged to join in conversation. In any event, you do not expect to be injured or insulted—at least not if the proper rules are in effect. In other words, you enter into a situation that is familiar (even if you do not know your host or hostess well), and you anticipate behavior that meets the standards of the company you ordinarily keep.

Similarly, when you enter a place of business, you step into not just a place but a pattern and standard of behavior. If you are in a doctor's office, you expect the receptionist and medical staff to treat you courteously and with due concern for your health. If you are in a bank, you take your place in line like everybody else and expect, when you reach the front of the line, to be served by a teller with attention, courtesy, and efficiency.

What does this have to do with the Internet? Exactly this: Think of your Web site as a place that others come to visit. Okay, it's not your living room or your showroom or your studio. But it is *your place* in cyberspace—your virtual office, parlor, research library. Interested readers and Internet cruisers will find this place, and when they do, they expect to encounter circumstances that make them feel welcome. They hope to understand clearly from the moment of their arrival what this place is all about, and they deserve to be treated with courtesy and efficiency.

How do you provide this? By understanding the overall culture of the Internet, observing a few general rules, and using your own common sense. Practicing etiquette on the World Wide Web offers you the flexibility that generally comes with new institutions. You are free to develop your own patterns of hospitality and your own style of presentation, and nobody will consider you an improper host so long as you show your visitors some common courtesies and give them all the encouragement they need to explore your premises.

**General ambiance.** We discussed the general look and feel of your Web site in chapter 6, where we explored the use of graphics as decoration and the desirability of branding your site. Your site's overall ambiance, like that of the home you choose to live in, can be a reflection of your own style and tastes. As with designing a business office, however, you would do well to attune your style and tastes to the comfort and tastes of your likely visitors. Hanging a skeleton in the lobby of a hospital's emergency unit is not likely to amuse patients and their loved ones; so, too, with your Web site—make sure the look and tone of it are appropriate to the company you expect to keep.

This will require some careful thought, and perhaps even some trial and error. Don't be hesitant about repairing mistakes, and do pay atten-

---

### Two very different ambiances

If you'd like to see two Web sites designed in completely different styles, each of them entirely appropriate for its audience, take a look at

`http://ucmpl.berkeley.edu/welcome.html` **and**
`http://www.hotwired.com`

The first of these is the Web site of the University of California's Museum of Paleontology. It's an elegant, realistically designed site that is thoughtfully laid out and easy to navigate. The visitor is immediately greeted by a large, thematic graphic linked to a text description of it, and a graphically embellished toolbar linked to the various departments of this virtual museum's exhibits. There is also an alternative home page for text-only browsers. The exhibits themselves include graphics and clearly written text discussions. The overall ambiance of this Web site is intelligent and tasteful; the site designers obviously respect their visitors and give them the kind of educational tour that is perfectly suited to the purposes of the site.

The second address is that of *HotWired,* the on-line Web site of *Wired* magazine. Its design, full of branding graphics that have been described as "Picassoesque," captures the spirited and even frenetic mindset of cyberspace pioneers. Full of jargon and references that are immediately recognized by the electronic "in" crowd, *HotWired* plays to an audience that it knows very well. It's a different audience from that of the California Museum of Paleontology, and the site was rightly designed with a different flair.

---

tion to any comments your audience sends back about the appearance and effectiveness of your Web design. But remember also that the graphical environment of the World Wide Web is new; it's a new stage, a new showroom, a new visual medium that offers you plenty of room to innovate. Chances are your readers will appreciate it if you use that freedom to innovate intelligently.

**What are we doing here?** The first rule of thumb is that you should let your readers know what your Web site is all about. Giving it a descriptive title, as we discussed earlier, is a good start. Just as importantly, you should include on your home page exactly the words and/or images that make the aim of your document clear. Knowing what to expect will not only help your readers understand where in cyberspace they've landed, it will also influence the way they browse your material.

Don't be afraid to be explicit. If your Web site is highly graphical, a small number of words, or none at all, may suffice to make the message and purpose apparent. And in any case, what you tell your readers up front doesn't need to be lengthy; it just needs to be clear. "A tutorial on the fundamentals of vegetarian cooking," or "an experiment in geometric designs," or "a work of hyperfiction," or "an opportunity to view and purchase the latest in windsurfing equipment"—such descriptions as these appearing on a home page would leave little question in the reader's mind what the document contains.

This does not mean World Wide Web documents are no place for subtlety. If subtlety is your style, by all means, use it—and if it's truly your style, we certainly don't need to tell you how. But just be sure that, on your home page, you do not confuse subtlety with obscurity.

**Is the welcome mat out for all browsers on all platforms?** Remember again what we said earlier in this chapter, about accommodating text-only browsers. If you decide to provide text alternatives for your graphics, be consistent about it. This does not necessarily mean providing a text-only track, or even detailed `alt`-attribute text for every single graphic, but it does mean that you should provide text alternatives for all *essential* content embodied in graphical images. This includes all navigational hot spots within image-mapped (ISMAP) graphics: because each hot spot is the anchor for a link to a specific destination, you will need a text alternative for each ISMAPped anchor. (We will discuss image mapping more in chapter 9.)

One possible rule of thumb is that wherever you provide a link from a graphic, you might also provide one by text. You do this not just with text-only browsers in mind; you do it also to accommodate readers who turn off their in-line image switch—and you do it for those times when even the most "graphical" of browsers are, for whatever reason (low memory, short time-out configuration, and so on), unable to load a particular graphics file. See figure 7-5 for a good example.

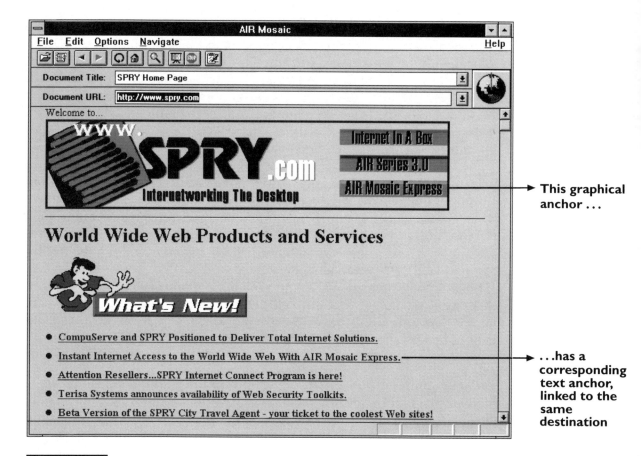

This graphical anchor . . .

. . .has a corresponding text anchor, linked to the same destination

**FIGURE 7-5**

Bear in mind that not all graphical browsers have the same capabilities. A banner graphic that is more than 500 pixels wide, for example, will run off the edge of the screen when displayed on some monitors, particularly some used with Apple Macintosh systems. When you write up your design spec, consider which browsers and platforms you intend to support and draw up your specifications accordingly.

**Status, authorship, and responsibility.** It's a matter of courtesy to provide your readers with information that identifies your project's creators and tells them its status. We recommend that you consider the following:

- Sign your work. Don't be shy—take credit for your creative effort! We recommend adding an author's signature at the end of each major segment of a document. One easy way to do it is simply to insert a horizontal rule (using the `<hr>` code), followed by an `<address>` block containing the name and e-mail address of the preceding segment's author.
- Include a point of contact for your readers so they can send you queries, comments, and other things they wish to communicate. This can take the form of a Webmaster alias, possibly printed together with your signature. A Webmaster alias tells your readers how to address e-mail messages to you, or to whoever is responsible for administering the Web site. An even better way of providing access to you is by providing an auto-email feature such as the one illustrated in figure 7-6.
- Make it clear what the status of the project is. Is this a completed work? A work in progress? A living document (that is, it's complete but subject to change because the content will need to be updated)? Especially in the latter two cases, it's a good idea to give the project status up front in your document set, on the home page or in the TOC. If the status is different from segment to segment, you might give the status of each segment at its beginning. If the material is "under construction," can you give a date for your grand opening?

**Size of documents and segments.** Aside from the practical limits of such elements as graphics and other non-textual files, which we discussed earlier, there are additional size considerations that require careful planning. Even "pure" text files can easily grow too long. If, for example, the chapters of your novel run to thirty pages or so, each chapter will cost your readers dearly in downloading time; some might not even be able to download a chapter because of memory limitations. Some readers may also have difficulty printing a lengthy chapter. It's more practical to break your files up into, say, six to eight pages each. (We know that this threatens to disturb the aesthetics of your narrative, but have pity on your gentle readers, and trust that they will stay with you from one segment to another.)

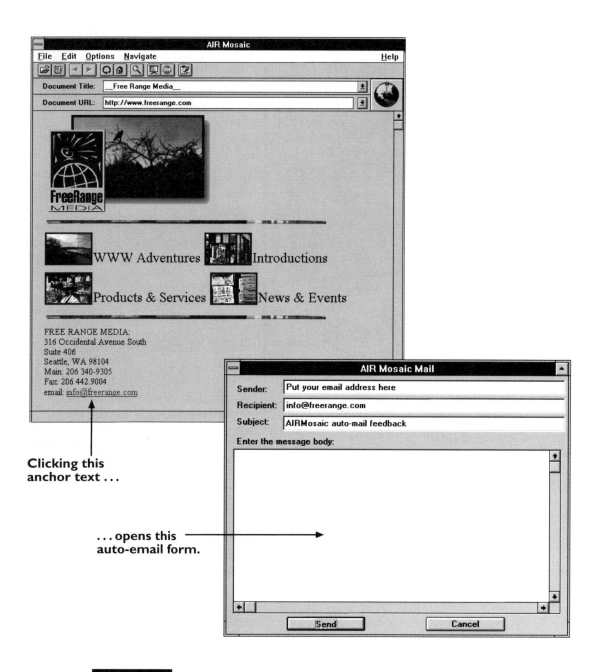

**Clicking this anchor text ...**

**... opens this auto-email form.**

**FIGURE 7-6**

We wish we could give you a specific guideline, but we can't. Judging the appropriate length of a document, or any individual part of it, is to some extent a matter of experience and to some extent a subjective feel. Surely the standards are different for an epic novel and for a virtual auto showroom.

Always keep your audience in mind. What do they expect? If the purpose of your Web site is to attract potential buyers of your product, give them all the information they need to pique their interest, including graphics that show off your merchandise in all its beauty; tell them how to order your goods or where to find your sales outlets; and then stop. If, by way of stark contrast, your purpose is to present a serious rebuttal of Hegel's *Science of Logic,* your readers are not likely to be satisfied by three pages of text (no matter how brilliant) and a JPEG graphic of yourself contemplating a bust of the philosopher.

If you're not certain whether you're giving your readers the right amount of information, by all means solicit their feedback and pay attention to it. Take time to analyze their input. Weed out the crackpots, and look for both general trends and singularly insightful comments. You should be able to tell how you're doing.

**Make your links appropriate to your content and audience.** This may seem an obvious point, but always try to stay in the minds of your audience when designing links. If your Web site is that of, say, the National Kennel Society, you don't need to link from Dog to a definition of a dog. However, you might want to link off to topics like Schedule of Events or Best in Show, 1995. If your document set is going to be read primarily by nuclear physicists, do not create a link to a high-school-level textbook topic on, say, The Components of an Atom. However, you might want to create just such a link if your intended audience is high-school students.

Avoid the temptation to link excessively or superfluously. Don't create links just to show off your link-making virtuosity. If impressing your audience is one of your objectives, you will have more success at it by including just the right number of links, in just the right locations, to just the right destination topics. This is a lot harder than it sounds, but work on it.

**FAQs, FYIs, and Notes.** Abbreviations are inevitable in cyberspace and already multiplying beyond control. FAQs (frequently asked questions) and FYIs ("for your information") are standard items in World Wide Web documents, and notes, too, can be a useful addition to a document set.

You can think of an FAQ as something that can save you, or your Webmaster, a fair amount of time once your Web site is up and running. And

FAQ is actually a *list* of frequently asked questions that you can include in an easily accessible place—for example, by linking from an anchor on your document's home page. In this list you should include answers to questions that come in as feedback from your readers. To be sure, it is hard to anticipate the questions you will get before they start coming in, and therefore you might not be able to include this feature in your document set's initial release. As you receive feedback, however, you will begin to see patterns in the questions, and you can start to post answers that may serve to head off similar questions in the future.

FYIs are pieces of information that are pertinent to a topic but do not exactly fit the flow of your content. They might include source references, for example; or citations from other material that is loosely related to your discussion; or wild tangents that you think your readers will appreciate. You may or may not want to include FYIs in one integrated topic; you can add an FYI link to every main section of your document if it seems appropriate.

Notes can be any of numerous specific additions to a document: footnotes, afterthoughts, marginalia. Again, you can put them together in one or more separate files and link them to your main document as appropriate. One possible use for notes is to publish the feedback that you receive in e-mail; you can do this quite simply, by saving e-mail messages as a plain text file (`.txt`) and creating a link to that file. This is a way of adding a sort of "Op-Ed" page to your document.

**Saying good-bye.** You may have seen some Web sites that include a "Thanks for visiting" or similar message. You may or may not choose to add a phrase of this sort. The present authors are of the opinion that it isn't necessary; like signing "Sincerely" or "Yours truly" to an e-mail message, this is a courtesy that has not made its way from the world outside cyberspace into standard practice on the Net. But certainly no one would be offended by such pleasantries. If it feels right for your style, go ahead. And come again.

## TESTING

Does it all work?

That is the crucial question you have to ask when you've completed your project. And before you release it, you must satisfy yourself that the answer is yes. The only way to do that is through testing.

If you've been doing the lab exercises in this book, you've already done a bit of testing. Such testing as you've done, however, has been limited to the one or two documents you've created to complete the exercises. Now you need to think about what it means to test an entire document or set of documents.

It means two complicated things, actually, because what you have created when you've finished an HTML document set is a cross between a published (or soon-to-be-published) work and a software program. Your readers will see your work as if it were a book or some other publication. However, they won't be able to read it as you've intended them to if the software features underlying the text and pictures do not work right—that is, if the links do not jump the reader from one topic to another, or if the image tags do not connect to files and bring the right graphics onto your reader's screen.

Because of this hybrid quality in HTML documents, you need to test your completed work from both angles: as software and as documentation.

## Testing the Software

Testing the software aspects of your HTML documents entails looking closely at a number of critical questions.

**Checking your work with multiple browsers.** Does your document or document set work right on Mosaic? On Netscape? On Cello? Try to get your hands on as many different browsers as you can, and run the project on each. If you find a problem, try to figure out why the feature isn't working, fix it in the source file, and test it again.

**Checking the links.** Do they all work? Does each link connect to the right destination? Do the text alternatives link to the same places as their corresponding anchor graphics? Be sure to check *all* links. Do not make the naive assumption that because one works, others do too. More often than not, a nonfunctioning link is caused by a small oversight or typographical error specific to that particular link.

The following are some of the most common causes of nonfunctioning links:

- No quotation marks on either side of destination text
- No ending angle bracket (>)
- Misspellings or typos in the anchor or destination tag
- Forward slash(es) missing in a URL pointing to a destination document

- Double backslash used instead of double forward slash following the colon separating the protocol from the server name (for example `http:\\srvr` instead of the correct `http://srvr`)
- Destination document is not located in the URL path specified

Remember that software is unforgiving: your codes must be letter-perfect, or the links will not work.

**Usability testing.** If you really want to be thorough, you should consider submitting your document(s) to neutral persons for usability testing. Usability testing is a standard procedure among producers of software programs. Companies like Microsoft and Lotus spend thousands of hours testing their products on typical users before packaging the programs and shipping them to market.

Your project, too, can benefit from usability testing. The point of usability testing is this: *You* know how to use the documents and navigate around them just fine, but will others who haven't been involved in building the files easily figure out how to use them?

Grab a co-worker who hasn't contributed to your project; or bring in a friend; or, better still, find someone Web-literate who has no personal stake in your document and has not worked with it. Best of all, find five or ten such testers for the task.

What task? Set your testers up at a computer, and open your document set for them with a browser. Start them on the home page, and ask them to find specific topics or specific pieces of information.

Referring, for example, to the hypothetical topic about dogs that we designed in lab 7, you might ask your testers to find some information about housebreaking. This is how to test the logic we used in structuring the material. If four out of five testers see a link to Training & Discipline and click on it, and then quickly find the link to Housebreaking, you can consider this part of the structure a success. Do the same with however many similar tasks you have time for, and repeat the same questions with all of your testers. If the results suggest a lot of problems in locating specific information, you might want to rethink and redesign some of your linkages before releasing the project as a completed work.

## Testing the Documents as Documents

This is the realm of more conventional publishing practices. "Testing" your documents as documents means giving them a thorough check in ways that are familiar to book publishers: editing, copy editing, and art

**How to Publish on the Internet**

checks in particular. Editing, as in conventional book publishing, should involve smoothing out inconsistencies of style and tone—including the sometimes challenging task of bringing disparate styles among multiple authors into a standard of consistency.

The nature of hypermedia, though, suggests another dimension to the usual editorial process. Your material needs to be read with a critical eye toward how the pieces you've linked up fit together logically. This is especially true if you link to external documents that are the work of other persons or teams. For example, you may have discovered that there is a document on `//www.xyzzyx.edu` about the internal organs of dogs and, in a hurry, assumed it to be relevant to your subtopic on caring for the health of the family pet. So without looking at it too closely, you created a link to it from your topic "Our Friend, the Dog," subtopic "Caring for the Family Pet." A critical editor who takes the time to follow the link and examine the document you've linked to might discover that it presents a series of vivid graphics showing a dog laid out and cut open on an autopsy table. This might not be the right type of article to be linked to your dog-lover's document set.

This may seem like an absurd example, but we think you can see how a critical reading of a document or document set can benefit the project. If you don't test your documents thoroughly before you release them, your users certainly will.

## How Important Is All This Testing?

How important is testing? It all depends on how important quality is to you. Now that might sound like a loaded answer, but it's true. "Garbage in, garbage out," the computer-age-old dictum about the data you feed into a program, has numerous equivalents in Internet publishing. We'll let you coin your own aphorism.

The most important single element in testing is checking the links. This is where the largest number of things can go wrong, where the slightest mistake can cause a structural or functional failure. Thoroughly checking links should be the bare minimum for any testing routine.

Just how important testing is may be conditioned by the purpose of your documents. If you need to get one out on the Net in a hurry and don't mind the likelihood that readers are going to stumble over your errors, you might want to let it go in a preliminary release. Be sure to specify clearly that it represents a work in progress. If the document is meant for a limited audience that wants the information badly and, by and large, will not be too critical of its presentation, that might be another reason for forgoing or postponing a thorough testing. If, on the other hand, you are preparing a Web site for a mass audience and the reputation of your work, or that of a paying client, is at stake, you will not want to stint on the testing effort.

## Coming Up

If you haven't done the lab exercises for this chapter, this is another reminder that they are there for your practice and amusement. Labs 7 and 7½ follow. Save your finished labs and then it's on to chapter 8, where we'll come full circle in Part Two by discussing how your published Web documents can contribute to the development of information communities.

# Lab 7

## Designing a Web Site

This is an exercise in designing a structure for a complex HTML document or a set of interrelated documents. You can do this exercise individually or together with your team, as a brainstorming session. For purposes of illustration, we've picked the topic—dogs—but of course you can choose another topic if you prefer. (We understand that some people don't like dogs; we don't understand why, but we admit the possibility.)

### Designing a Web site

1. In a conference room or another place, preferably one with a table on which you can organize your work, gather together the following materials:
   - 50 index cards
   - Pad and paper (or use a white board or chalkboard)
   - A pad or two of Post-it Notes
   - Paper clips or rubber bands
2. If you're working with a team, assemble the members around the table, announce the topic, and ask them to free-associate about the topic. For example, ask them to name everything they know about dogs.
3. On the white board, chalkboard, or notepad, list all the things that come to mind. At this stage, the only rule is: *Anything goes.* Whatever comes to mind goes onto the list. It doesn't have to be nouns, doesn't have to be logical. Let's say these are some of the things that come to mind on the subject of dogs:

| | | | |
|---|---|---|---|
| man's best friend | dog shows | hunting | pooper scoops |
| fetch newspaper | puppies | Poodles | leash laws |
| doghouses | rubber toys | chew slippers | German Shepherds |
| Samoyeds | digging in the yard | barking | housebreaking |
| dog doors | floppy ears | wet tongues | chase cars |

This is only a representative sample; try to come up with at least fifty items in your list.

**4.** Now sort through the list and select those items that would be good candidates for inclusion in your document set. From the first row above, for example, you might decide that *dog shows, hunting,* and *pooper scoops* are good material for subtopics, but *man's best friend* is too abstract or all-encompassing.

Try to include about forty good items, and delete those you think aren't so useful.

**5.** Take another look at the list, and try to think of anything important that isn't there. For example, you might see *German Shepherd* in the list and think of adding *Doberman Pinscher.* You might see *digging in the yard* and think of *jumping up on house guests.*

Continue thinking about your list until you again have about fifty items.

**6.** Now write each item on a separate index card.

**7.** Sort and stack the index cards into logical groups of like subjects, such as the following:

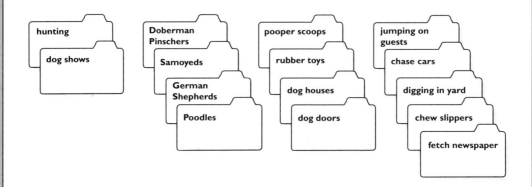

**8.** Count the stacks. If you have more than five, rethink them; try to consolidate the cards into five groups, or six at most. Consider:

☐ Do you have only one card in any one stack? For example, if *leash laws* is in its own separate stack, could you move it into the same stack as *jumping on guests* (because they both have to do with discipline)?

**How to Publish on the Internet**

❑ Can any of your stacks be combined? For example, if you have a stack with two cards in it, say, *large dogs* and *small dogs,* can you logically include them with *Poodles, German Shepherds, Samoyeds,* and *Doberman Pinschers?*

9.  Paper-clip each card stack, or use rubber bands, and then name each stack and stick a Post-it Notes label on each.

    For example, you might name the four stacks illustrated in step 7 *Dog activities, Breeds, Paraphernalia,* and *Training & Discipline.*

10. Arrange the stacks on the table in a logical progression.

    Does the content of any stack lend itself to an overview topic? If not, have another brainstorming session until you come up with an overview topic. You might, for example, recall the item *man's best friend,* which you rejected earlier; maybe if you rename it *Our Friend, the Dog,* to make it gender-inclusive, you could use this as the title and heading of an overview that can serve as your first screen topic. Or you might just decide to use the heading *Overview.*

11. Whichever title/heading you decide to use, write it on another index card and place that index card on the table above the others.

    Perhaps you now have a layout of the card stacks that looks something like this:

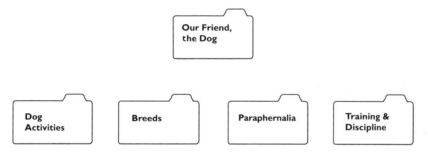

**A working model.** You now have the basis for a working model that you can use to structure your document or Web site. Can you begin to see it? In your imagination, draw lines that represent links between topics—or write the topics on the white board and draw the lines there. If you're not satisfied with the organization, play with it; rearrange the cards, rethink the topic names. And by all means, keep an open mind even after you've decided on the overall structure, for you will get more ideas as you build your document set.

# Lab 7½

## Unhelpful Document Titles and Unsubtle Anchor Text

*Surprise!* This isn't really a lab, it's a pop quiz. If you've done your homework and put on your thinking cap, you'll do just fine. There are two parts to the quiz. In a fit of originality, we decided to call them Part A and Part B. To make the exercise as much fun as possible, we've made it a multiple-choice quiz. We hate to tell you this, but if you're stumped, the answers appear on the next page.

### A. Unhelpful Document Titles

1. While performing a search on the Internet, you've discovered a document with the following title:

   **Part Two, Section Five**

   What is this document about?
   - (a) A play by William Shakespeare
   - (b) Assembly instructions for a mower
   - (c) An inventory at a morgue
   - (d) Part Two, Section Five

2. Same situation, different title:

   **The Importance of Accurate Title Wording**

   What is the document about?
   - (a) A play by William Shakespeare
   - (b) Assembly instructions for a mower
   - (c) An inventory at a morgue
   - (d) The importance of accurate title wording

### B. Unsubtle Anchor Text

1. You are reading through a document about dogs, and you come upon the following text (anchor text is displayed as underlined):

Another breed that has its enthusiastic admirers as well as its sworn enemies is the Doberman Pinscher. For information about Doberman Pinschers, Click here.

Which of the following is/are true of this text?

(a) It's pretty clear what the anchor links to
(b) It wastes words (and bytes)
(c) It's not very subtle
(d) All of the above

2. Same situation, different wording:

Another breed that has its enthusiastic admirers as well as its sworn enemies is the Doberman Pinscher.

Which of the following is/are true of this text?

(a) It's pretty clear what the anchor links to
(b) It wastes words (and bytes)
(c) It's not very subtle
(d) All of the above

## Answers

(and a little gratuitous commentary)

### A. Unhelpful Document Titles

1. (d). Sadly enough, this is all you have to go on. You'll have to load the document to find out whether or not it's Part Five, Section Two of something you actually want to read.
2. (d). Sounds like a sure cure for insomnia, but at least you know pretty well what to expect.

### B. Unsubtle Anchor Text

1. (d). And you know how the authors feel about being unsubtle.
2. (a). Ha! Fooled you if you thought all the answers were the same.

# 8 Information Communities:

## Reaching and Sustaining Your Audience

Y ou now know everything you need to know about planning and assembling a document, linking it to other documents, enhancing it with graphics, and maintaining consistency in your style and process. You're now ready to publish.

In the following section, you'll learn the steps to post a document or set of documents on the World Wide Web. There is more than one way to do this, and we'll give you some suggestions about different approaches.

But this chapter is about more than just putting a document out on the Net. After we discuss how to do the actual publishing, we're going to move on to the larger issue: How do you promote, extend, and continue your work? How do you get the right people interested in it? And how do you keep them interested enough to revisit your Web site, contribute their input, and perhaps even be stimulated to link up their own projects to yours?

The answer lies in building an *information community,* a community of Internet users who share your interests or develop a sustained reason for visiting your Web site. That reason can be intellectual, commercial, cultural, or quirky—but it serves to bind you and your Web audience together in a relationship that will persist over time. Now, doesn't this sound better than just putting a document out there and hoping that now and then someone, anyone, will take a look at it?

## PUBLISHING YOUR DOCUMENTS

If you've ever set out to publish in the traditional media, you probably know that it isn't so easy. Which magazine will be interested in your travel article on Patagonia? Which publishing house will buy your manuscript on *Becoming a Piano Virtuoso in 1,000 Hours*? Both beginning and experienced writers write a lot of query letters, suffer a lot of rejections, follow up on a lot of leads that turn into dead ends. Those that get their work published usually succeed only after months or years of trying. The reward of success is all the sweeter because the effort was so exhausting.

One option in the traditional publishing business is self-publishing. Self-publishing involves either paying a commercial printer/publisher to produce your book or setting up your own desktop enterprise. Either way, you can spend a lot of money and end up with a tall stack of books that you don't know how to get rid of. But it *is* a way of publishing your work, and if that is what's important to you, then you will naturally consider it an alternative.

The World Wide Web is different from other publishing markets, although it does have its analogies to traditional publishing. Because the Web is a new medium, the rules and methods for publishing on it are few and the barriers to having your work circulated are less fearsome than in the traditional publishing world. The opportunities for publishing on the Internet are only beginning to show their potential, and so far they suggest that this newest of the mass media is much more open and democratic than most of the older media. While it is not risk or cost free, if you have a positive attitude and a sense of adventure, we think you will discover exciting opportunities.

## Post Your Work on a Web Server

To publish on the World Wide Web, you post your documents on a server that is:

❑ Connected to the Internet
❑ Configured for the Web

**Connected to the Internet.** Obviously, the server you post your work on has to be connected to the Internet. Obvious, however, does not mean simple—unless you are on the staff of an organization that can set you up on one of its own servers. In all other cases, you will have to find a server that you can use or set one up yourself. We'll discuss the alternatives in a minute.

**Configured for the Web.** A server configured for the Web means one that's programmed to operate according to the standard protocols used by the World Wide Web project—HTTP, of course, but also e-mail, newsgroups, and any other Web protocols your documents may support. We've been referring to HTTP throughout this book, and it should be obvious that this is the most important protocol for your purposes, because it's the one governing the transfer and display of your HTML documents. Later in this chapter, we'll discuss how you might use the various other Web protocols in your documents.

## Where Do You Find a Server to Post Your Documents On?

Gaining access to a Web server is the hypermedia equivalent of finding a publisher for your book, article, or story, in the functional sense of securing an outlet for your work. It's not like overcoming what can sometimes be the Dante's *Purgatorio* of obstacles on the road to publishing in the traditional media.

**If your organization provides you with server space.** If you are connected to an organization that provides you with Internet access, you may in fact have no worry about securing your outlet on the Web. You might have to apply for an allocation of space on one of your organization's servers, and you will probably have to obtain permission from your network administrator. You may have to battle your way through a few yards of red tape or take your network administrator to lunch. But you will not have to beg or contract for space on someone else's server, nor will you have to buy or program a server yourself. You are among the lucky ones.

**Getting published in an established electronic publication.** There are already a number of established Web sites whose purpose is to publish content of certain types—the electronic magazine *HotWired,* for example, or any of the growing number of other electronic magazines covering a variety of subject areas. Many of these electronic magazines accept submissions, so you might give them a try.

You can use Internet services to research the existing electronic magazines, which are often referred to by the familiar term *zines.* The following are some sources of information (by no means exhaustive) about what is available:

- The Global Network Navigator (GNN) list of electronic publications, at `http://gnn.com/gnn/wic/art.toc.html`
- The WELL (Whole Earth 'Lectronic Link) list of electronic magazines, at `gopher://gopher.well.sf.ca.us:70/11/Publications`
- Discussions and announcements in the newsgroup `alt.zines`

| A small sampling of electronic magazines being published as of the beginning of 1995 | |
|---|---|
| *The Blue Penny Quarterly* | An electronic journal of fine writing and art |
| *Collectors Network* | A world-wide information exchange for devotees of antiques and collectibles |
| *Fine Art Forum* | A monthly magazine of arts announcements |
| *Pete and Bernie's Philosophical Steakhouse* | Surreal and straight humor, and humorous articles of a general nature |
| *Pure Sheng* | A celebrity fans' electronic magazine |
| *Quanta Magazine* | An on-line magazine of science fiction and fantasy |
| *Telegraph* | An electronic magazine dedicated to discussions of "indie" (non-mainstream) music |
| *The Terrorist Profile Weekly* | Electronic magazine dedicated to discussions of current terrorist groups and their activities |

—Information from the Global Network Navigator's list of electronic magazines, at `http://gnn.com/gnn/wic/art.toc.html`

**FIGURE 8-1**

On the horizon, we see a widening field of electronic publishers who will be looking for quality material—not just articles and short stories, but book-length pieces and other major works. Indeed, we may see the flourishing of new creative forms that defy description in such conventional terms as "a book," "an article," or "a story." It is not unlikely that, at some point in the future, having a hypermedia work published through one of these outlets will be much like having one published by a traditional press or magazine. That is, your work will be accepted on its merits, read and discussed by the publication's regular readership, and respected for having been issued in that particular publication. You may even be paid for it! (But don't quit your day job.)

**Posting on somebody else's Web server.** Another way to publish your work is to find an existing Web server, other than that of an established publication, that offers hosting services (that is, accepts materials for publication). This is the hypertext equivalent of self-publishing, and it usually means incurring some expense. There are Web sites that will contract with you to publish your work for a fee. Such fees are analogous to the charges you would pay to a printing company for printing and binding copies of your self-published book. The Web site, however, provides the built-in distribution service of the World Wide Web.

Because this is such a new medium, you might find a wide variety of fee schedules for publishing your work on a Web server. Some providers might charge by the size of your documents; some might charge by the month. And some might charge you a variable fee depending on the traffic: the more visitors to your site, the higher the fee. The market for Internet publishing has not yet reached its adolescence, so we can expect some erratic behavior before fee schedules settle into a predictable pattern. Don't be put off if the first offer you encounter seems out of line; shop around.

If you're really lucky, you might find an organization that will post your material for free. Look around; you may discover a Web site dedicated to the subject matter of your own work, and its owner happens to be looking for new material. In the long run, a Web site will lose its audience and die if it does not refresh its content periodically. Many Web site administrators are therefore interested in attracting new material that complements what they already have and enhances their overall audience appeal.

The first place you might check is with the provider of your Internet service. Contact your provider and ask if there is a way for you to post Web documents on one of their servers. Explain exactly what you have in mind, and be prepared to talk about the size of your document (in bytes) as well as the period of time you have in mind for posting it. If you are publishing a seasonal topic, for example, you may need to post it for only a few weeks. If you have an ongoing project, on the other hand, you may want to make a deal for a certain amount of server space that is guaranteed over some longer stretch of time.

If the answer from your provider is "No, we're sorry," you should follow up by asking if they can suggest a list of other providers that may offer hosting services for Web documents.

You may find that certain Web servers offer space only for single, sim-

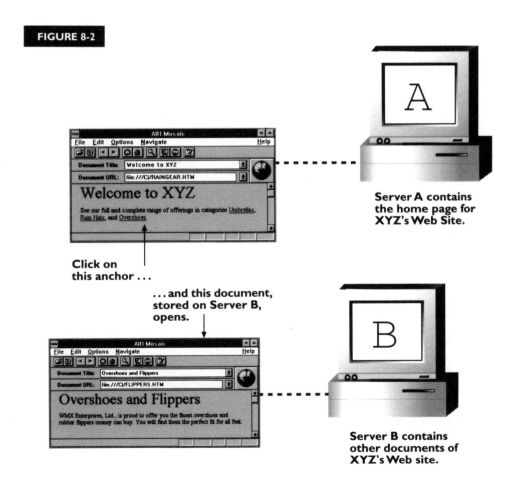

FIGURE 8-2

Server A contains
the home page for
XYZ's Web Site.

Click on
this anchor ...

... and this document,
stored on Server B,
opens.

Server B contains
other documents of
XYZ's Web site.

ple HTML documents containing a home or introductory page. Although your initial reaction to this might be, "Huh, I need more than that," in fact this is not to be sneezed at. The more places there are with an entry page to your publication, the larger the audience that is likely to find your material. We may see an evolving trend of high-traffic servers that specialize in home pages; many Web browsers will frequent them, looking for interesting subject matter. Once they find your home page on such a server, they simply click on an anchor and link to another server to bring up the rest of your document set. Of course, you still have to find a host server for the rest of your document set, which probably makes it seem like twice the hassle and expense; however, it may prove worthwhile because multiple postings of your home page will increase your visibility on the Internet.

One possibility you might want to consider is a free home-page service offered by Ohio State University at `http://www.mps.ohio-state.edu/Home Page/HPPinfo.html`.

For more possibilities, go to the Internet. Some Web sites offering space are listed at `http://union.nsca.uiuc.edu/HyperNews/get/www/leasing.html`. In addition, you might check out the announcements and discussions in any of several newsgroups, such as:

- `comp.infosystems.www./announce`
- `comp.infosystems.www.providers`
- `comp.infosystems`

You can post your own query through these newsgroups, hoping to get a reply from another newsgroup user who has a Web site available or knows of one.

You can also use your browser to read the "What's New" page of certain Web sites, for example that of NCSA (the National Center for Supercomputing Applications).

Yet another approach is to find one or more Web sites that you like and get in touch with the Webmaster or administrator of the site. Most World Wide Web sites have a Webmaster whom you can contact by e-mail. Usually—although not always—you can address the Webmaster as webmaster@*domain* (where *domain* represents the specific name of the Web site's domain, including any three-letter descriptive extension, for example .com or .edu, or two-letter locative extensions such as .ca, for Canada, or .uk, for United Kingdom). Ask the Webmaster if there are any opportunities for you to post documents at the site, and if not, whether the Webmaster knows of any hosting services that might be appropriate for your particular work.

**Doing it yourself.** A second method of self-publishing on the Internet is by setting up your own Web site. This can be an expensive way of doing it, but it might be the right way for you. If your project is related to your business and your company or organization has the resources to set up an independent Web site, then you might very well want to make the investment. Having your own Web site gives you complete control over your documents, and your file-storage space is limited only by the capacity of your server.

And if you have in mind an ambitious, ongoing project of the sort we've frequently alluded to in this book, sooner or later you are probably going to need your own server. You will need it for your encyclopedia of music theory, your guidebooks on dog ownership, your interactive catalogue of merchandise, or your Beatles/Rolling Stones Web site. You will need your own server for anything that requires more file space than you can contract for on someone else's server; and may very well want your own server for any project with the capacity to expand continuously over time.

What are the costs? First of all, you'll need hardware and software. That means, of course, a server: a computer powerful enough to handle the file processing, together with the programming that constitutes the brainwork of the server. In addition, you'll need various other bits and pieces of hardware, including your connecting line—generally a T1, fractional T1, or ISDN line. (These are lines that equip your computer for digital data transfer.)

For the server, you have several choices:

- Set up your own personal computer as a server
- Buy or lease a higher-powered computer, specially built for use as a server, and configure it yourself (or hire someone to configure it)
- Buy or lease a computer that comes pre-configured as a World Wide Web server

As you may have guessed, these three alternatives are listed in ascending order of their likely cost; buying a pre-configured server probably sounds like the easiest approach (and it is), but it is generally also the most expensive. Even so, as more and more manufacturers enter the market with pre-configured Web servers, the cost of buying your own may decline. Of course, costs can vary widely depending on the class of computer you use, as well as the traffic and maintenance on it after you've put it into service.

All of these approaches carry with them the fact that servers require maintenance of a highly technical order, and this becomes another cost of owning your own Web site. Remember Murphy's law? Things *will* go wrong and need fixing. Somebody who knows how to program and debug a Web server must be available. And even when things are going just fine, somebody must be able to work with form scripts, image mapping and indexing programs, and other specialized server programs that are essential to a fully functioning Web site. (We'll discuss some of these issues in Part Three of this book.) In short, a Web server requires a technician—either you, if you have the technical knowledge, or someone you hire for the job.

Third, connection to the Internet does not come without cost. You will need to contract with a service provider, who will of course bill you regularly for your Internet connection. If your connection uses high-speed, digital transmission (T1 or ISDN), expect to pay more for it than for a standard analog telephone-line connection.

**Enlist collaborators.** Don't think you can afford your own Web server? What if you worked with others, pooled your resources and formed an Internet publishing alliance? Let's say, for example, that your encyclopedia of music theory sparks the interest of another team who is engaged in a project on the great composers of the nineteenth century. And another team that's building a set of documents on musical instruments. And yet another working on an encyclopedia of ethnomusicology. Why not get everybody together, integrate your projects, and split the costs of your own server? Or think even further: write up a series of grant proposals, and solicit sponsors.

Reaching out and gathering together a group of participants who share your enthusiasm for a project can serve more than one purpose. Obviously, sharing the costs of owning and maintaining a Web server is one big benefit. In addition, your project can profit from those that are associated with it, capitalizing on the spin-off of energy and inspiration that results from a cooperative effort. Finally, your larger cooperative project will draw in a wider audience to your Web site.

## Choose Your Approach and Go for It

Whether you form a global Internet publishing consortium or work solo on a limited project, be prepared to move off into uncharted territory, for even if you follow in the footsteps of others, the terrain where you will be working is constantly shifting. The methods and technology of cyberspace change rapidly, and you will want to keep abreast of the latest breakthroughs that make your work easier, less costly, and more flexible.

We should add a note of caution: If you are not prepared to handle the technical tasks of administering and maintaining a server, and if you cannot hire or beg someone to do it, you should not consider purchasing your own Web server. Try one of the other ideas we've suggested for publishing your work.

## WHAT IS AN INFORMATION COMMUNITY?

Remember the old philosophical question: If a tree falls in the forest and no one is there to hear it, does it make a sound?

Well, try this cyberspace analogy: If you publish the greatest piece of creative work ever posted on the World Wide Web and nobody visits your Web site, is your work really the greatest piece ever posted?

The true answer to the first question is yes, the tree does make a sound. The physical definition of a sound is that it is a vibratory disturbance that is *capable of being heard.* If no one is around to hear it—not even forest animals (which seems unlikely)—the falling tree makes a sound nonetheless.

In the case of publishing the greatest piece of creative work to a nonexistent audience, though, we're not so sure the answer is the same. After going to the trouble and expense of publishing your work, you want people to see it, respond to it, and return to the Web site where your work is published. To a large extent, this requires you to keep your content fresh and engaging, or to encourage your audience's participation.

But more than that. In the era of cyberspace travel, you are inevitably competing against a galaxy of other Web sites, many of them new, exciting, and innovative. How do you reach *your* audience, and how do you hold them?

By building an information community around your Web site.

An information community, as we've described it, is an audience that is drawn to the content of your Web publications and brought into a continuing relationship to it. The members of this audience are attracted to your Web site because they share your interest in the subject matter, or they admire the writing or graphical style of your content, or they love the products you sell. You retain their interest by continuing to satisfy their expectations, giving them an opportunity to interact with you or your content, and making them feel connected to you and your work.

Building an information community is like building a circulation base for a magazine, an audience for a television program, or a listenership for a radio system. You don't need an information community to publish, but you do need one to sustain an ongoing *program* of publishing.

## Virtual Communities

Howard Rheingold, editor of *The Whole Earth Review* and well-known guru on virtual communities, has often argued that it is not information that attracts people into cyberspace, but *other people*—the communities that are forming around the new electronic media. When we talk about these communities, we are talking about something new under the sun. They are not communities in every sense of the word as we traditionally know it; Rheingold himself has acknowledged, for example, that the members of a virtual community do not necessarily share the same level of commitment to each other as members of a conventional community do.

---

### Howard Rheingold on virtual communities

Howard Rheingold has written about, and promoted, a range of issues on the cutting edge of American society ever since he helped put together the original *Whole Earth Catalog* in 1968. As an associate of the WELL since its inception in 1985, he has participated in the development of this networking experiment, which he points to as a prime example of a virtual community.

Rheingold has had so much to say about virtual communities that we could not begin to summarize it adequately. His work is always interesting and provocative. We recommend that you take a look at his book *The Virtual Community: Homesteading on the Electronic Frontier* (Reading, PA: Addison-Wesley, 1993, 1994).

---

There are other, more obvious, anomalies about virtual communities. We're not speaking of people who share the same streets, sidewalks, and walk-in cafés abuzz with conversation and pervaded by the aroma of freshly ground coffee. But we are speaking of a community, or quasi community, that exists by virtue of human interactions. These interactions do not occur face to face; they occur computer monitor to computer monitor. We don't see people in the electronic community physically shaking hands, shrugging shoulders, or casting meaningful glances. We do, however, see them practicing certain evolving rules of conduct and doing their best to communicate through words and images.

And even though we are definitely not talking about a geographical community, in its own way the electronic community allows people an opportunity to "gather." They engage in real-time chat sessions, contribute to newsgroups or conferences on topics of mutual interest, or participate in joint projects involving research and data exchange. They send e-mail messages, often more readily than they answer their telephones and almost always more readily than they write letters. And they participate in special-interest events organized around individual Web sites.

Specialized communities have grown up on the basis of particular interests. If you've followed one or more newsgroups, you might have noticed some of the same contributors returning regularly. Even more so, if you are a member of the WELL, you've undoubtedly found "regulars" who tend to gather within some of the WELL's conferences. People can be welcomed into a given community by its existing members—and sometimes ostracized from one—according to how well they fit in or how deeply they offend others. (You may be familiar with what is called the *kill file*—a kind of electronic dumping ground created by an automated "kill" feature that deletes communications coming from a specific sender or on a particular subject. Now there is an even more "lethal" Internet weapon: the dreaded *Cancelbot*—a robot-like program that seeks out Net postings and deletes them.)

## Virtual people in a virtual community?

Just as there are virtual communities that exist only in the electronic world, so too are there virtual inhabitants of those communities. That is, there are personalities who exist only as members of virtual communities.

Of course there are flesh-and-blood people behind these virtual personalities, people who choose to present themselves on the Internet as their virtual alter egos. Virtual personalities may be known only by aliases such as Webspinner, DarkCloud, or Pickpock, and never by the names of the actual people behind them. To make things even more interesting, men may identify themselves by female aliases, and women by male aliases. (Gender switching is not necessarily something we advocate; we merely want to mention that it has been done electronically.)

Whether using aliases or their own names, people have already engaged in a fascinating array of interactions on the Internet. Many have debated politics, religion, or social issues; some have collaborated on books or articles; some have made business deals; some have carried on virtual romances— and without even having met in person!

No doubt those who operate under aliases experience a certain thrill of freedom, or feel inspiration when they don the electronic clothing of their Internet persona. And who is to say that it's just a weird game? After all, think of the contributions made in other media by individuals who applied their creative talents under pseudonyms or stage names, from Samuel L. Clemens, ordinary Missourian who became Mark Twain, the great American writer, to Norma Jean Baker, girl next door who became Marilyn Monroe, screen star and immortal sex idol.

Virtual communities are made up of people who "come together" because they are wired together—brought into contact by electronic telecommunications media. It is a uniquely contemporary phenomenon, and some say it is the beginning of a new societal realignment.

## The World Wide Virtual World

The advent of hypermedia makes possible the evolving communities of the World Wide Web, a virtual place with its own neighborhoods that people can explore. As in physical-geographical neighborhoods, when you explore the Web you frequently stumble onto something you didn't know was there—a newsgroup, a forum, a virtual museum. You may find things for sale and decide you want to buy them. If you like, you can find locations on the Web where you can post your own wares for sale by purchasing advertising space or, in effect, renting a booth. You will encounter people with specific jobs—the Webmaster at this or that Web site, the moderator of this or that newsgroup, the host of a WELL conference. And most importantly, you will encounter people who share your interests; you can discuss all sorts of things with them—a movie you've recently seen, a book you've read, a new Web site you've discovered.

**Some examples.** It's not hard to find examples of communities that are forming around specific Web sites. Let's briefly consider a few.

- *HotWired.* This is the on-line version of the computer magazine *Wired,* but it's also a club of sorts that offers you an opportunity to become a member and participate interactively. When you read an article in *HotWired,* you don't have to just digest it and then move on to something else; you can react to it by expressing your opinion on-line and then check back periodically to see if others join in the discussion. If so, you've started a conversation, which can sometimes go on until the conversation, like conversations in the physical world, exhausts itself. It's hard to predict where something that starts in *HotWired* will go; an article might generate a multilateral discussion between you and other interested participants, and then lead to ideas about products you can buy or events you might want to take part in. The thread might even lead, by way of an anchor in a reader's contribution, to another Web site.
- **The WELL.** The WELL calls itself "a conferencing system on the Internet." It's a connecting point for people who discuss hundreds of special-interest topics within *conferences* built around general subject

areas: computer-related issues, politics, parenting, the environment, arts and letters, cultures and languages, the Grateful Dead, and many more. Each conference has its own ambiance; one may have the feel of a seminar, another a neighborhood pub. The WELL was established in 1985 (before the World Wide Web) by a number of people associated with the *Whole Earth Catalog.* Participants pay a monthly membership fee.

□ **Gramercy Press.** This is an interactive marketing tool for MCI Communications in the form of a fictional publishing company, with a virtual staff, a catalog of (fictitious) books, and even a means of making book submissions. The intricate graphics of the Gramercy Press Web site lead you into a virtual building that houses the press, with a reception desk, production quarters, and staff offices. If you send an e-mail message to one of the staff members, you will receive a reply from that virtual person. Why not make a submission? You may just find your work virtually published.

□ **CommerceNet.** This is a business community, accessible by paid membership. It is another club, in a way, with membership benefits that are related to business purposes. Chief among them is a yellow-pages-like listing of a member company's products or services.

Other communities are springing up here and there on the Web, ranging in purpose from forums for special computer-interest groups such as IBM OS/2 users to linking together fans of the television show "The X-Files." Some of the groups that are forming will prove to be lasting communities and some passing fads.

## How Do Web Communities Form?

A Web community might form in any of several different ways. We'd like to describe two interesting models. The first is that of a community forming around a dedicated, single Web site, and the second is that of a community composed of Web sites linked to each other because their creators or administrators "discovered" each other's concern with a topic of mutual interest. Both models are instructional for planning a strategy of reaching your maximum Web audience.

**The dedicated Web site.** The model of the special-interest Web site draws a loyal audience on the basis of being dedicated to a subject with distinctive appeal. Two good examples are Web sites dedicated to rock music: the Grateful Dead Web site and the Elvis Aron Presley Web site.

Both sites have attracted thousands of visitors who view the exhibits and follow discussions and events associated with these popular icons of American rock.

Among other topics, the Grateful Dead site includes an FAQ about the group's music and personalities, a schedule of tour dates, and a vast collection of lyrics from songs the Dead have performed in the course of their long career. The Elvis site features a virtual tour of Graceland as its centerpiece, plus a variety of other items such as sound clips from some of the King's recordings. In each case, the visitors who periodically return to the Web site constitute a kind of community based on their mutual attraction to the site's subject matter.

## Legal problems in CyberGraceland — and a caveat

In November 1994 the creators of the Elvis Web site ran into a snag. Attorneys for Elvis Presley Enterprises, Inc. (EPE), the organization that owns trademarks and copyrights associated with the late rock 'n' roll star's estate, threatened legal action against the owners of the Elvis Web site for copyright infringement and other alleged violations. The Web site was obliged to stop its display of Graceland, its sound clips from Elvis recordings, and other features subject to the legal challenge. As of this writing, the creators of the Elvis site had vowed to bring back the exhibit minus all materials that infringed upon EPE's rights — provided these could be sorted out. Elvis fans, stay tuned.

This case points out a very important issue of Internet publishing. Many aspects of law regarding the circulation of Internet content are still nebulous, owing to the fact that the Internet is a relatively young communications platform; thus, it is often hard to determine who owns the rights to what, when it comes to content circulated via the Internet. When it comes to content of various kinds drawn from other media, however, Internet publishers are subject to the same laws governing rights and trademarks that apply to traditional publishers. A registered copyright is a registered copyright, and a registered trademark is a registered trademark. All who would publish on the Internet must be cognizant of the laws governing materials they wish to borrow or cite. Without the appropriate permission, reproducing material that has been published, exhibited, recorded, projected, or otherwise circulated in another medium is at least risky and usually illegal. Reproducing material originally created for the Internet is likewise risky and possibly illegal, unless prior permission is received from the legal owner of the material.

**Topical communities.** The other model we want to mention is best described by relating a discovery one of the authors made while cruising the Web in 1994. A discussion about software that followed an article published in *HotWired* drew a comment from one participant who wondered why IBM's OS/2 operating system had not been mentioned. In that comment, the characters *OS/2* were coded as an anchor linking to a Web site dedicated to information about OS/2. Anchors in material contained in that Web site linked to other Web sites containing further discussions of OS/2—including at least one link to IBM's Web site. The IBM site contained a frequently asked questions list (FAQ) and other advice for OS/2 users. Thus an incipient OS/2 users' network, a mini-Web of Web sites, sprang into being for the benefit of a community consisting of OS/2 users.

Obviously, the Web sites had to be already in place before the OS/2 network could be created. The main difference between this model and

---

### Frontier towns on the World Wide Web?

You are, in a sense, entering a frontier: an electronic frontier. What does this frontier have in common with earlier frontiers? Pioneers who moved west across America in the nineteenth century discovered that the towns they built along rivers, or located above the mother lode of a gold mine, or at the intersections of covered wagon routes, flourished for a while but did not persevere unless they kept up with the demands of new times and new technologies. When the mother lode ran out, mining towns without another industry became ghost towns. When the railroads were built, towns located on the wagon trails disintegrated unless the iron tracks ran through them; and the iron tracks did not run through them unless they had something to trade—cattle or grain or manufactured goods.

But it was not all a tale of destitution and woe. Cities such as St. Louis, Denver, and San Francisco survived the transformation of their frontiers. They moved with the times, developed diversified industrial bases, established themselves as hub cities for airlines, and sprouted suburban satellites that both fed off and contributed to the activities of the urban core. Linked to the rest of the world by ever-modernizing transportaiton and communication lines, these onetime frontier cities have survived to play important roles in world commerce and world culture at the end of the twentieth century.

But whoa!, as they used to say in the American West. Is the electronic frontier the same? Not quite. But it is a frontier, and there is something to be learned from that earlier, geographic frontier. You don't need to build your Web site on a riverbank or a railroad line. You do need to build it on an electronic line—telephone, ISDN, or TI—and when the transport technology changes, you'll be well advised to keep up with it. You also need to move with the interests of the community that builds around your Web site, so that you do not lose your audience when its demands start to shift. And, like the frontier cities that have grown into large urban-suburban complexes, you need to forge connections with other communities and support each other reciprocally.

---

that of the Elvis or Grateful Dead community is that the OS/2 community gathers around a collection of Web sites, none of which has quite the individual visibility of the Elvis or Grateful Dead Web site. Together, however, they comprise the basis for a true information community that will last as long as there are OS/2 users seeking information—and as long as the Web sites continue to satisfy their community's need for such information.

There's a practical lesson in this example. Given the general lack of organization characterizing the Internet, the readers you want to attract might not find your Web site unless you strategically place links in a variety of other Web locations. Unless you have a document set with the allure of Graceland and the Elvis legend, you cannot assume that people will follow their instincts right to your home page. Some may discover your material through a purposeful search (assuming you have in place the right signposts on the appropriate Gopher servers and other Web vehicles), but many others will encounter your material by chance while browsing on the Net. We'll come back to this matter of hooking up to other Web protocols in the next section.

## Community Interaction

At the heart of any community is human interaction. The more positive human interaction takes place, the more cohesive are the bonds of community. This is as true of an electronic community as it is of a geographic community.

In a geographic community, human interaction takes myriad forms. But within the electronic community structured interactions take fewer forms, owing to the limitations of what can be done over the wire. However, the seemingly inexhaustible human imagination continues to invent new methods and patterns by which electronic interaction can take place. Some of the patterns supported by Internet protocols include:

- Contact information
- Interactive forms
- E-mail
- Newsgroups
- Chat sessions

We've listed these more or less in increasing complexity of their interactive potential. Contact information, the first in the list, means simply a posting of your name and point of contact (e-mail address, telephone number, and/or postal address); anyone who sees this information can contact

**How to Publish on the Internet**

you. Although the possibilities for interaction widen once someone gets in touch with you, say, by telephone, there is no further potential for interaction on the Internet itself.

Interactive forms give other Internet users an opportunity to send you their reactions to your posting. This makes your connection through cyberspace a two-way channel but limits your respondents to the structure of the form you've posted for them to use.

E-mail provides a freer range of give and take, as well as the potential for widening the number of participants through forwarding and the use of group aliases. Newsgroups widen the participation a big step further, opening up a conversation that can be joined by anyone who wanders onto the Net. Chat sessions, on the other hand, may be limited to a manageable number of participants at one time, but the fact that they are indeed participating *at one time* adds another dimension to the interactivity of the medium: Chat participants interact in real time.

**Special events.**  You can add still another dimension to electronic interaction by presenting special-feature programs for people who have a general interest in your Web site. For example, say your Web site focuses generally on automobiles, with ratings of current makes and models, a topic on classic and antique cars, and do-it-yourself repair hints. To spice up the appeal of your Web site, you decide to hold on-line special events periodically, and you invite your audience to participate. So you announce a sports-car rally in the summertime, asking your readers to send you bitmaps or photos of their beloved XKEs, Alfa Romeos, Morgan M4s, and so on—and then you create your event around these audience submissions. Events like this add the dimension of special-interest enthusiasm. If you plan them well and hold them regularly, you can't help but add to the cohesiveness of your electronic community—and the appeal of your Web site.

## CREATING AND SUSTAINING AN INFORMATION COMMUNITY

While discussing and describing electronic communities in the preceding section, we touched upon several ideas about how communities are created and kept going. Let's look at these questions more directly now.

### Advice About Creating Community

As you plan your strategy for creating an information community based around your Web publications, here are some suggestions to keep in mind.

**Maintain topical cohesion.** Keep your subject matter under control. This doesn't necessarily mean you have to stick with one specific interest or idea. You could have a Web site that starts with discussions of Shakespearean plays, add a set of documents about the plays of Chekhov, and plan another related project about the Beijing Opera. You're still working with an identifiable theme, and interested readers would know what they are likely to find at your Web site.

As another example, let's say you are a clothing manufacturer specializing in outerwear. You might start with a set of documents displaying the rain gear you're offering for sale and then add more featuring the latest in skiing outfits.

The point is to maintain cohesion among the documents that make up your publication. You want to avoid going off on tangents or throwing in something unrelated to your main interest area. If your topic is cooking, you don't want to introduce a discussion about professional football—unless you have a subtopic about, say, snacks for Superbowl Sunday. Maintaining a central theme gives people a reason for gathering around your publications. Unexpected tangents make them wonder why they're spending their time in your section of cyberspace.

**Create content that is dynamic.** This is something we touched upon earlier in the chapter when discussing how geographic communities grew up and survived. If your material is static, it may have an initial appeal but it will not continue to draw visitors to your Web site. If it keeps pace with the evolving interests of your audience, however, it is likely to continue attracting them. Like all communities, information communities are organic; they are composed of human individuals who change and grow, and your published work also needs to change and grow with them if you are to retain their loyalty.

**Foster participatory content construction.** Interaction, as we've been stressing, is vital to an information community. Give your audience opportunities to participate. Provide feedback forms so your readers can send you suggestions—and pay attention to what they tell you. Plan events, like the sports-car rally we mentioned, and invite your audience to participate. Encourage newsgroups or chats on your subject matter, and let it be known that you are open to ideas about the further development of your Web site. Any way you can give people the feeling that they are more than just passive readers will contribute to the sense of community you're trying to build. And you may also get some great ideas.

**Choose helpful domain and document names.** We discussed document titles in chapter 7. To summarize the point, it's important to help your audience identify what is in your documents by assigning succinct and descriptive titles. Beyond this point, if you are in charge of naming your Web domain, you can ease your audience's way to your Web site by giving the domain a name that is immediately recognizable. A domain name like `//www.baseball.com` or `//www.doglover.org` is both identifiable and memorable.

Of course, if you are using space on someone else's Web server, you will probably not have any influence on the choice of domain names. In this case, you need to make doubly sure that your document titles are descriptive—especially the title of the entry, or home page, document. You also need to put out an ample supply of announcements and notices on the Internet so that your intended audience will make it to your neighborhood in cyberspace. This means, in part, making full use of World Wide Web services to beat the drum for your Web site.

**Make use of Web services.** Post information about your publications in other places on the Web—that is, by using other Internet services. Look around, first of all, for bulletin boards where you can post an announcement. For example, one very good bulletin board that exists specifically for announcing new Web sites is `http://mirror.com/mirror/newsites/newsites.html`.

Newsgroups organized around related subjects are another excellent place to spread the word. You've probably seen announcements about Web sites in many newsgroups; add your own to inform newsgroup readers of something they might want to see. (See figure 8-3.) Start a new newsgroup on your topic if you have to.

Another good resource is Gopher service. Post a listing of your Web site on a Gopher server so that Internet users who use the Gopher search mechanisms will find you. To identify a Gopher server that is available for your posting, look around within your Gopher directories. You will quickly discover numerous ways of gaining the information you need. You can consult a directory of Gopher sites, for example, or open a file labeled "How to get your information into Gopher," "How to list a resource," "Frequently asked questions about Gopher," or the like.

**Publicity, publicity, publicity.** Spread the word as widely as you can. If you've ever run a shop or staged a public event, you know that carefully targeted publicity is essential to its success. Ask any book publisher, and

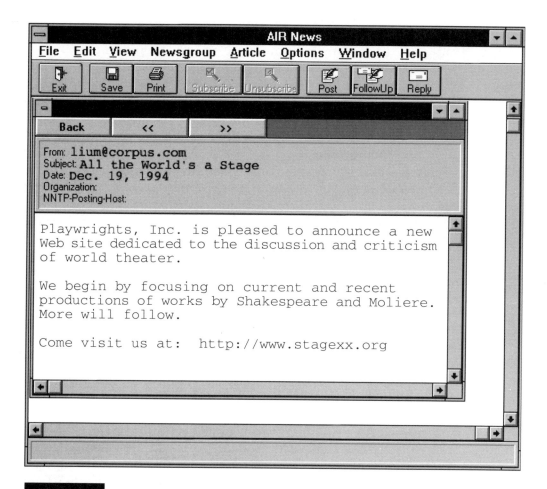

From: lium@corpus.com
Subject: All the World's a Stage
Date: Dec. 19, 1994
Organization:
NNTP-Posting-Host:

Playwrights, Inc. is pleased to announce a new
Web site dedicated to the discussion and criticism
of world theater.

We begin by focusing on current and recent
productions of works by Shakespeare and Moliere.
More will follow.

Come visit us at:  http://www.stagexx.org

**FIGURE 8-3**

he or she will tell you that people need to be told about a new work before
they will buy it in mass numbers.

Think of your Internet publications similarly. Get the word out, or you
will never attract your maximum audience. Look around for conventional
publications and other media information aimed at the audience you want
to attract, and post announcements about your Web site: not just what it
is, but also *where* it is and how to access it. We know of a major book
publisher, for example, who plans to print the URL for its corporate Web
site on every book it publishes. Do the same in your publicity: Always add
"You can find this on the World Wide Web at //www.hottime.com", or
the like.

**How to Publish on the Internet**

Think big. Can you persuade a national sports magazine to do a short piece on your baseball Web site? It's worth a try, isn't it? How about printing up announcements and distributing them at the gates of Yankee Stadium? Or for your classical music site, standing in front of Symphony Hall and giving out handbills? For your on-line film lovers' symposium, why not buy an ad in an entertainment magazine or, again, see if they will print a story or notice for free?

As in so many aspects of Internet publishing, creativity is the key. Make use of any good opportunity to publicize your work. Do adhere to the non-intrusiveness etiquette of the Internet, but don't be shy. Be honest about what you have to offer, and by all means stay within the bounds of ethical responsibility. But get the word out. Figure out where your potential audience browses and, wherever you are likely to capture their attention, give them the message: *We've got something for you.*

**Design for good access.** There are a number of ways you can make it easy for your audience to find and use your Web site. Here is a quick list of easy-access design points:

- Develop an interface that works well and is easily understood. This point embraces many design issues that we discussed in detail in chapter 7, and we recommend that you refer back to that chapter for specific recommendations.
- Create a QuickTour page (again, something we discussed in chapter 7).
- Include a searching mechanism, for example by using the ISINDEX feature or adding a form-based search. (There are server-based features that we'll discuss in chapters 9–10.)

## Web Sites: Building Up, Building Down

So far, we've discussed community building by focusing mainly on your potential audience. There is another aspect of community building that can be very important in this process: bringing together a diversified group of people who are presenting the material—that is, talented collaborators of the type we described earlier in this chapter. Not only is this a good way to raise the financial and personnel resources for your own Web server, as we pointed out, but it can also help your audience appeal by capitalizing on your collaborators' ideas and broadening your subject area.

**Building up.** Suppose you want to create a Web site on poetry. You don't have a grand scheme or concept, but your favorite poet is Emily Dickinson.

So you gather together a representative sampling of her works. Then you decide you're not really interested in publishing yet another *"Collected Works of . . ."* type of piece; rather, you decide to focus on the poet herself. You create a timeline of Emily Dickinson's life, including samples of her work at various stages. You add graphics and text descriptions of where she lived, discuss the important events of her life, and mention the people who influenced her. When you complete your study, you test the document set, feel a wonderful surge of pride when it works, and start thinking about where to go from here. Maybe Edna St. Vincent Millay?

Now you get wind of another project: Someone else is thinking about doing similar work on Ralph Waldo Emerson and Walt Whitman. You get in touch with that team and agree to join forces. Now you've got the ball rolling. Maybe eventually your project will include more teams. Maybe

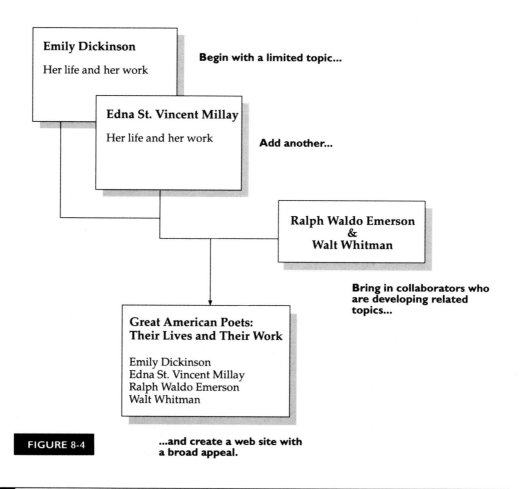

you will add to your study not just more poets but additional topic dimensions: Approaches to the Analysis of Poetry, or Poetry and the American Dream, and so on.

This is what we mean by *building up*. You've started with a limited topic and added more topics that are closely related. If you maintain this momentum and keep the quality of your work at a high level—and, importantly, maintain the cohesion of your subject matter—you will produce something quite wonderful. If you then make sure you're getting the word out to your public, you are on the way to creating an information community that will be the envy of the Internet.

**Building down.** Suppose you start from the opposite end. You have a vision of a project, grand in its scope and ambitious in its objective. You're willing to start anywhere, depending on what materials are available and who is ready to contribute to the project.

This is the model on which Project Gutenberg was begun. Born with the intent of putting as much great literature on-line as possible, Project Gutenberg built downward from this imposing goal. Contributions are solicited from anyone willing to send appropriately formatted copies of his or her favorite classic. In the beginning, the project was assembled in archives on several Web servers located at different universities. The display files were accessed via links from a set of welcome and index pages located on still another server. (As of this writing, plans about these file locations are in flux.) As the project develops, texts are included not on the basis of any overall intellectual design, but rather as they are submitted by contributors.

**Hybrids.** Project Gutenberg started from a grand vision and has been building downward in the sense that the Web servers exist and all contributions are made in response to the overall objective. In practice, however, the ultimate shape and scope of the project will not be known (if ever) until all contributions are in: that is, until an *up-building* process has been completed. There is a sense in which every publishing activity is an up-building process, for neither books nor magazines nor HTML document sets begin intact; they come into being character by character, word by word. Thus any project that begins "from the top down" must of course be constructed piece by piece.

Many up-building processes undergo a similar "hybridization." One interesting example is DealerNet, which began as a single Web site presenting the automobile products and services of Rood Nissan/Volvo, a new-car dealership in Lynnwood, Washington. When the results were seen, it became apparent that this was something that might interest other dealers. Suddenly, a larger vision emerged: a network of auto dealerships across the country, represented in a complex Web site. The vision engendered a logical design that encompassed not only the wares of auto dealers but also information from insurance companies and institutions that offer auto loans. Thus, what started as a single set of documents generated the outline of a massive project. The overall plan then needed to be filled in with specific pieces of the publishing venture. *Voila!* Both up-building and down-building.

## Sustaining a Community

We've touched upon some of the tactics involved in keeping an information community going once you've gotten it started. To a large extent, the success of your community over the longer run will depend on how well you've built the sustaining factors into your original document set: the cohesion and dynamism of your content, the degree and ease of audience participation, and the effectiveness of your publicity. However, the job is not over once you've launched your Web site. If you want to keep your audience and expand it to its maximum potential, you need to keep working.

**The casino principle.** Do you know how a successful casino achieves its success? It offers something people want, and makes it very easy for them to get in but more difficult for them to leave. The successful casino owner makes certain his guests have a great time while they're there and gives them plenty of reasons for wanting to come back. And if they happen to leave a little something behind, fantastic.

The same can be said about your Web publications. Now we don't propose that you offer your prospective guests the exact same enticements—cocktails, dancers in skimpy costumes, and the dream of striking it rich—but you do need to hit them with the right appeal and make it easy for them to get to your Web site. Once you have them there, you want them to stay; your linking strategy should encourage them to explore your content rather than jump out to something else. Like a casino owner, you want to keep them interested without feeling like prisoners, so don't make it impossible to leave; just try to make your premises so hospitable and engaging that they won't think about leaving until it really is time to go.

**Strategic linking.** When you create links to documents outside your Web site, bear in mind that you are doing two things for your readers: giving them ready access to other related materials and ushering them away from your Web site. The first thing, giving access to related materials, is something you want to do for them; the second, ushering them off your premises, is something you want to do with caution.

A good rule of thumb: Don't place anchors to outside documents on your home page. Remember the casino principle, and don't give your guests the encouragement to turn right around and leave immediately after entering.

How should you give your readers such links? One way is to create a separate region of your document set for linking to other resources. This could be a specific screen that serves as a kind of reference page, analogous to a bibliography in a book (except that the reader can immediately jump to the resources listed). On that page, it would be a good idea to repeat the name and URL of your Web site so that your readers will know they are leaving and know where to find your material when they want to come back to it. For example, you might say, "Thanks for visiting *The Web Ant Farm* at www.myweb.com. Come back soon."

An even better idea is to contact the owner or Webmaster of each outside Web site you want to link to, and reach an agreement about mutual cross-linking. This should be a proposition that is in the interest of both sides; you're essentially saying, "I'll send my readers to you if you'll send yours to me." With the confidence that your readers will have an easy time linking back to your content, you can give them access to the other Web sites whenever it makes sense to do so.

For those of you who like moral quandaries, here's one: What if you know of another Web site that contains much the same information as yours—and does a better job of presenting it? If you've followed our advice on creating your own documents, you should have a good idea about how to avoid a predicament of this sort, but sometimes it happens. Other teams may have greater resources, build their documents with the benefit of more recent information or newer production technologies, or have some other advantage. Do you tell your readers?

We would. Or at least we think we would. And then we'd get to work figuring out a way to improve our own documents. We like to think of the World Wide Web not so much as a place of cutthroat competition as of mutual encouragement. And *community,* of course.

## Advice About Sustaining a Community

You've done everything right. Your publications are out there on the Web. They are brilliantly designed, well publicized, and satisfyingly interactive.

You're already attracting a crowd, and the feedback is positive. How do you keep up the momentum?

**Review your design, from its appearance to its functional layout.** Make sure you have branded your Web site well, so that your readers recognize it and feel comfortable with it. Add new links to outside documents when new, related materials appear on the Web—and continue to forge new cross-linking alliances with other Web sites. (See our earlier discussion of strategic linking in this chapter.)

**Make sure you give something to your readers.** Interesting, accurate, up-to-date information is the first requirement of your presentation. Review your information, update it when needed, do not hesitate to correct inaccuracies, and by all means, respond to feedback. Respond by sending your readers e-mail acknowledgments, introducing their suggestions into your content, or both. Do all you can to make your audience more than readers: give them the opportunity to be participants.

**Expand your content in scope or detail.** Like a good stock portfolio, a Web site can profit from diversification. Cast your net further. More poetry lovers will be attracted if, in addition to Dickinson and Millay, you add Emerson and Whitman, and then Edgar Allan Poe, and . . . well, you get the picture.

As you expand your content in scope or detail, do not forget to maintain the cohesion that is so important to your overall presentation. Think carefully about how you should expand your content. If you have a Beatles site, you may not want to expand by adding the Rolling Stones or any other rock group that began during the sixties; you might instead want to move more specifically within the content you've begun, for example by going into the lives and careers of the "Fab Four" individually after the breakup of the Beatles.

Build upon material that you have while maintaining a focus. If your topic appears to be developing into American poets from the mid-nineteenth to the mid-twentieth century, go with it. But know where to draw the line. Avoid veering off the topic in a way that explodes it into senseless fragments.

**Be willing to move with your audience.** Sometimes you make a mistake, or you misread what's going to have lasting appeal. Let's say, for example, you've developed a Web site based around the hottest new musical group, called The Webspinners. You publish the documents, get the word out in

**How to Publish on the Internet**

all the right places, and it's a smashing success. Three months later, however, The Webspinners split up. You try to keep the Web site going in the hope that they'll get together again or that the magic of their music will live on, but soon it's clear that your audience is dropping off. The Webspinners Web site was a great idea, but let's face it: it's over. But your first foray into Internet publishing was popular, and you had a lot of fun making it work. How about trying something else?

This time, you might try structuring your topic differently. What have you learned from your readers' feedback? Did some of them tell you they'd like to see something about the Webspinners' rival group, The Electronixx? Maybe you should feature more groups; that way, if something happens to one, you've got others to work with. Were any of your readers interested in a revolving topic, like a "CD of the month" feature? You already have a nascent Net community—follow their interests. They know who you are and where to find you, so give them what they want.

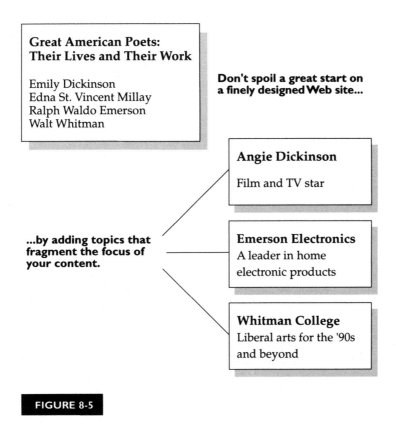

**Great American Poets: Their Lives and Their Work**

Emily Dickinson
Edna St. Vincent Millay
Ralph Waldo Emerson
Walt Whitman

**Don't spoil a great start on a finely designed Web site...**

**Angie Dickinson**

Film and TV star

**...by adding topics that fragment the focus of your content.**

**Emerson Electronics**
A leader in home electronic products

**Whitman College**
Liberal arts for the '90s and beyond

**FIGURE 8-5**

Or maybe nothing catastrophic has happened; your material—whatever its subject matter—just needs to be updated because it has exhausted your audience's interest. That happens. It's not that audiences are hopelessly fickle, but we live in a rapidly changing world and sometimes it's necessary to move with the current.

Here's another scenario: You know the topic of your Web publication is going to be good for only so long, but once you catch the fever you want to go with it. Let's say you're developing a Web site based around the Summer Olympic Games. This is a big topic, but it's something that actually happens only once every four years. Still, you love the Olympics and you really want to do it. And you have corporate sponsorship. (You don't have to have corporate sponsorship for this general scenario on other topics, but let's say you have.) So you build the snazziest Web site any sports fan ever saw.

Come 1996, and it's a smash hit throughout the weeks heading up to, during, and immediately following the Games. Then your audience drops off—as you expected. It was a lot of fun, though, wasn't it? You got tremendous feedback from your audience; there were write-ups in the major international sports magazines, and you attracted an enthusiastic following. Not only that, but your sponsor is begging you to follow up your success with something new. How about the Goodwill Games? The annual world championships in track and field, swimming, gymnastics, and other international sports? Think about it. You've won over an audience; do you want to keep them?

Maybe your audience will provide you with the winning idea. Read their feedback. Take a survey. Raise the issue in a newsgroup forum.

This advice applies to any kind of topical material. Again, *pay attention to your readers' feedback,* and be prepared to shift with them if necessary. Although it is tempting to think of yourself as the reigning monarch of your Web domain, you might do better to see yourself as its mayor, providing leadership but also bound by duty to understand and serve the interests of your citizens.

## HOOKING UP TO OTHER INTERNET PROTOCOLS

Your World Wide Web documents use HTTP as their governing protocol, of course. As we explained in chapter 1, this means they are capable of being transported along the Internet and interpreted by Web browsers. Earlier, we mentioned other World Wide Web protocols that govern services such as file transfer (file transfer protocol, or FTP), Gopher, newsgroups, and electronic mail (e-mail). Although you don't need to use other protocols in HTML documents, you may find it useful to link your documents to them.

**What does it mean to hook up to other protocols?** If you provide a link to another Internet service within your HTML document, it means the user can click on the anchor for that link and jump directly to the other service. The reader starts by viewing your document with a browser. If you provide a link to a Gopher server, for example, the user clicks on the anchor and jumps into a Gopher menu without having to back out of the browser and open the Gopher application. Similarly, a link to a newsgroup jumps the user right to a newsgroup page.

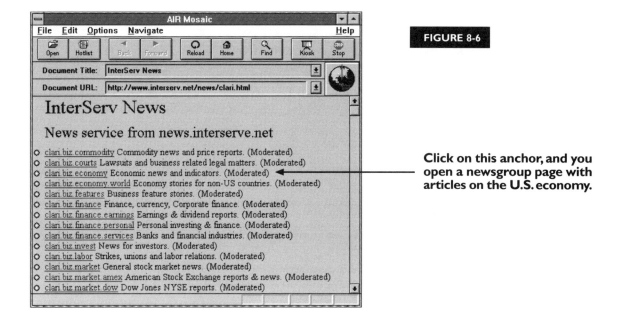

FIGURE 8-6

Click on this anchor, and you open a newsgroup page with articles on the U.S. economy.

The beauty of this capability is that you can put into your HTML documents links to *specific* newsgroups, Gopher servers, or FTP servers. You choose the resources you believe will be most useful for your readers. They don't have to search Gopherspace or wander through a hundred newsgroups to find the relevant information.

Allowing your readers easy access to other Web services might not add to their use of your HTML document, but it shows them that you want to give them a way of getting still more information.

You can also provide links to an auto-email service that opens an e-mail form which your readers can use to send you feedback about your Web site. Your e-mail address is built into the form, so your readers do not have to add it; all they have to do is type in their message and click on a Send button.

> **N O T E** Not all browsers support all Web protocols. Some do not support the newsgroup or the auto-email connections, for example. This means readers using such browsers will not be able to use those features. Don't let this stop you from adding them to your HTML documents, anyway. Someday, all browsers probably will support all Web protocols. In the meantime, just be prepared to answer complaints if you hear from readers about this problem.

## Anchor Codes for Links to Other Internet Services

To link an HTML document to a Gopher server, an FTP server, a newsgroup, or an auto-email form, you use the same general anchor tags that you would use to create a link to an external document:

| | |
|---|---|
| **\<a href=** "*URL*"**\>**<br>**\</a\>** | **Anchor tags for an external link.** These tags mark the beginning and end of an anchor for a link to another Web service. The text that you type between the two tags (the anchor text) should in some way describe the specific destination the reader will jump to by clicking here. |

Generally speaking, you use an Absolute URL to link to an Internet service located on another server, and a Relative URL to link to a service on the same server as your HTML document. The specific components within the anchor start tag differ somewhat depending on the type of service you link to. These differences are subtle, but, like all coding elements, they must be entered perfectly if the links are to work.

**Links to Gopher servers.** The following is an example of an anchor to a Gopher server designated by an Absolute URL:

```
<a href="gopher://gopher.interserv.com">
InterServ Gopher</a>
```

Notice that this conforms in every respect to the conventions used in linking to external files, except that no file name is used. That's because the link takes the reader not to a specific file, but to the menu for the InterServ Gopher server. The first element in the URL is the protocol, gopher, which appears just before the colon. The server name, which in this case is gopher.interserv.com, follows the conventional double slash.

You can use a link to a Gopher server as a way of helping your readers find more Internet resources on topics related to that of your HTML document—or any Internet resources. By linking to a Gopher server, your readers have access to the typical searching mechanism of a Gopher site.

**Links to FTP servers.** The following is an example of an anchor to an FTP server designated by an Absolute URL:

```
<a href="ftp://ftp.spry.com/filename.ext">File to
Download</a>
```

Notice that this URL takes the same components as the Gopher example we cited, plus a file name. The whole point of opening an FTP server is to download a file, so you want to include the exact file name, including its extension, where the placeholder *filename.ext* appears in this example.

You use a link to an FTP server to enable your readers to download a specific file to their own computers. If you have some files on an FTP server that you'd like to share with your readers, you can make them immediately available by linking that server to your HTML document.

**Links to newsgroups.** The following is an example of an anchor to a newsgroups designated by an Absolute URL:

```
<a href="news:alt.rock-n-roll.stones">
Rolling Stones newsgroup</a>
```

Notice that this URL uses no double slash (//). By clicking on the anchor text, in this case Rolling Stones newsgroup, the reader jumps directly to the newsgroup dedicated to discussions of the Rolling Stones.

You can use a link to a newsgroup to connect your readers to a specific newsgroup, or a list of newsgroups, that carry discussions of subjects related to your Web site's content.

**Opening an auto-email form.** The following is an example of an anchor that opens an auto-email form:

```
<a href="mailto:myname@domain">feedback</a>
```

In this anchor, *myname@domain* stands for the specific e-mail address at which you want to receive messages.

You use a link to an auto-email form, as we've suggested, to give your readers the means for an immediate response to your Web site.

## FROM THE ELEMENTAL TO THE COMMUNAL

Throughout this book, we've stressed the point that human interaction is central to the promise of the World Wide Web. What you've learned in Part Two is a strategy of building progressive levels of interactivity into published documents. We started with the basic elements of HTML text codes, from setting up headings, paragraphs, and other blocks of text through the formatting of characters, lists, and other features. At this *elemental* level, we focused on pieces of information. A single line of text with a coherent idea became the title of a document. Additional lines and additional codes were added, giving the document substance and shape. But all we had was something for our readers to read: a flat document that could be retrieved and displayed by a browser.

As soon as we started to introduce links and graphical elements we were dealing with something more than just a flat piece of writing. Now we could assemble a fully operative hypertext document with complex formatting and graphics, and links both internal and external to the document. These elements allowed readers to *interact* with our content by making navigational choices. Links brought into play other documents that supported and added information to the original document. They also changed the shape and dimensionality of the work so that we were able to describe the documents we were creating in terms of numerous conventional publishing models, including the article and the brochure. No longer working on the elemental level, we had moved onto a *structural* level of presentation.

Next we discussed how we might develop or adapt models to fit a specific purpose: What would be the best structure for displaying a catalog of clothing or a manual for woodworking? We were discussing strategic enhancements, and we had entered a new level of presentation, the *functional level.* What we were constructing with links and navigational graphics began to perform specific functions. And the models we were working with offered readers a further dimension of interaction. Not only could they click on this anchor text or that anchor graphic to get around in the document set, they could use such links for immediate access to specific information required to fulfill their immediate functional needs.

A full strategy of Internet publishing requires only one more step, but it's a big one. The full potential of publishing on the World Wide Web will be realized only when the interactive qualities of hypermedia documents are exploited on the *communal* level. When you, as an Internet publisher, successfully involve your audience in participatory actions, and when you work to expand that audience and give Internet users a continuing reason to return to your Web site, you are operating on the communal level.

And this is what, at its best, the World Wide Web is all about: community. Building a mass audience for your publications, and keeping that audience, is a matter of building information communities.

## WHAT'S NEXT?

Two lab exercises, for starters. Labs 8 and 9 help you through some of the processes we've discussed in chapter 8.

After that, it's on to Part Three to learn about indexing, image mapping, and forms. These are more advanced Web publishing processes that involve working with server programs.

# Lab 8

## Designing Access to Other Internet Services

This is an exercise in building links within an HTML document that connect to other Internet services via World Wide Web protocols. Specifically, the services these links will connect to include Gopher, file transfer protocol (FTP), and newsgroups. For information about linking to an auto-email feature, see chapter 10, "Forms Support and Server Scripting."

### Designing access to a Gopher site, an FTP server, and a newsgroup

1. Open any HTML document you've created. You can use a document you created in an earlier lab exercise, or any other document that functions correctly.

2. Near the end of the document, place your cursor at the beginning of the line containing the end tag `</body>`, and then press ENTER.

3. Move the cursor up to the beginning of the blank line you just created, and then type the following text:

   ```
   <p>For more resources, you might want to search through
   <a href="gopher://gopher.interserv.com">a Gopher
   site.</a>
   ```

4. Press ENTER, and then add the following text:

   ```
   <p>If you want to download an interesting graphics file
   and don't mind waiting for one that is quite large,
   take a look at this lovely <a href="ftp://ftp.uwtc.
   washington.edu/pub/Japanese/Pictures/Ukiyo-e/
   abeauty.gif">Japanese picture.</a>
   ```

5. Press ENTER, and then add the following text:

   ```
   If you'd rather get in on a newsgroup discussion about
   art, <a href="news:rec.arts.fine">here's one.</a>
   ```

6. Save your document in the usual way (text-only format, with the extension `.html` or `.htm`), and close the file.

**7.** Test the links by opening the document with your browser and clicking, one by one, on the anchor texts:

a Gopher site

Japanese picture

here's one

**Note:** The actual Gopher, FTP, and newsgroup resources used in this exercise were active at the time of this writing. Be aware, however, that Internet resources change so frequently, we cannot guarantee that the ones used in our examples are current. If your links are typed and coded correctly and they still do not work, check to see if the resources are still available.

# Lab 9

## Building an Information Community

In this exercise, you go through some of the steps you would take if you were actually seeking to build an information community around your set of documents. You can do this exercise individually or with a working team.

Begin by assuming that you already have a working document set posted at a Web site.

### Planning to Build an Information Community

1. In the upper-left corner of a notepad sheet, white board, or chalk-board, write the overall title of your document set or a brief description of your topic area.
   For purposes of illustration, we'll use the topic "All the World's a Stage." But you use your own topic in this exercise.

2. In a column running down the left edge of your writing surface, write very brief descriptions of the next-level topics in your document set. By "very brief," we mean one to three words.
   For our "Stage" topic, we might write *Shakespeare* and *Molière.*

3. In a column running down the right edge of your writing surface, write very brief descriptions of additional topics you think might appeal to the type of audience you have in mind.
   For our "Stage" topic, we write *Chekhov, Ibsen,* and *Beijing Opera.*

4. Consider the topics you've written in the right column, and eliminate any that you think might be moving too far away from your theme.

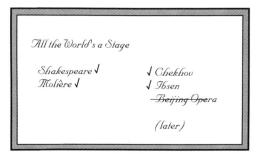

**How to Publish on the Internet**

We love the idea of the Beijing Opera, but we decide this topic might be stretching the boundaries a bit farther than we want to go. So we're deleting the Beijing Opera.

5. Now think again about the title: Is it descriptive? succinct? How will it look as a line on a Gopher server's list?

We decide "All the World's a Stage" is a great name, but maybe our title line should be more explicit. So we're going to use "All the World's a Stage" in our banner heading, but for the title we show elsewhere, we're changing it to "World Drama: Shakespeare, Molière, and Company". That allows room for adding more playwrights.

6. File away the ideas you've written in the right column. Next week or next month, you can start looking around to see if anybody else is working on projects such as these. Use Internet newsgroups and other forms of contact to ask around. Consider your own workload and think about beginning some of these additional projects yourself. In the meantime, there's more to be done for the document set you've already published.

7. Go back to your computer and explore the newsgroups out on the Net. Is there one related to the subject area of your document set? Are there more than one? If so, post an announcement.

Aha—for ours, we've discovered `rec.arts.theatre`. Just the place to post an announcement about our Web site on Shakespeare and Molière. We decide to post one there, and we also post one in the newsgroup `comp.infosystems.announce`.

8. From your browser, open `http://web.nexor.co.uk/aliweb/doc/aliweb.html`. This is a cataloguing service you can use to post your new site. Read the instructions, and contact the Webmaster to register your site.

9. Now open your Gopher application and check for Gopher servers that you might apply to for a listing. Follow their instructions about how to list with them.

10. Think about all of the conventional publications you know of that relate to the subject matter of your document set. Pick those you think might be good places to place an ad.

Remember that many professional and special-interest magazines have classified or "kiosk" sections that provide listing space at low cost.

11. Now put your thinking cap on, and try to come up with other ways of getting the word out about your document set.

   For our "Stage" topic, we've decided to print handbills and seek permission from theater managers in our hometown to leave the fliers in the theater lobbies.

   We're also sending packets to all of our friends in other cities and asking that they help us out by doing the same.

12. Continue to think and brainstorm until you're satisfied that you have all bases covered.

   Okay, put these processes into action and you're off to a great start!

   **Note:** The newsgroups cited in this exercise, as well as the HTTP newsites bulletin board, were active at the time of this writing. Be aware, however, that newsgroups and other Internet resources change so frequently, we cannot guarantee that the ones used in our examples are current.

# PART THREE

# INTERACTING WITH THE SERVER

**N**ow that you know how to create a publishable set of HTML documents, and what to do with your finished work, you're all set to publish on the Internet.

We haven't quite told you everything, however. There are some additional HTML tools that we've put off telling you about: indexing, image mapping, and interactive forms building. We've mentioned the features you can create by using two of these tools—image maps and feedback forms—but we've postponed discussing them in detail until now because they introduce some further complications. Adding these features takes you beyond the assembly of an HTML document and requires you to work with programs that run on a Web server (an HTTP server).

To do this, HTML codes are still necessary. Now, however, you will be using HTML to create an interface for actions that the server takes. And in addition, you will be instructing the server about how to take the actions. Thus, if you want to add indexing capability, image maps, and interactive forms to your documents, you have to work with executable programs and scripts on the server that process the actions your readers will take.

What we will be discussing now are interactive features you can add to an HTML document that require specific server-based programs for their implementation. To make these features work, you also have to create or modify existing files on your HTTP server.

 To work with the server-based programs, you must have read/write access to the server on which you post your documents. If you are posting your documents on somebody else's Web server, you probably do not have read-write access to the server. If in such cases you want to use indexing, image mapping, or interactive forms support, you might discuss your needs with the server administrator, who may be able to help you add the features.

## Server-Based Programs and CGI Scripts

Generally, the programs we're talking about are contained in a special directory on your Web server; on a UNIX-based server, this directory is usually called the cgi-bin. *CGI* stands for *common gateway interface.* This refers to interfacing software that facilitates communication between an HTTP server and programs operating outside the server (client programs, for example). The specific server-based programs that serve such interface functions are generally referred to as *scripts.*

Many such scripts already exist and are available for your use, either because they are already in place on your Web server or because you can find copies in Internet resources and download them. To make the scripts work with your HTML documents, you may need to modify or contour them in specific ways to fit both your server configuration and your document structures.

Note that we do not discuss in detail how you create these programs; programming languages and server configurations are beyond the scope of this book. What we discuss in Part Three is how you can use existing programs, and how you can contour scripts and create or modify other server-based files that the programs must use.

**CGI scripts and additional server-based files.** The HTML codes we discuss in Part Three are those that trigger the actions of the server-based programs to carry out indexing, image-map linking, and forms interactions. Generally, for these actions to take place, one or more additional files are needed—either another server script or, in the case of image mapping, a *configuration file* and a *map file.* It is up to you to create these additional files or to add specific information to them.

## More About CGI Programs and Scripts

The features and methods we discuss in Part Three are relatively simple examples of CGI programming. If you want to develop more complex interactive features for your HTML documents, you need to do more sophisticated programming. If you don't have the necessary skills, we suggest that you either take instruction in programming (preferably in PERL or C), or consult any of the standard reference books about PERL or C programming. These are widely available in book stores and computer stores.

If you already know your programming essentials, you're in luck—there are a number of Internet resources you can consult for help on setting up and configuring a Web server. Here is a great connection to many such resources:

```
http://www.charm.net:80/~web/
```

You need to keep in mind that CGI programs and scripts must be contoured to fit the system and platform they work on. A CGI script written for a UNIX-based server will not necessarily work on a Macintosh or a Windows NT server, and vice versa. Already there are a growing number of resources written especially for non-UNIX servers. The following is a connection to some of them:

```
http://www.charm.net/~cyber/
```

## WHAT'S IN PART THREE

The following chapters make up Part Three:

9. **ISINDEX and ISMAP: Indexing and Image Mapping.** How to add a keyword-based indexing feature to your documents, and how to create image maps, or graphics that contain anchors to multiple destinations.
10. **Forms: Increasing the Interactive Quality of Your Documents.** How to create simple interactive forms that allow user input in various formats.
11. **The Next Chapter.** A few words about things to come, and a good contact point on the World Wide Web for keeping up to date with changes in HTML.

# 9 ISINDEX and ISMAP:

## Indexing and Image Mapping

Indexing and image mapping are two valuable tools you can use to enhance the interactive quality of your HTML documents. When you add indexing capability to a document, you enable your readers to perform searches by keyword. When you add image maps, you give your readers another graphical tool for navigating. The code elements used in your documents for these purposes are <isindex> (for indexing) and the ismap attribute (for image mapping).

These two features both rely on server-based programs to make them work. The reader's browser does not itself perform a keyword search on a document; it carries the reader's search command back to the server, and the server performs the search. Likewise, when a reader clicks on a hot spot in an image map, the browser must pass the command back to the server, because that is where the program that activates an image map and the information about the link destinations are stored.

To add either of these features to your HTML documents, you must have access to files located on your Web server.

> **N O T E** Because many Web servers are UNIX-based, much of the following discussion uses constructs that apply specifically to UNIX. All server files must, of course, be contoured for compatibility with the platform on which the server runs. You can use the Internet to find information on working with both UNIX and non-UNIX platforms. Refer back to the introductory pages of Part Three for references to some generally related Internet resources. An additional resource for information specifically about using ismap and isindex with Macintosh servers can be found at:
> `http://www.biap.com/machttp/howto_maps.html`

# ADDING THE ⟨ISINDEX⟩ INDEXING CAPABILITY TO A DOCUMENT

There is more than one way to add a searching capability to an HTML document, of which the ⟨isindex⟩ method is one. We are focusing on ⟨isindex⟩ because discussing this method also provides a good introduction to server scripts. For information about other search methods, we suggest that you consult the Internet resource: `http://wwwrlg.stanford.edu/home/jpl/websearch.html`

**Important:** It is best *not* to insert the ⟨isindex⟩ code into your HTML document manually. If you have the appropriate server script in place, the server generates an HTML document with the ⟨isindex⟩ element auto-

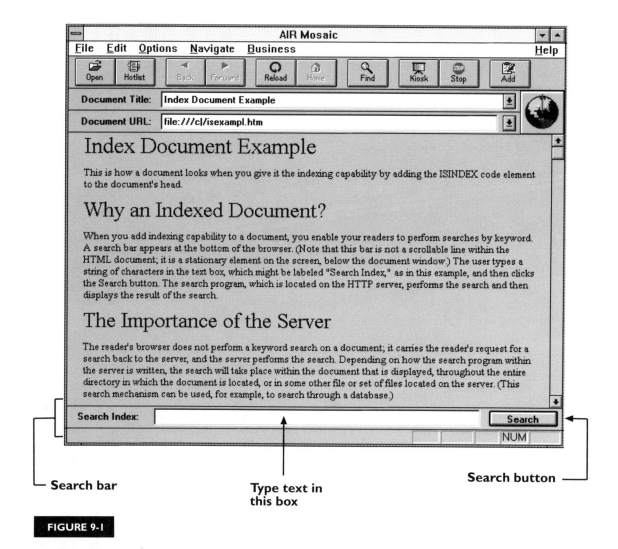

**Search bar**      **Type text in this box**      **Search button**

**FIGURE 9-1**

matically included in the document's head. You can, of course, add the <isindex> element to a document manually, but if there is no server script in place to receive the user's input, no search will be performed and the client software may freeze.

## How the Indexing Feature Works

When the reader opens an index document, a search bar appears at the bottom of the browser. Note that this bar is not a scrollable line within the HTML document; it is a stationary element on the screen, below the document window.

The search bar contains a text box, which might be labeled "Search Index," as in the example in figure 9-1. The user types a string of characters in the text box and then clicks on the Search button. The search program, which is located on the HTTP server, performs the search and then displays the result.

A *server script* acts as interface between the server and the browser. Depending on how the server script is written, the search will take place either within the document that is displayed, throughout the entire directory in which the document is located, or in some other file or set of files located on the server. The search mechanism can be used, for example, to search through a database such as a company employee list.

The result of the search appears in a window similar to the one illustrated in figure 9-2. In this example, the character string the reader has typed in the search box is *fry*. Note that <isindex> searches are case-insensitive and will generally return all instances of the character string entered, whether complete words or not.

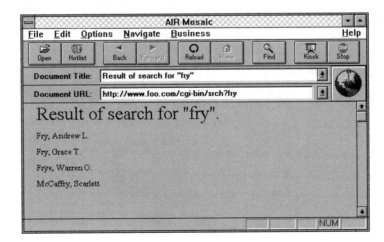

**FIGURE 9-2**

## The ISINDEX Code Element

The existence of the `<isindex>` code element in the head of an HTML document acts as a signal to the server that the document is an index document.

---

**‹isindex›**    **Indexing element.** `<isindex>` is automatically inserted into the head of an HTML document by a server script written to create that document. This element is then used to inform the server that the document is an index document. This means that readers can use keywords to search the document or other files on the server.

**Example**
```
<html><head>
<title>Index HTML Document</title>
<isindex>
</head>
```

---

That's all there is to the ‹isindex› feature, as far as your HTML documents are concerned. To make it all work, you need to create the server script.

## The Server-Based Program and the Server Script

For the ‹isindex› feature to work, your Web server must contain a search program that's written in an interpreted or compiled computer language such as C, PERL, or TCL. In our examples below, we will be referring to one widely used search program called Grep. This program is triggered by action that a user takes within the client (that is, the browser). In other words, when the user clicks on the Search button illustrated in figure 9-1, the server-based program runs.

**The server script.** The browser reports the user's action (clicking on the Search button) and the information the user has supplied (the character string the user has typed in the text box) to the server. For the browser to communicate with the server-based program, however, it's necessary to add an executable CGI script that you create specifically.

We do not intend to teach you how to write an `isindex` server script from scratch. On the Internet, you can find a number of server scripts as models. See, for example, those offered in the following files, bearing in mind that server scripts must generally be contoured to work with the specific configuration of a server:

http://www.utirc.utoronto.ca/HTMLdocs/NewHTML/
server-isindex.html
http://iamwww.unibe.ch/~scg/Src/PerlLib/

Figure 9-3 shows our own example of a simple server script, which you can also use as a guide to creating or adapting your own script.

```
#!/bin/sh
echo Content-type: text/html
echo
if [ $# = 0 ]
then
  echo "<head>"
  echo "<title>Index Document Example</title>"
  echo "<isindex>"
  echo "</head>"
  echo "<h1>Index Document Example</h1>"
  echo "Enter your search in the search field.<p>
  echo "This is a case-insensitive substring search: thus"
  echo "searching for 'fry' will find 'Fry' and 'McCaffry'."
  echo "</body>
else
  echo "<head>"
  echo "<title>Result of search for \"$*\".</title>"
  echo "</head>"
  echo "<body>"
  echo "<h1>Result of search for \"$*\".</h1>"
  echo "<pre>"
  grep -I "$*" /Foo/Personnel.mdb
  echo "</pre>"
  echo "</body>"
fi
```

**FIGURE 9-3**

This script calls the search program Grep, seen at the beginning of the fourth line from the bottom of the script sample. Again, this program must be in place on the server for the indexing feature to work. We've set up this code example so that the Grep program acts upon the directory path /Foo/Personnel.mdb, which means that the file to be searched is Personnel.mdb in the directory /Foo. Searching this file, then, might yield a result like the example shown in figure 9-2, assuming the reader searches for the keyword *fry*.

**More information about server scripts.** This is as far as we're going to go in discussing <isindex> server scripts. If we went any further, we would soon be in technically complex territory on the server side of the client-server relationship. For more information about writing scripts for the <isindex> feature, we recommend that you check the //www. utirc.utoronto.ca and //iamwww.unibe.ch resources cited earlier, together with further references given within the former document.

## CREATING AN IMAGE MAP

In chapter 6, we mentioned that you can create an image map and use it as a modular navigational graphic. Doing this enables you to include multiple anchor destinations within a single in-line image. This means that a mouse click on one area of the image jumps the reader to one topic, and a mouse click on another area jumps to a different topic. The term *image map* thus refers to a graphical image mapped so that different, graphically active parts of the image (called *hot spots*) are coded for different results when acted upon by a user.

To add an image map to your HTML document, you use the <img> code together with the ismap attribute. As with indexing, however, you must also set up corresponding files on the server.

### What the Reader Sees

Figure 9-4 shows an image-mapped graphic that we've seen before. It's from the navigational page of a Web site we visited in chapter 2, The Palace of Diocletian at Split (Spalato), in Croatia.

The Palace of Diocletian document set, you may recall, describes the architecture of a magnificent palace complex from the late Roman era. It also includes short essays on the Emperor Diocletian and his time.

The graphic shown in figure 9-4 contains two different uses of image mapping:

- The image of the palace itself contains hot spots. A reader can click on any of several areas in the picture to jump to a topic about that section of the palace.
- At the bottom of the graphic is a navigational toolbar. Each button links to a separate subtopic: Introduction, Diocletian (an essay about the em-

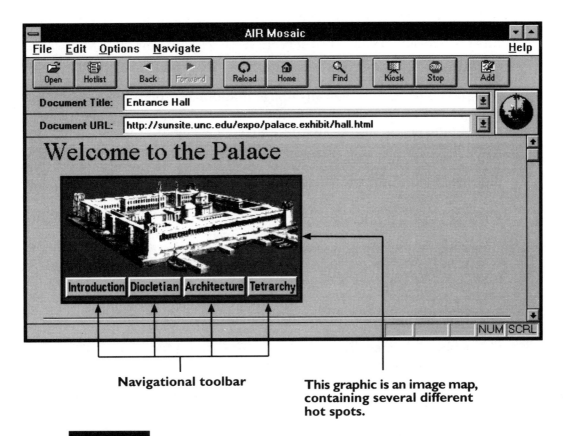

**Navigational toolbar**

**This graphic is an image map, containing several different hot spots.**

**FIGURE 9-4**

peror), Architecture (about the architecture of the palace), and Tetrarchy (about the governmental form of Diocletian's day).

## How to Do It

First, you need a graphics file containing the overall image you want to use. Generally speaking, this should be a GIF file that graphical browsers can download as an in-line image. As with other graphics, you do not add the file itself to your HTML document. Rather, you insert a pointer to it within your document, using an `<img>` tag with the `ismap` attribute. We'll demonstrate this coding below, but you may also want to refer back to chapter 6 for a general discussion about using the `<img>` tag.

Next, you set up this graphic as an image map by defining specific areas within it as anchors. You create a *map file* that identifies the areas by their pixel coordinates and maps them to specific destinations. The map file must be stored on your Web server. We'll explain how you create the map file later in this chapter.

*Imagemap* **program.** For any image mapping in your documents to work, your HTTP server must contain an executable program that is usually called *imagemap* and located in a directory called /cgi-bin. This program processes information about the reader's mouse clicks sent by the browser and returns information that instructs the browser to display a specific new document or location.

> **N O T E** As with the server-based program that runs the isindex search mechanism, you cannot create the imagemap program with HTML codes. The imagemap program should be in place on any server configured for HTTP.

**Configuration file.** In addition to the imagemap program, your server also needs to include a file called imagemap.conf. This configuration file, which is generally located in the /httpd/conf directory of your server, contains the names of all mapped images and the directory paths (URLs) to their corresponding map files. You need to make sure that the imagemap.conf file contains the name and path of your map file.

## The ISMAP Attribute and the Anchor Tags

To create an image map within your HTML document, you add the ismap attribute to the <img> code that marks the overall graphic. You also need to specify the URL of the map file within the anchor tag.

| | |
|---|---|
| **ismap** | ismap **attribute.** Insert this attribute into an <img> (image) code to designate an in-line image as an image map. |
| **<a href = "***URL***">**<br>**</a>** | **Anchor tags.** These are familiar from all our previous work with anchors. The URL is the path to the map file on the server. It is important to know the following specific characteristics of the URL:<br>  ❑ The server name is the name of your HTTP server.<br>  ❑ The directory (for UNIX servers) is /cgi-bin.<br>  ❑ The URL includes the name of the executable program, imagemap (no file name extension).<br>  ❑ The file name of the map file also has no extension. |

**How to Publish on the Internet**

***Example***

```
<a href="http://www.test.com/cgi-bin/imagemap/
map_clas"><img src=clas.gif ismap>
</a>
```

In the anchor start tag of this example, map_clas is the name of the map file. In the <img> tag, clas.gif is the file name of the overall graphic.

## The Map File: Precise Coordinates and Destinations

The map file contains precise information about the location of hot-spotted areas in your image map and the URLs for the destinations to which the hot spots are linked.

Before you create the map file, you need to determine the exact locations, in pixel coordinates, of the hot spots you want to build into your image map. How you define the coordinates of a given hot spot depends on the shape of the hot spot you want to create. There are three different shapes you can use:

- A circle
- A rectangle (including a square)
- A polygon (maximum 100 vertices)

In all cases, we assume a rectangular overall graphic on which we plot the $x$ and $y$ coordinates, starting from the upper-left corner (0,0). The coordinates are measured by pixel count to the right (the $x$ coordinate) and downward (the $y$ coordinate) from the 0,0 point. Thus, the four corners of a graphic that measures 200 × 80 pixels would be as shown in figure 9-5.

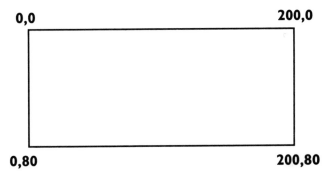

0,0          200,0

0,80         200,80

**FIGURE 9-5**

It is a relatively simple matter to map a rectangular or circular hot spot, but rather more complicated to map a polygon. Let's look at them one at a time.

**Rectangular hot spot.** A rectangle is the simplest mapping shape to define. Two pairs of coordinates are required: One pair defines the upper-left corner of the hot spot, and the other pair defines the lower-right corner. In figure 9-6, which uses an image map the same size as in figure 9-5 (200 × 80 pixels), hot spot #1 occupies the left one-third of the overall graphic and is defined by the coordinates 0,0 and 67,80. Hot spot #2 is defined by the coordinates 100,20 and 150,60.

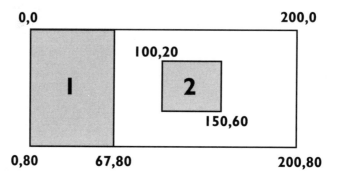

**FIGURE 9-6**

**Circular hot spot.** Two pairs of coordinates are required to define a circle: the center of the circle and any point on the circle's circumference. Figure 9-7 illustrates two circles in a graphic of 200 × 80 pixels overall. Circle #1 is defined by the coordinates 20,20 (the circle's center) and 20,0 (where the circumference touches the top edge of the graphic). This circle could also be defined by the coordinates 20,20 and 0,20 (where the circumference touches the left edge). Circle #2 is defined by 160,20 (the center) and 160,60 (one point on the circumference).

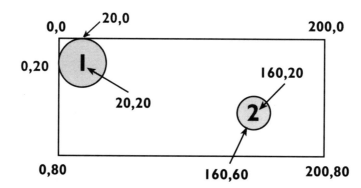

**FIGURE 9-7**

**How to Publish on the Internet**

**Polygonal hot spot.** You can map a polygon of almost any shape imaginable. Each vertex is defined by a pair of coordinates, to a maximum of 100 vertices. The example shown in figure 9-8 has five vertices that map to the following coordinates:

0,80    45,30    60,40    110,20    80,80

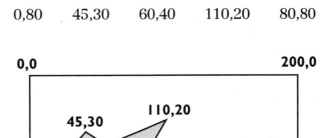

FIGURE 9-8

As you can see from this illustration, mapping a polygon is analogous to drawing a picture by connecting numbered dots. Polygons are useful for defining as hot spots images that do not easily map to circles or rectangles. If your graphic contains a picture of a running Greyhound dog, for example, you might want to define a polygon along the edges of the Greyhound as the anchor to a document on the topic of Greyhounds.

**Default destination.** It is likely that not every point or area within your graphic will map to a destination document or location. You need to specify a default destination that is anchored to all undefined coordinates in your image map. Let's say, for example, that your image map contains pictures of twenty or so people posing for a group portrait, and you've defined each person's image as a hot spot that links to a biography of that person. The space around the people, however, doesn't link to any particular topic. In the map file, you need to specify the location (as a URL) to which the browser defaults when the user clicks on an area not defined as a hot spot. In the example of the group portrait, this could be to a document that discusses the group as a whole; or it could be the document and location that the user is already viewing—that is, no jump at all.

**Creating the map file.** To create a map file, you can use any text-editing or word-processing program that is capable of saving files in plain-text (ASCII) format. Open a new file, and type the following lines:

❑ A line specifying the default destination, including Relative or Absolute URL.

❑ One line for each set of coordiantes defining a hot spot in your image map. Each of these lines should follow this format:

*shape URL x1,y1 x2,y2 . . . xn,yn*

where *shape* specifies the shape of the hot spot (rect, circ, or poly); *URL* is the location and file name of the destination; and *xn,yn* are the *x* and *y* coordinates defining the location of the hot spot.

Thus, a map file that includes the rectangular, circular, and polygonal hot spots illustrated in figures 9-6 through 9-8 above might look like figure 9-9.

```
default http://www.website.com/samples/mydoc.html
rect http://www.website.com/samples/yourdoc.html 0,0 67,80
rect http://www.website.com/samples/herdoc.html 100,20 150,60
circ http://www.website.com/samples/hisdoc.html 20,20 20,0
circ http://www.website.com/samples/theirdoc.html 160,20 160,60
poly http://www.website.com/samples/anydoc.html 0,80 45,30 60,40
110,20 80,80
```

**FIGURE 9-9**

**Naming and storing the map file.** You save the map file as text only and give it a name with the extension .map. For example, we might name the map file illustrated above ourmap.map.

You can store the map file in any directory of your Web server as long as your configuration file (imagemap.conf) lists it, along with its Relative URL.

## The Configuration File

Now all you have to do is add the name of your map file to the imagemap.conf file. This file, as we've said, is generally located in the /httpd/conf directory of your Web server. You can open imagemap.conf in any text-editing and word-processing application capable of saving a file as plain text (ASCII, or text only).

**How to Publish on the Internet**

The format for entering a map file is *name: path_of_map*. For example, we would enter the map file from our sample above as:

```
ourmap: /httpd/conf/ourmap.map
```

and then save and close the file.

## How It All Works

The process by which an image map works as a navigational feature takes place in the following steps:

1.  The reader clicks on an area within the image map.
2.  The browser reports the pixel coordinates of the mouse position to the server.
3.  The imagemap program gets the location of the map file from `imagemap.conf`, reads the map file, determines the destination of the link according to the pixel coordinates, and acts upon displaying that destination document or location as if the initial HTML document simply contained an anchor.
4.  The browser then displays the new document or location.

## One Final Point of Etiquette

When you create an image map, you should be sure to add a text alternative for each hot spot in the graphic within your HTML document. You do this as a courtesy to readers who are using non-graphical browsers or who choose to work with their in-line image feature turned off. Set up your text alternative so that the reader can click on a word for each separate anchor within the image map. It is best to do this by adding a text paragraph, generally right below the image map. Do not try to add text alternatives by using the `alt` attribute within the `<img>` tag; this method works only for a simple navigational graphic with a single destination, because the `alt` attribute cannot be mapped to more than one location.

## Precision and Testing

You probably don't have to think very hard to realize that getting the coordinates right is crucial to the functionality of your image map. As with every other feature that you build into your documents, you should be sure to test your image maps thoroughly before sending them out into the wide world of the World Wide Web.

**FIGURE 9-10**

## AN EXAMPLE: A VIRTUAL CLASS REUNION

Here's an example of a use for an image map. Let's imagine holding a virtual class reunion on the Internet. To make it interesting, we're not going to hold a reunion of our graduating class, but of the first-grade class from our illustrious alma mater, the Web School. We'll contact all of our erstwhile classmates, and ask each of them to send us a recent personal photo and a brief account of their lives during the intervening years. We might also offer each person the opportunity to add a message to one or more classmates. Once we have all the data, we'll create a set of documents with a separate page for each classmate. We'll post the document set on a Web server and inform all of the relevant people where to find it. Let's hope they all have good browsers!

As it happens, we have a photo of that original first-grade class, under the tutelage of the redoubtable Mrs. Harbottle. We've been hit by a thunderbolt of inspiration: with the photographer's permission, we're going to scan that photo and make it into an image map. We'll put it on the first page of our document set, and we'll map it so that when you click on any face in the photo, you'll bring up the page containing the current-day data for that person. Cool, huh?

Figure 9-10 illustrates this image map and the current photos that appear on two of the data pages it is linked to. We want to be sure the full image fits into the view of all possible browsers, so we've decided to make it 480 × 320 pixels overall.

This makes for a pretty complicated map file, with more than twenty coordinates to plot, but we can at least simplify the hot spots by drawing them as rectangles. Thus, the spirited little fellow on the left end of the middle row, Andy, can be defined by the coordinates 59,96 and 87,135. Davy, the demure tyke in the top row, second from the right, can be defined by the coordinates 328,45 and 355,80. As figure 9-10 illustrates, when you click on either Andy or Davy in the overall picture, you bring up his current photo and biographical data.

**NEXT**

We've concluded our discussion of indexing and image mapping, but we haven't finished with our Web class reunion. We'll refer to it again in the next chapter, where we discuss how to create interactive forms for your HTML documents.

# 10 Forms:

## Increasing the Interactive Quality of Your HTML Documents

The third HTML feature that utilizes a server-based program is the interactive form. By using forms, you substantially increase your audience's interaction with your documents, because forms give your readers the means to send you specific input—from comments to purchase orders. This input can take any of several formats: text strings, option checkboxes, or selections from a drop-down list.

As you might expect, server scripts for HTML forms are a little more complicated than those for indexing or image maps. When you work with the `isindex` and `ismap` features, you can get away without having to write complex server programs from scratch, because there are programs and scripts available that you can adapt to your specific implementation. When you create interactive forms and their accompanying scripts, on the other hand, you have to do a bit more programming.

As in chapter 9, we are not going to teach you all you have to know to write the applicable server-based programs. What we are going to do is to show you an example of a form, as viewed with a browser, and explain how it works from both the client side and the server side. Then we'll examine the HTML codes that create the form itself. Next, we'll look at an example of the feedback data that we might expect to get from respondents. Finally, we'll lay out for you the CGI script, written in PERL, that retrieves and processes the data that our readers enter in the example form.

## CREATING THE HTML FORM

Let's return to our Web School virtual class reunion, which we started to work with in chapter 9. Suppose we've collected the photos and biographical data from our classmates, created our document set, and got everything ready to post at our Web site. Now, however, we have another idea: We'd really like to know our classmates' reactions once they've "attended" the virtual reunion. To encourage their participation, we're going to offer them a couple of mementos: a commemorative T-shirt and a copy of that original class photo, autographed by none other than the redoubtable Mrs. Harbottle, whom we have located in a retirement center in Florida.

We create a new page for our document set, using HTML codes, and build into it the form that you see illustrated in figure 10-1.

The large, white space in the center of the form is a text box where the reader can type in any comments he or she wishes to send as feedback. Below that is a smaller text box for the respondent's name, a checkbox

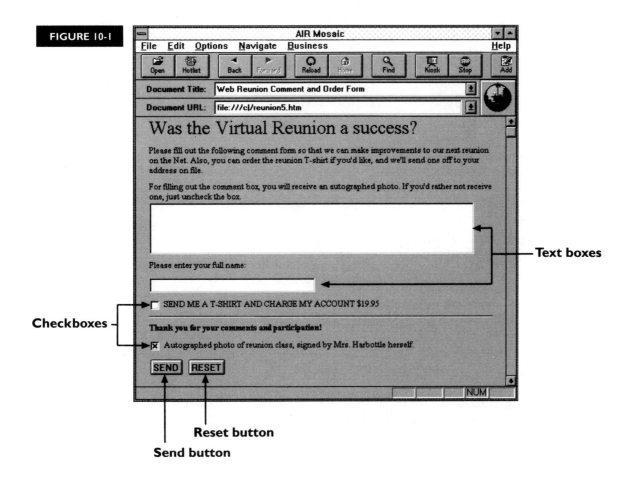

**FIGURE 10-1**

**Text boxes**

**Checkboxes**

**Reset button**

**Send button**

for ordering the official class T-shirt, and another checkbox for a free, autographed photo. Finally, there is a Send button for submitting the form and a Reset button for starting over again.

Now we need to write a server script that will process the feedback our readers send. The script will place all responses in a text file that we can refer to (for filling the T-shirt orders and sending the photos, for example). And it will immediately send a reply back to our readers' browsers, like the acknowledgment message illustrated in figure 10-2.

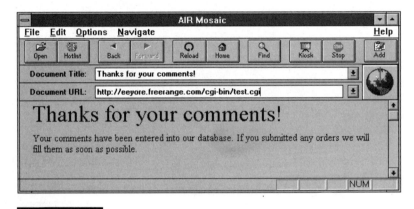

**FIGURE 10-2**

To produce this form, we create an HTML document, using many of the code elements you're already familiar with—plus a few more. The new elements and their attributes are summarized in the next section. Later in this chapter, we'll show you the script that processes this form and sends back the acknowledgment message.

## HTML Codes for a Form

The three tag elements used to create the Reunion form are ⟨form⟩, ⟨textarea⟩, and ⟨input⟩. We'll look at these elements one at a time, together with their attributes.

**The ⟨form⟩ element.** The ⟨form⟩ element marks the beginning and end of a form. It also defines where the information that a reader enters in the form is to be delivered (server, directory, and file), and by what method.

**How to Publish on the Internet**

<table>
<tr>
<td>

**&lt;form method = "*method*" action = "*URL*"&gt;**
**&lt;/form&gt;**

</td>
<td>

**Form tags.** These tags define the beginning and end of a form. The start tag takes the following attributes:

*method*  specifies how the data entered in the form is delivered to the server.

*action*  specifies the location to which the data is delivered for processing.

***Example***

```
<form method = "post" action = "http://
eeyore.freerange.com/cgi-bin/
reunion.cgi">
```

</td>
</tr>
</table>

This example code specifies that the information a user enters into the form will be delivered by the `post` method to the `/cgi-bin` directory of the server named `eeyore.freerange.com`. There it will be processed by a script file named `reunion.cgi`. The URL refers to the location where the executable file is stored.

There are two alternative delivery methods, described as follows:

- `post`: Using this method, the server script places the input information into a packet as a body of data, and delivers it to the executable file on the server. (This is the method we recommend.)
- `get`: The server script appends the information to the URL as a string and carries it back to the server in that form (rather than as a body of data).

**The `<textarea>` element.** The `<textarea>` element creates a text box. Readers can type in multiple lines of text as comments, an address, and so on. The attributes `rows` and `cols` delimit the exact size of the box.

<table>
<tr>
<td>

**&lt;textarea name = "*name*" rows = *n* cols = *n*&gt;**
**&lt;/textarea&gt;**

</td>
<td>

**Text area tags.** These tags define a data field as a text box and specify its size. The start tag takes the following attributes:

`name`  symbolic identifier used by the server script in processing the data field (must be included)

`rows`  vertical dimension of the text box (number of lines)

`cols`  width of the text box (number of characters)

</td>
</tr>
</table>

```
<textarea name="comments" rows=5
cols=60>
```

This example creates a text box named *comments* that is five lines high by sixty characters wide.

**The** `<input>` **element.** The `<input>` element defines the nature of a data field within a form—whether it is a text box, a checkbox, and so on—and how the reader will use it.

**`<input type = "`*type*`" attr 2 = "`*str*`". . .>`**

**Input tag.** This element identifies a data field, and defines its appearance and how readers will use it. It does not require an end tag.

Note that `type` is the first attribute listed here; the placeholder `attr2` stands for a second attribute, and `str` stands for a character string defining the attribute. You may use more than two attributes.

The following attributes are used in the Web Reunion form:

| | |
|---|---|
| `type` | specifies the type of data entered by the user (default is "text") |
| `name` | symbolic identifier used by the server script in processing the data field (must be included) |
| `size` | size of the field (number of characters: used only for "text" and "password" type fields) |
| `checked` | specifies that a checkbox or radio button is *checked* by default |
| `value` | the value displayed by the field; can be either SEND or RESET |

*Examples*
```
<input type = "text" name = "fullname" size=30>
<input type = "checkbox" name = "photo" checked>
<input type = "submit" value = "SEND">
```

The first example specifies that the type of input is *text;* this creates a one-line text box, 30 characters wide, for the reader to type in. (Notice that you do not use quotation marks around the size value.) The second example specifies that the type of input is a *checkbox* and that the box is checked by default. The third example defines a button that, when clicked, *submits* the data the reader has entered in the form; the value "SEND" represents the lettering that will be displayed on the button.

The following are the most commonly used `type` choices:

- `text`  Produces a text box limited to one line (horizontally scrollable if used together with the maxlength attribute).
- `checkbox`  Produces a checkbox; any number of checkboxes can be checked.
- `radio`  Creates a round checkbox. Used for attributes that can take only one value from a set of alternatives; that is, only one radio field can be checked.
- `password`  For use as password submission. Text typed into the box is not displayed.
- `submit`  Creates a button for submitting the form.
- `reset`  Creates a button that resets all input fields to their defaults (as they were before the reader started filling them in).

For text boxes, there is another commonly used attribute that we have not included in our Web Reunion form: `maxlength`. This attribute specifies the maximum number of characters a reader can type into the text box, irrespective of the size of the box. Any characters that exceed the size of the box will be displayed by scrolling to the right within the box.

**The** `<select>` **and** `<option>` **elements.** There's one important feature that we haven't used in the Web Reunion form. The `<select>` element defines a field as a list box. If there are two or more alternatives in the list, the field becomes a drop-down list box. The `<option>` element defines each of the selectable alternatives.

Here are the codes:

| | |
|---|---|
| **\<select name = "*selectname*">**<br>**\</select>** | **Select tags.** These tags identify a field as a selectable option box. If there are two or more options, the field defines a drop-down list box. The start tag takes the `name` attribute. |
| `<option>`***selectoption*** | **Option element.** Use the tab to identify each possible choice within a selectable option box. Note that the value does not require quotation marks. |

```
<select name="colors">
<option>White
<option>Navy
<option>Puce
<option>Hunter green
</select>
```

This example defines a box with a drop-down list containing four options, *White, Navy, Puce,* and *Hunter green.* Notice that the `<select>` and `<option>` elements work together much as the various types of list elements that we discussed in chapter 4.

Figure 10-3 shows how this drop-down list box looks.

**FIGURE 10-3**

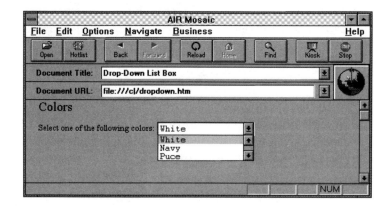

## More Information

The discussion in the preceding few pages gives you the basic HTML elements for creating forms. There are a few elements and attributes we haven't covered, plus some that have been proposed but not yet implemented at the time we are writing this. For complete and periodically updated information, we recommend that you consult the on-line spec published on the Web by CERN and the HTML primer published by NCSA. We've cited these references before, and here again are their URLs:

```
http://info.cern.ch/hypertext/WWW/MarkUp/
HTML.html
http://www.ncsa.uiuc.edu/General/Internet/WWW/
HTMLPrimer.html
```

## The Codes in Our Example

Figure 10-4 shows the complete HTML document that contains our Web Reunion form (the form shown earlier in figure 10-1).

```
<html>
<head>
<title>Web Reunion Comment and Order Form</title>
</head>
<body>
<h1>Was the Virtual Reunion a success?</h1>
<p>Please fill out the following comment form so that we can make
improvements to our next reunion on the Net. Also, you can order the reunion
T-shirt if you are so inclined and we'll send one off to your address on
file.</p>
<p>
For filling out the comment box, an autographed photo will be sent to you.
If you'd rather not receive one, simply uncheck the box.
</p>
<form method="post" action="http://eeyore.freerange.com/cgi-bin/
reunion.cgi">
<textarea name="comments" rows=5 cols=60></textarea>
<p>
Please enter your full name:
<p>
<input type=text name="fullname" size=30>
<p>
<input type=checkbox name="tshirt"> SEND ME A T-SHIRT AND CHARGE MY
ACCOUNT $19.95
<hr>
<strong>Thank you for your comments and participation!</strong>
<p>
<input type=checkbox name="photo" checked> Autographed photo of reunion
class, signed by Mrs. Harbottle herself.
<p>
<input type="submit" value="SEND"> <input type="RESET" value="RESET">
</form>
</body>
</html>
```

**FIGURE 10-4**

## THE SERVER SCRIPT

The next step is writing the server script. This is the executable file that processes data entered in an HTML form. The server script is triggered when the reader clicks the Send button. The script accepts the data from the client (the reader's browser) and processes it on the server. Our script appends the data to an output file that has been specifically created to assemble the data gathered by the HTML form.

To implement the Web Reunion form, we use PERL to write a CGI script contoured for this specific form. The script will use the post method of delivering the data from the form (because that is what we specified in the HTML file for the form) and deliver it to a file on the server named feedback.txt. In addition, the script will immediately send back to the client the acknowledgment message that we illustrated in figure 10-2.

Figure 10-5 shows an example of what we might expect to see in the output file, feedback.txt. Remember, this file contains the data from each respondent, stacked one response on top of the other. You'll notice that the data includes not only the respondents' names and comments but also how they responded to the checkboxes for ordering the T-shirt and for receiving a free photo.

```
-----------------------------

Person's name is: Bobby Jo Whiplash.
Person's comments are:

i loved the reunion

Photo ordered.
T-shirt ordered.


-----------------------------

Person's name is: Andrew R. Free.
Person's comments are:

I enjoyed visiting with all my fellow classmates, at least in
the realm of Cyberspace. I look forward to the next online
gathering, and will keep in touch with several of those I
was reintroduced to recently as well.

Photo not ordered
T-shirt ordered.


-----------------------------

Person's name is: David Q. Pauley.
Person's comments are:

They let us use the computer facility here now and then and
so I showed the reunion to my prison mates. I don't
understand what they were laughing at.

Photo not ordered
T-shirt not ordered.
```

**FIGURE 10-5**

## The CGI Script

Figure 10-6 displays the CGI script that retrieves and processes the data.

```perl
#!/usr/bin/perl

#reunion.cgi
#This script will retrieve and process the information entered in the
#form 'reunion.html'.

print "Content-type: text/html\n\n";

read(STDIN,$in,$ENV{'CONTENT_LENGTH'});
@pairs=split(/\&/, $in);
foreach $pair (@pairs) {
  ($name,$valu) = split(/\=/,$pair);
  $valu =~tr/+/ /;
  $valu =~ s/%([a-fA-F0-9][a-fA-F0-9])/pack("C", hex($1))/eg;
  $form{$name} = $valu;
}
open (OUTPUTFILE, ">>feedback.txt");

print OUTPUTFILE "--------------------------\n";
print OUTPUTFILE "Person's name is: $form{'fullname'}.\n";
print OUTPUTFILE "Person's comments are:\n\n$form{'comments'}\n\n";

if (defined($form{'photo'}))
{
        print OUTPUTFILE "Photo ordered.\n";
}
else
{
        print OUTPUTFILE "Photo not ordered\n";
}

if (defined($form{'tshirt'}))
{
        print OUTPUTFILE "T-shirt ordered.\n\n";
}
else
{
        print OUTPUTFILE "T-shirt not ordered.\n\n";
}

close (OUTPUTFILE);

print "<head><title>Thanks for your comments!</title></head>\n";
print "<body><h1>Thanks for your comments!</h1>\n";
print "Your comments have been entered into our database. If you \n";
print "submitted any orders we will fill them as soon as possible.<p>\n";
print "</body>";
```

**FIGURE 10-6**

**How to Publish on the Internet**

**What this script represents.** We want to emphasize that the script shown in figure 10-6 is a *scenario* for CGI forms scripts. This script happens to work, running on a UNIX-based server and collecting data from certain widely used client applications. However, we are in treacherous technical territory and need to point out, once again, that different server platforms operate according to different standards. To be sure that your script will work, you need to consult up-to-date documentation pertaining to the platform(s) you are writing the script for.

## THAT'S ALL, FOLKS

Well, what more can we say? A lot, as it happens, but not without abandoning our stream of logic and veering off into the world of code. We've moved into more complicated subject matter in Part Three, ending up with our discussion of forms. Interactive forms are a valuable addition to HTML documents, but they do require some knowledge of programming.

If you don't feel confident about working in PERL, C, or another appropriate programming language, you can still make use of other interactive features we've discussed in earlier chapters. Instead of a server-scripted form, you can use an auto-email form that channels audience feedback to your e-mail address. (See our discussion of this in chapter 8.) This method lacks the elegance of a server-scripted form and requires you to assemble the feedback data manually, but it can get a part of the job done. Or, if you really want to do things the old-fashioned way, just give your telephone number and/or postal address. (We doubt that you will want to get your feedback by telephone or regular mail, nor will you receive as much, but they are still options.)

But if you can do the server scripting—or get somebody to do it for you—you will maximize your feedback and have it processed automatically. And you will be firmly in command of the newest of the mass media.

# 11 The Next Chapter

*Once long ago, in an Eastern land, a young wanderer in search of the ultimate Truth consulted a sage. The wanderer traveled for many days and nights, and when he finally encountered the sage, he asked the sage the question that had troubled him all of his young life: "Master, can you tell me one great Truth that is eternal?" The sage combed his long beard with his fingers and answered: "And this too shall pass."*

Well, fellow seekers of the Truth, you've landed here. It's the last chapter—at least, the last chapter you'll find in this book. But you didn't really believe it would end, did you?

In fact, it doesn't. The technology of the Internet and the World Wide Web is so dynamic, so much in flux, that new changes are taking place every day. The next chapter is already being written, and will be in place by the time you pick this book off a shelf in your neighborhood book store.

We don't mean this in the metaphorical sense. We have developed an on-line update page that contains information about new code elements, new features, and new publishing ideas for the World Wide Web.

We've told you throughout the book that the technology is changing, that URLs to your favorite Web sites (other than your own—and maybe even your own) can change, and that new software and hardware are emerging. You're probably tired of hearing this, but be comforted: we're going to keep you up-to-date.

**Where to look for updates.** Here is our World Wide Web address, where you can look for the on-line version of *How to Publish on the Internet: The Next Chapter:*

```
http://pathfinder.com/twep/Features/How_Pub_Web/
How_Pub_Web.html
```

So please go to your computer, fire up your browser, and open this document to see what has changed in the wide world of World Wide Web publishing in the time it has taken you to read this book.

## A Preview of Coming Attractions: Heading and Paragraph Alignment

Here is one thing that is unavailable as we write but will most likely be available as you read these words: the ability to use the `align` attribute with certain block codes—paragraph and heading tags in particular. This will enable you to center these blocks of text on a browser screen or to justify the right margin (leaving the left margin ragged). We think this will be especially useful to you in designing headings, but you will probably also find ways to use the feature for text paragraphs, too.

The following describes how you can use the `align` attribute for these purposes.

---

**\<h1 align = right\>**
**\</h1\>**
**\<h2 align = center\>**
**\</h2\>**
*etc.*

**Heading tags with the** `align` **attribute.** The `align` attribute can be used with any heading element to specify its alignment: flush left, flush right, or centered. The `align` attribute is followed by an *equal sign* (=) and the specific alignment designation.

The following example shows a centered heading.

*If you write this:*

```
<h2 align = center>Aligned
Headings</h2>
<p>A centered heading is aligned midway ...
```

*It will be displayed similar to this:*

**Aligned Headings**
A centered heading is aligned midway between

**\<p align = left\>**
**\</p\>**
**\<p align = right\>**
**\</p\>**
**\<p align = center\>**
**\</p\>**

**Paragraph tags with the** `align` **attribute.** The align attribute used with the \<p\> start and end tags specifies paragraph alignment: flush left, flush right, or centered. The align attribute is followed by an *equal sign* (=) and the specific alignment designation. Notice the space between \<p and `align`.

The following example shows a right-aligned (flush right) paragraph.

---

| *If you write this:* | *It will be displayed similar to this:* |
|---|---|
| `<p align=right> This right-aligned paragraph will be displayed with its right edge flush (straight) and its left edge ragged.</p>` | This right-aligned paragraph will be displayed with its right edge flush (straight) and its left edge ragged. |

## Good Luck, and Stay Tuned!

We'd like to say we've told you everything we know about publishing on the World Wide Web, but modesty prohibits us from doing so. We hope you've found in this book everything you need to know to get started, as well as how to find some useful on-line information.

And we welcome you as fellow publishers on the Internet!

See you on the Net . . .

# Glossary

**Absolute URL**

A *uniform resource locator* that designates an absolute location for a file. It specifies the full path for a file, including server name and all subdirectories. An Absolute URL directs the reader's browser to retrieve the file from the specified server and path, and from nowhere else. Cf. *Relative URL*.

**anchor**

An HTML code, consisting of the elements `<a>` and `</a>` plus the attribute `href` and an identifier, that marks text or a graphic linked to another location in an HTML document or in another document.

**anchor graphic**

A graphical image that contains an anchor.

**attribute**

A part of an HTML code that adds specific information to a code tag. In the code `<img src="`*URL*`">`, for example, `src="`*URL*`"` is an attribute that defines the name and location of a graphics file.

**banner graphic**

A graphic image at the beginning of a Web page, roughly analogous to the flag, or nameplate, of a newspaper.

**Block formatting codes**

HTML codes used to identify blocks of text that represent specific structural elements of your document, for example the head, title, body text, headings, and paragraphs.

### branding

Giving your Web documents a distinctive look and feel by applying graphic images, colors, formatting, and other decorative techniques according to a common style and conscious design.

### browser

A client software program that you use to search networks, retrieve copies of files, and display them in an easy-to-read format. Examples of popular browsers are Mosaic, NetScape, and Cello.

### CGI

See *common gateway interface.*

### cgi-bin

A commonly used directory on a UNIX-based Web server that contains server scripts and other programs used to carry out interactions between the server and clients.

### CGI script

See *server script.*

### client

Software programs that enable a user to access network resources by working with the information stored on a server. A browser is an example of a client. Cf. *server.*

### common gateway interface (CGI)

Interfacing software that facilitates communication between a Web server and programs operating outside the server. Examples include server scripts for image maps and forms.

### destination

The point, either elsewhere in a document or in a different document, that an *anchor* connects to—that is, the location to which a reader jumps by clicking on anchor text or graphics.

**directional graphics**

> A type of navigational graphics, such as arrow graphics, which, when clicked on, move the reader forward or backward in a document.

**document type definition (DTD)**

> A methodology used in SGML (Standard General Markup Language) to define codes for a specific usage of the markup language. HTML (Hypertext Markup Language) is based on a DTD that identifies a marked-up document as one that can be transported on the World Wide Web and read by browsers.

**DTD**

> See *document type definition.*

**etiquette**

> Forms, manners, and customs. Specifically with reference to the Internet, etiquette (a.k.a. *netiquette*) refers to the application of stylistic and other features that please readers and aid their use of Internet documents.

**external image**

> A graphical image that is stored and loaded separately from an HTML document. Unlike an *in-line image,* an external image is not loaded and displayed on a browser screen until the reader clicks on an anchor associated with either text or an in-line graphic. External images are often much larger files than in-line images and are generally displayed not by the browser but by a separate program, such as ImageView. A common graphics format for external images is JPEG.

**external link**

> A link that jumps from an anchor within one HTML document to another document. When clicked on, an external link can either open a second document at its beginning or jump the reader to a particular location within the destination document.

**FAQ**

> A list of frequently asked questions and their answers.

### Font codes

HTML codes that change the appearance of text characters. Examples are the italics code <i>, the bold code <b>, and their logical counterparts <em> for emphasis and <strong> for strong emphasis.

### FYI

"For your information"—a piece of information that is pertinent to a topic but might not exactly fit the content flow. An FYI might include source references or a citation from another document that is loosely related to a discussion.

### gateway

A computer system, or sometimes a program or set of programs, that provides a link between two different networks, systems, or programs. On the Internet, a *gateway* often means software connecting two networks governed by different protocols.

### GIF

Abbreviation for Graphics Interchange Format, a standard graphics format for in-line images transported by HTTP. GIF files are identified by the file name extension .gif.

### home page

The opening page of a Web document, sometimes alternatively called the *welcome page*.

### HTML

See *Hypertext Markup Language*.

### HTTP

See *Hypertext Transfer Protocol*.

### HTTP server

See *Web server*.

### hypermedia

Hypertext combined with *anchor graphics* and/or other media in a hypertext document. Hypertext offers the possibility of jumping to a new destination from a single media file, or of accessing sound, video, or a graphic image.

## hypertext

Electronic text in a format that provides instant access, via *links,* to other hypertext elsewhere in a document or within a separate document.

## Hypertext Markup Language (HTML)

A set of codes that form the standard of documents capable of being transported on the World Wide Web and read by a browser. The codes are used to identify the different parts of a document, specify the appearance of text and graphics, and form links between related topics. HTML is a subset of the Standard General Markup Language (SGML). HTML was originally developed at the CERN institute in Switzerland and continues to undergo further development by a working group of the Internet Engineering Task Force.

## Hypertext Transfer Protocol (HTTP)

The *protocol* that forms the basis of the World Wide Web technology. HTTP is the set of rules governing the software that transports hypertext along the Internet.

## image map

A graphical image mapped so that different, graphically active parts of the image (called *hot spots*) are coded for different results when acted upon by a reader. Typically, this means that a mouse click on one area of the image jumps a reader to one topic, and a mouse click on another area jumps to a different topic.

## *imagemap* program

An executable program that runs from a Web server. The *imagemap* program processes information about the reader's mouse clicks sent by the browser and returns information that instructs the browser to display a specific new document or location.

## imagemap.conf file

A configuration file, located on a Web server, that is used by the *imagemap* program to process image mapping actions. imagemap.conf contains the names of all mapped images and the directory paths (URLs) to their corresponding map files.

### in-line image

Images that are displayed within an HTML document itself. In-line images are loaded and displayed when you open an HTML document in your browser. The most common format for an in-line image is GIF.

### information community

A community of Internet users who develop a sustained interest in a given content area or a particular Web site.

### integrated services digital network (ISDN)

A network that acts as a digital connection service for telephones and other communication devices. An ISDN connection (not widely obtainable yet at the time of this writing, but probably coming soon to your area) can provide high-speed access to the Internet.

### internal link

A link that connects an anchor in an HTML document to another location within the same document.

### Internet

A global "network of networks" that connects individual computers and many computer networks for the purpose of exchanging information among people. Any two or more computers anywhere in the world are capable of communicating via the Internet, as long as the computers are connected to the Internet and can operate according to TCP/IP.

### Internet Protocol (IP)

The *protocol,* or set of rules, that governs the movement of information over the Internet. It is from the Internet Protocol that the Internet derives its name.

### IP

See *Internet Protocol.*

### ISDN

See *integrated services digital network.*

# `<isindex>`

An HTML code element which indicates that the user can enter a search string attached to an HTML document. That is, the reader can use keywords for searching the document or other files on the server.

# JPEG

A frequently used format for graphics files used as *external images*. *JPEG* is the abbreviation for the Joint Photographic Experts Group, which developed the JPEG standard. JPEG files are identified by the filename extension `.jpg`.

# kill file

An automatic procedure a user can set up to delete communications coming from a specific name, alias, or e-mail address, or communications that meet specified criteria pertaining to the subject line.

# link

Sets of HTML code that enable a reader to jump from place to place within a document, or from one document to another. Technically, a link consists of an *anchor* at the location of origin and a *destination* at the point the reader jumps to.

# list codes

HTML codes used to identify listed text items. Commonly used list codes include those for unordered lists, ordered lists, and definition lists.

# logical code types

HTML codes written so as to give the browser general, rather than specific, instructions about how to display characters. Logical font types, for example, leave it up to the browser configuration as to exactly how the designated text will be displayed—whether to make the characters bold, italic, a different color, or distinct in some other way. Cf. *physical code types*.

# map file

A file, stored on a Web server, that identifies the areas of an *image map* by their pixel coordinates and maps them to specific destinations.

## modular graphics

Graphic images that are composed of multiple button-like elements representing anchors for several related links.

## navigational graphics

Graphics that are used for moving around in hypermedia. The code for navigational graphics consists of an image tag enclosed within anchor tags. When a reader clicks on a navigational image in a browser, it acts as a link to another document or location.

## netiquette

See *etiquette.*

## network

Two or more computers connected to each other for the purpose of communication. They may be connected by permanent devices, such as cables, or by temporary links over a telephone or other communications line. Many networks consist of computers connected to each other through one or more *servers* that transport information and control access to network resources.

## PERL

Abbreviation for Practical Extraction and Report Language, a programming language commonly used for system management. PERL is well suited to writing scripts needed for Web server processes.

## physical code types

HTML codes written so as to instruct the browser to format text specifically. Physical font types, for example, dictate that browsers display marked characters as boldface, italics, or typewriter (monospace) font.

## protocol

A set of rules that computer programmers apply when writing code for a specific software. Computers and networks interact according to standard protocols, which determine the behavior that each side of a network connection expects from the other side.

## Relative URL

A *uniform resource locator* which designates a file location that is relative to another file. Generally, this means the two files are located at the same Web site—that is, on the hard disk of the same computer. To specify a relative URL for an anchor destination, for example, you specify the destination path only to the extent that it is different from that of the file containing the anchor. Cf. *Absolute URL.*

## server

A computer (or its software) that "serves" other computers by administering network files and network operations. Cf. *client.* Three types of Internet servers are *Web servers,* WAIS servers, and Gopher servers.

## server script

A specific server-based program that facilitates communication between a Web server and programs operating outside the server (client programs, for example). Server scripts are needed, for example, to run search features and to process information from interactive forms.

## T1

A high-speed, relatively high-bandwidth, digital electronic communication carrier.

## Transmission Control Protocol (TCP)

The *protocol,* or set of rules, that governs how computers and networks manage the flow of information among themselves. TCP works together with the *Internet Protocol (IP).* Functionally, TCP (a) divides information into packets that can be transmitted over electronic connections between computers, and (b) at the receiving end, reassembles the packets of information and checks them for errors.

## uniform resource locator (URL)

The path to an Internet file, including file name and extension. URLs are used to guide Internet readers to the exact loctions of Net resources, and to complete links between HTML anchors and external destinations. See also *Absolute URL* and *Relative URL.*

## Web server

A server on the World Wide Web which, by definition, offers hypertext-based access to documents. Web servers are governed by the *Hypertext Transfer Protocol (HTTP).*

## Web site

The location of published hypertext content. Physically, a Web site can occupy an entire Web server or a part of a server; or it can be spread out among different servers as long as its sections are all linked, directly or indirectly, to the same home or opening page.

## welcome page

A page of a Web document (frequently the opening, or *home page*) that welcomes visitors to a Web site and gives basic information describing the site's contents.

## World Wide Web

A medium of communication built around the goal of seamless information delivery over the Internet through *hypertext* links. The World Wide Web was first developed by a team of scientists at the CERN Research Center in Switzerland around 1990. Subsequent modifications have made possible the use of graphics and other media to enhance ease of use and deliver multiple forms of information—qualities we now commonly associate with the Web.

# Index

*Page numbers of graphics and illustrations appear in italics*

Art museums, 31
"Arts & Crafts," 38
ASCII files, 18, 50–51, 57, 233, 234
Attributes
   Align, 126–27, 251–52
   Alt, 125–26, *126,* 165, 235
   defined, 253
   href, 82, 210
   identifier, 82, 86
   ismap, 126–27, 230
Audience. *See also* Information community
   character of, 46–47
   as "driver," 81
   growth, 43–44
Auto dealerships on line, 19, 35–37, *36, 37,* 46, 203–4

## B

Banners, 33, *34,* 121, 136, *137,* 153, 156, 166, 253
Berners-Lee, Tim, 11, 54
Bignall, Rosina, 81
Bitmaps, 124
Block codes, 61–62, 253
   address tags, 63
   block quotation tags, 65
   body tags, 63
   heading tags, 64, 72, *73*
   head tags, 62
   horizontal rule, 65–66, 167
   HTML tags, 62
   line break, 65
   paragraph tags, 64
   title tags, 63
Block quotation tags, 65
Body tags, 63
Bold fonts
   and logical code, 67
   tags, 68
Bond, Dalinda, 81
Bookstore, Online (OBS), 40
Branding, 121, 135–36, 145, 153, 206, 254
Breast cancer, information source for, 32
Broadcast media (television/radio), 3, 10, 44–45

Brochure model, 99, *100,* 101, 104
   creating (Lab 4), 115–18
Browser, 12–13, *13,* 17–18, 31, 43, 55, 122–23, 166–67, 254
   testing documents using multiple, 171
   text-only, 126, 151, 165–66
Bulletin boards, 199
Business information, 32
Business models on Internet, 46

## C

*Cancelbot,* 191
Case sensitivity
   in file names, 56*n*
   in Isindex, 225
   in URLs, 89
Case, Steve, 47
Catalog model, 106–7, *106*
CancerNet, 32
Cello, 18, 51, 122, 126, 151
*Center de Données Astronomiques de Strasbourg* (CDS), 32–33
Cerf, Vinton, 42–43
CERN Research Center, 11, 123, 244
CGI (common gateway interface), 220, 221, 254
   -bin, 220, 230, 241, 254
   script, 238, 246, *248,* 249, 254
Charts and graphs, 132–33, *133*
Chats, 196–97, 198
Checkbox, creating, 243
   round (radio), 243
*Chicago Manual of Style,* 152, 157
Citation tags, 67
Clients, 7, *8,* 9, 16–17, 55, 254
Codes, 61, 62–73, 79, 82–83, *83,* 85–87, 88, 93–94, 95–96, 121–22, *122,* 126, 130, *130,* 138–42, *139, 140, 141,* 143–44, 151, 165–66, *166,* 210–12, 214–15, 223, 223*n,* 226, 230–31, *234,* 240–46. *See also* specific code types
Cognitive elaboration, 81
Color use, 127–28, 128*n,* 153, 155–56, 157
   for anchors, 159

HTML (*cont.*)
"raw" text sample document, *71*
and SGML, 55, 57–58
showcase for creative works, 38
software for HTML, 51, 57–58, *73*
spacing, 60–61, 89
strategies for linking, 96–97, *97,* 98, *98,*
99, *100,* 101, *101,* 102, *102,* 103–4
tags, 59, 59*n,* 62–72
text editors that will handle, 57–58
text samples, *54, 71*
tips for using text codes, 72
URLs, 88–92, 93, 95–96
HTML tags, 62. *See also* Codes
HTTP (Hypertext Transfer Protocol), 11,
16–17, 18, 53, 55, 89, 123, 208, 219,
257
Hypermedia, 256–57
Hypertext, 12, 13–15, 257. *See also* HTML
building, 53–74
as interactive document, 16, 28–29,
80–82, 104, 196–97, 212–13, 238–49
nontextual data, 12, *15. See also*
Graphics
and on-line help, 80, 107
text, 12
text editors, 17

# I

IBM, 43. *See also* OS/2
compatibles, 50
Icons, 12
Identifier of the attribute, 82, 86
Image mapped graphics (ISMAP), *26,* 27,
157, 165, 228–29, *229,* 257
circular hot spot, 232–33, *232*
configuration file, 220, 230, 234–35, 257
creating map file, 233–35
default destination, 233
example, 236–37, *236*
linking, 220
naming file, 234
map file, 220, 229–35
polygonal hot spot, 233, *233*
rectangular hot spot, 232, *232*

saving file, 233, 234
text alternative for, 151, 165–66, *166,*
235
Imagemap program, 257
Image tag, 125–26, *125, 126*
Indexing. *See* Isindex
Index pages, 203
Information community, 44–45, 180,
189–92, 258
advice about creating, 197–201, 206
and anchors to other servers, 205
cross-linking, 205
dedicated Web site, 193–94
hooking up to other Internet protocols,
208–12, *209*
interaction between, 196–97, 207–8,
212–13
specific Web sites, 192–93
sustaining, *202,* 204–9, *207*
topical communities, 194–96
Information superhighway, 11
In-line image, 25, 123, 124, 228, 258
In-line image switch, 126
Input element (<input>), 242
Instructional documents, creating, 107–8,
*108*
Intellitag, 57
Interactive communication, 38, 81, 196–97,
199, 212–13
Interactive documents, 16, 28–29, 80–81,
212–13, 219, 223–37, 238–249
Interactive forms, 196–97, 238–40
CGI script, *248,* 249
codes, 240–46
drop-down list box in, 243–44, *244*
feedback returned to server, 246, *247,*
*248*
response to feedback, *240*
sample, *239*
Interactive learning, 81
Internal links, 85–87, 258
codes for external links to internal destinations, 93–94
external links to, 92–93, *93*
when to use, 86–87
International Standards Organization
(ISO), 53

Internet. *See also* Archie; Browsers; Gopher servers; WAISes; Web servers; Web sites; World Wide Web
  access, 43
  clients, 7, 9, 16–17
  commercial use of, 46–47
  connecting with, 49–50
  as decentralized media, 10
  defined, 258
  etiquette, 47
  global aspects of, 5, 6, *6*, 79
  as means for communicating ideas, 3
  origins and history, 9–11, 11*n*
  protocols, 4, 5–6, 11, 55, 123, 208–12, *209*, 214–15
  providers, 185, 188
  publishing companies, 37–38, *39*
  servers, 7, 9, 18
  software, new, 11, 18
  software packages, 18, 43
  technology of, 3–4
  user base, 13, 42–43
  web sites, 10
Internet Shopping Network, 46
Internet Society, 42
ISDN lines, 50, 187, 188, 195, 258
Isindex (<isindex>), 201, 223, 223*n*, 224–28, *224, 225, 227*, 259
  case sensitivity, 225
  code, 223, 223*n*, 226
Ismap attribute, 126–27, 230
Italic fonts
  and logical code types, 57
  tags, 69

# J

JPEG (Joint Photographic Experts Group), 124, 127, 128, *129*, 157, 255, 259

# K

Kill file, 191, 259

# L

Labs
  adding navigational graphics, 143–44
  designing access to other Internet services, 214–15
  designing a web site, 175–77
  document titles and unsubtle anchor text, 178–79
  electronic brochure, 115–18
  external links, 113–14
  first HTML document, 75–78, *78*
  internal links, 110–12
  planning linked documents, 119–20
LAN (local-area network), 5, 7
Length of documents, 167, 169. *See also* Downloading
Libraries on Internet, 11
Line break, 65
Lines, connecting, 187, 195
Links (hypertext), *14*, 18, *21*, 22, *22*, 23, *25*, 79–80, 161, 259
  accessibility for text-only browsers, 151, 165–66, *166*
  appropriateness of content and audience, 169
  common causes of nonfunctioning, 171–72
  cross-linking (to other servers), 205
  electronic brochure, creating (Lab 4), 115–18
  external, 87–88, 91–96, *93, 95*, 205
  external, exercise for creating (Lab 3), 113–14
  functional models, 104–9, *105, 106, 108*
  internal, 85–87
  internal, exercise for creating (Lab 2), 110–12
  number of in document, 150
  planning linked documents (Lab 5), 119–20
  Quick Tour page, 154–55, *154*
  strategic, 204–5
  structural models, 96–97, *97*, 98, *98*, 99, *100*, 101, *101*, 102, *102*, 103–4
  testing, 171–72, 173

O'Reilly and Associates' Global Network
    Navigator (GNN), 32
OS/2, 18, 49, 53
    community, 193, 195–96
    HTML file extensions, 56, 57

# P

"Palace of Diocletian at Split, The" (Green-
    halgh) 24–27, *25, 26*
Paragraphs
    align attribute, 251–52
    and block quotations, 65, 65*n*
    conventions, 159–60, *160*
    indentation, 64
    optional end tag, why to use, 64
    tags, 64
Password creation, 243
PBS, 10
Periodicals on-line, 182–83, *183*
    *Time* Magazine on-line, 40
PERL, 221, 226, 238, 246, *248,* 249, 260
Peters, Mike, 21
Photos, 133–34
    exhibits on-line, 133–34
Physical code types, 260
    bold tags, 68
    italic tags, 68
    typewriter font tags, 68
    vs. logical code types, 66, 72
Platforms. *See* UNIX; Servers
Post delivery method, 241
Print media, 3, 10, 44
Programming, 221
Project Gutenberg, 32, 96, 203
Protocols, 4, 260
    e-mail, 209–12
    FTP, 18, 55, 162, 208–11, 214–15
    Gopher, 7, 32, 196, 199, 208–11, 214–15
    HTML, 16–17
    HTTP, 11, 16, 208
    newsgroups, 208–9, *209,* 210, 211–12,
        214–15
    TCP/IP, 4, 5–6, 11, 258
Publishing companies on World Wide
    Web, 37–38, *39,* 200

Publishing on World Wide Web. *See also*
    Branding; Graphics; HTML; Interac-
    tive communication; Interactive docu-
    ments; Style; Web sites
    appropriateness of, 47
    author's signature/byline, 167
    central motifs, 148, *148,* 149
    clarifying concepts of work, 147
    collaborators and staff, 149–50, *200,*
        201–3
    and comments in hypertext document,
        70–71
    computer and network access, 49–50,
        181, 208–12, *209*
    consulting and training, 40
    creating a server (and web site), 187–89
    creating/sustaining an information com-
        munity, 194–96, 197–208, *202,* 207,
        212–13
    distribution, 16, 19, 182–89
    electronic publications, 182–83, *183*
    feedback, 167, *168,* 170, 208
    finding a server, 182–86
    hooking up to other Internet protocols,
        208–12, *209*
    and hypertext, 13–15. *See also* HTML
    hypertext links, *14. See also* Links
    legal pitfalls, 84, 91, 134, 194
    nontextual elements in content, 15–16,
        *15. See also* Graphics
    overall structure and design, 150–51
    post your work on a web server, 181–82
    project specs, 146, 151–52
    showcase for work, 38
    software, 50–51
    and software development, 70–71
    status of work (complete vs. in-
        progress), 167
    testing documents before distributing,
        170–74, 235
    text editors, 17

# Q

Qudralay QHWIS, 51

editing and copy editing, 172–73
editorial style guides, 146, 152–53, 157
project "specs," 146, 151–52, 166–67
Subdirectories, 90
Subheads and subtopics. *See also* Headings
in brochure model, 99, *100*
codes for external links to internal destinations, 93–94
and internal links, 86, 92–93, *93*
and number of links, 150
Submit button, creation of, 243

## T

Table of contents
Quick Tour on, 154–55, *154*
using internal links on, 86, 107
Tags, 59, 59*n*, 62–72. *See also* Anchors
TCP/IP (Transmission Control Protocol/Internet Protocol), 4, 5–6, 11, 55, 258, 261
Technical manual/Help file model, 107–8, *108*
as structural model, 108–9
Testing your documents, 170–74, 235
Textarea element (<textarea>), 241–42
Text box, 241–42, 243
maxlength attribute, 243
Text editors, 17
Text options, 28, *28*
Thurber, Bonnie, 81
Tibbetts, Todd, 27
TIFF, 124, 127
*Time* Magazine on-line, 40
Time Warner, 10
Titles
directions for creating, 157–59, *158*, 199
lengthy, 158, 159
map file, 234–35
recognizable, 199
restrictions on, 63
tags, 63
TLC, 226
T1 line, 187, 188, 195, 261
Tracks, creating for text-only browsers, 151
Travel Agents, 31, 40

Typewriter font
as monospace font, 68
tags, 68

## U

University of California's Museum of Paleontology, 164
University of Illinois/Urbana-Champaign, 12
UNIX, 13, 43, 53
case sensitivity, 56*n*, 89
CGI-bin, 220, 230
CGI servers/scripts, 220, 221, 223*n*, *248*, 249
HTML file extensions, 56
slashes and backslashes, 90
URL (uniform resource locator), 20, 261. *See also* Addresses; URL addresses to access
absolute, 89, 92, 95–96, 210, 253
as address, 89
components of, 88, *88*
in document header, *62*
errors in, 172
relative, 89–91, 91*n*, 210, 261
slashes and backslashes, 90, 211, 212
two rules about, 89
URL (uniform resource locator) addresses to access
Andy Warhol Museum, 134
bulletin board that announces new web sites, 199, 217
DealerNet, 35
Free Range Media, Inc., 37–38, *39*
freeware for HTML, 51
French Painting in the Eighteenth Century, 134
Global Network Navigator (GNN), 182, 183*n*
Gopher, 214
Horror, Fantasy, and the Grotesque in Art, 134
*HotWired*, 164
HTML codes, complete, 54, 244
ismap and isindex with Macintosh

WELL (Whole Earth 'Lectronic Link), 182, 191, 192–93
"What's New" pages, 186
*Whole Earth Catalog*, 190
*Whole Earth Review, The* (Rheingold, ed.), 190
Whosis, 55
Wilson, Chris, 123
Windley, Phillip J., 81
WinWeb, 51
*Wired* magazine, 164
Word for Windows. *See* Microsoft Word
WordPerfect, 51
   SGML add-on software, 57
   for Windows, 57
World Cup USA '94, 44–45, *45*
World Wide Web (WWW), 262. *See also* Web sites
   audience growth, 43–44
   browser for, 12–13, *13*
   commercial uses, 33–40, *34, 35, 36, 37, 38, 39,* 46–47

   content growth, 43–44
   creating a hypertext document, 53–74
   culture of, 46–47
   history of, 11
   and interactive learning, 81
   protocols, 11, 55
   publishing on, 13–16, 47
   search tools, 10
   servers, 9, 18–19, 55
   service pages, 10
   size, 41–43
   URLs, 20
   web growth, 42
"WWW Adventures," 38, *39*
WWW Conference '94, 81

## Z

Zakon, Robert H., 11$n$

# SPRY Mosaic Quick Start Guide
## *Use this Quick Start Guide to get going fast!*

## I. Installing SPRY Mosaic

1. Start Windows. Insert the HOW TO PUBLISH ON THE INTERNET/SPRY Mosaic diskette into your floppy drive a: or b:.

2. In Program Manager, choose Run from the File menu; in the <Run> dialog box, type a:setup or b:setup and press Enter.

3. The installation will ask you for a destination directory. Click OK to choose the default directory, SPRY.

## II. Helpful hints for configuring SPRY Mosaic

After you've installed the software to your computer's hard drive, you will be prompted for information regarding your computer's setup.

### COMMUNICATIONS PORT SETUP AND SPEED

Choose the port and speed settings for your modem if the default settings are not correct. If your modem speed is not listed, specify the closest speed of greater value (e.g. select 19,200 if you own a 14,400 baud modem). The "Port Status" message indicates which ports are available. If you have a PCMCIA card or multiple COM ports in use, this message may not indicate the correct COM port status. If you are unsure of your PC's COM port status, you should consult your modem documentation.

### MODEM TYPE

Choose your modem from the Modem Type drop-down list. If your modem isn't listed, choose a compatible modem (see your modem documentation, or contact your modem manufacturer), or choose Hayes. Most modems are compatible with the Hayes settings.

### DIAL MODIFIERS

If you need to use any dial modifiers (such as to access an outside line or to enter a long-distance code) enter them in this dialog box. The most common modifiers are: "9" to access an outside line. "," to pause during dialing, and "*70" to disable Call Waiting.

## III. Registering SPRY Mosaic

After configuring your modem, you'll be prompted to enter information necessary for registering your software. You must register the software in order to use SPRY Mosaic.

### INTERNET ACCESS PHONEBOOK

Specify your country, area code, city and preferred Internet access number from the drop-down lists. The dialog box is progressive: You must make a selection in the area code drop-down list before you can proceed to the city drop-down list. If you need to change your access number (or your dial modifiers) at a later time, you can access the phonebook by double-clicking the Internet Access Phonebook icon.

After prompting you for billing information, SPRY Mosaic will initiate a call to register your software.

Following registration, you will be asked to update your Internet identity. SPRY Mosaic is configured to use "anonymous@interserv.com" as the default e-mail address (for outgoing messages only). If you have a current Internet e-mail account, you can change the anonymous e-mail address. Note: if you do not have an Internet e-mail account, do not change the anonymous return address. Without the anonymous e-mail address, readers may think they can respond to your messages with personal e-mail replies. Their mail will not be delivered.

### STARTING MOSAIC

You can start Mosaic from the registration screen that displays your User ID, or you can start the application by double-clicking the Mosaic icon in your new windows program group.

### TECHNICAL SUPPORT

You can contact SPRY's technical support engineers by calling (206) 447-0958 during the hours of 8:00 a.m. to 5:00 p.m. PST.

### LICENSE AGREEMENT

Your use of SPRY Mosaic software is subject to a license agreement between you and SPRY, Inc. The full text of the license agreement is contained in the file "LICENSE.TXT" on the diskette. Please read it carefully before installing the software on your computer. Installation of the software on your computer constitutes your acceptance of the terms of the license agreement.

SPRY, Inc.
316 Occidental Avenue South
Seattle, WA 98104